HV7936.P8 M67 2009
Beyond no comment : speaking with
 the press as a police officer /
33663004438244

DATE DUE

NOV 0 2 2011	
OCT 2 3 2014	

BEYOND NO COMMENT

SPEAKING WITH THE PRESS AS A POLICE OFFICER

PATRICK MORLEY

KAPLAN) PUBLISHING

New York

Published by Kaplan Publishing, a division of Kaplan, Inc.
1 Liberty Plaza, 24th Floor
New York, NY 10006

Printed in the United States of America

Library of Congress Cataloging-in-Publication Data
Morley, Patrick (Patrick J.)
   Beyond no comment: speaking with the press as a police officer/Patrick Morley.
      p. cm.
   ISBN 978–1–4277–9962–3
   1. Police-community relations. 2. Police and the press. 3. Police and mass media.
   I. Title.
   HV7936.P8M67 2009
   659.2'93632–dc22
   2008054009

10 9 8 7 6 5 4 3 2 1

ISBN-13: 978-1-4277-9962-3

Kaplan Publishing books are available at special quantity discounts to use for sales promotions, employee premiums, or educational purposes. Please email our Special Sales Department to order or for more information at *kaplanpublishing@kaplan.com*, or write to Kaplan Publishing, 1 Liberty Plaza, 24th Floor, New York, NY 10006.

TABLE OF CONTENTS

ACKNOWLEDGMENTS

I would like to thank my wife, Chantall, my mother, my father (especially for his patient proofreading and assistance with this book), and the rest of my family.

I would like to thank the wonderful men and women that I have met in the criminal justice system. I would like to thank the Chicago Police Department and the Cook County State Attorney's Office, two organizations I am proud and privileged to have worked for. I would like to thank all those who I have worked with, who I have worked for, who have taught me, and who have mentored me.

Thank you to Kaplan Publishing for allowing me the opportunity to do this second textbook, especially Michael Sprague and Fred Urfer, who were both helpful and a pleasure to work with.

I would especially like to thank the following talented professionals who contributed their expertise to this book:

Assistant State Attorney Arunas Buntinas, Cook County, Illinois

Deputy Director (Retired) Patrick T. Camden, News Affairs, Chicago Police Department

Assistant State Attorney Joe Cataldo, Cook County, Illinois

Assistant State Attorney Patrick Coughlin, Cook County, Illinois

Lieutenant (Retired) Thomas A. Dreffein, LaGrange Park, Illinois Police Department

Detective Mark DiMeo, Chicago Police Department

Attorney Daniel Herbert

Federal Bureau of Investigation Agent (Retired) Francis Marrocco

Chicago Police Officer (Retired) James Marsh

Assistant State Attorney David R. Navarro, Cook County, Illinois

Chief Paul Rigsby, Nolensville, Tennessee, Police Department

Supervisory Inspector Shannon M. Robinson, United States Marshals Service

Sergeant (Retired) Joe J. Santercier, Illinois State Police

Commander Mike Ruth, Skokie Police Department

Cook County Sheriff (Retired) Michael F. Sheahan

Attorney Terrence J. "T. J." Sheahan

Assistant State Attorney Fabio Valentini, Cook County, Illinois

INTRODUCTION

POLICE AND THE MEDIA

The role of the police is to serve and protect the public. Part of that role is maintaining public order. A large part is the investigation of and prevention of crime. The goal in any law enforcement investigation is to find out the truth.

The media is the means by which information is transmitted to the public. The definition of media and the means by which people get their information has changed over the years. Today's media includes newspapers, television, radio, and the Internet. The job of the media is to report the news, but the goal is also to entertain and make a profit.

Turn on your television, pick up a newspaper, or go to the movies, and chances are that the subject being featured will be crime. Cops and robbers are big business with the media: a homicide, a rapist terrorizing the community, a police scandal, or a new policing program. Law enforcement and the police need the media. Media need the police. Sometimes they are at odds, sometimes arm in arm, but in many ways the two are inseparable.

It has been said that the media is the most powerful man-made phenomena created on this earth, for they determine what you eat, buy, and drive. For police, you do not have to seek out the media for it will hunt you down.[1]

It has also been said, "It is the cops' role to nail the suspect, find the body, and catch the bad guys. It is the media's role ... to cover that process, to report the facts, act as check and balance. It is not [the media's job] to aid in the investigation, a distinction both sides are generally clear in making."[2]

The police and the media have a love-hate relationship. Media can cite examples of overly secretive police, while police cite negative reporting and interference with investigations. Despite their differences, the police and the media both need and rely on each other. The police officer or law enforcement official who has lost his or her reputation for credibility with the news media is an individual in serious trouble.[3]

The media can publicize the good work the police do, focus attention on deserving personnel, assist with selling police programs, educate and inform the public, and supply a public forum.[4] The media needs the police because the police are often their best source of information, have the inside track on many good stories, are a great source for quotes and expert advice, and good relations with the police make its job easier.[5] A positive police-media relationship leads to increased public confidence in the department. This can help the police when it comes to budgeting and contractual issues.

Police departments should have a media policy and should have personnel designated to deal with the media. They should be accessible, prompt, respectful, and candid. They should be versed in speaking to the media and providing for the needs of the media.

According to the Iowa City Police Department, the duties of the public information officer are to "be present at the scene of major incidents; assist the news media; prepare and distribute media releases; arrange for, and assist at, news conferences; coordinate and authorize the release of information about victims, witnesses, and suspects; assist in crisis situations within the agency; and coordinate the release of authorized information concerning confidential agency investigations and operations."[6]

Some larger departments, including the Chicago Police Department, have an Office of News Affairs and allow the media to make inquiries to the office seven days a week during all watches, all hours of the day and night.[7]

Among the chief complaints of the news media toward the police are as follows:

- The police are obsessed with secrecy.
- They lie to the media.
- They stick together and cover up their misdeeds.
- They are arrogant and exaggerate their own importance.
- They are discourteous and obstructive.
- They see everyone except police as ignorant liberals who cannot understand.
- They oversimplify issues.
- They expect favors and special treatment.[8]

Among the chief complaints of the police towards the news media are:

- Reporters always believe the crook over the cop.
- They only report part of the story.
- They despoil crime scenes and create a circus.
- They violate confidences and screw up cases.
- They demand attention when the police are busiest.
- They are arrogant and exaggerate their own importance.
- They edit and cut to quote you out of context.
- They exaggerate and make big deals out of nonstories.[9]

The police and the media should work together to develop a mutual understanding. Reaching that understanding can help eliminate biases that may be present on both sides. It can also help eliminate personal confrontations and personality conflicts.

It should be noted that there are many philosophies and strategies on how to deal with the media as a law enforcement officer. While there may be many wrong ways to deal with the media, there is also no singular correct way. Some officers will be better and more comfortable than others in dealing with the media. Throughout this book, you will hear from a variety of experts in the "What the Pros Say" sections. All of the persons who shared their wisdom are highly qualified in law enforcement, media relations, or the legal field. There are differences in their beliefs and advice. Each of these individuals has experience with the media or media-related issues. They are all top professionals in the field. While some of the advice may vary, there is something that can be learned from all of these experts. Each can add something of great value to your learning experience.

Today's police officers and departments as a whole should possess the following prerequisites, both in general and in media relations: a reputation for credibility, an ability to communicate, common sense, technical knowledge, pride in professionalism, a positive outlook, emotional maturity and control, tact, modesty, and sensitivity.[10]

Big Story or a Big Potato?

"I was taught years ago that every reporter hates slow days. On slow days they call you up and ask if there is anything going on or any special story you want to run. One crusty old reporter I knew referred to these as 'big potato days.' If you are the reporter and it is a slow news day, your local sources (you) can be their lifeline to something newsworthy. If not, the film crew is doing a story on a farmer who grew a sweet potato that looks like Richard Nixon; hence 'big potato days.' Once you have a reporter's ear, you can now be in an advantageous situation when dealing with this

station. You may have had a new program started once, tried to get media attention, and nothing. Even if they filmed it, the story was not aired. You were bumped by the train wreck. Now is the time for the new program to be filmed. You will be surprised how much more air time you get this way. Patience on your part and big potatoes on theirs makes a winning combination for you.

They alone can make you a hero or shame you. Are they your enemy or friend? Neither, but do not get lulled in by them . . . this is a love-hate relationship that every chief must dance with in [his] tenure in office."[11]

WHAT THE PROS SAY

"The media can be used as a valuable tool for crime prevention and detection. In my experience, the media can be used most effectively to disseminate information to the public. They can be very helpful in getting out messages to the public on both a small and large scale. For example, on a small scale, we often worked with senior citizen groups, community groups, schools, and churches on community awareness programs. We would use the media to assist us with publicizing these crime prevention programs.

In particular, the media helped us educate the public about crimes that are specific to senior citizens, women, and school children. We also would use the media to advise the public about identity theft, Internet scams, and recent criminal activity in the community. We requested various media outlets to run special segments on home and personal security tips, how to properly secure your home while on vacation, and how to prepare for criminal activity that occurs during the summer months or the Christmas season.

Local media outlets can be used to give information regarding crimes that occur in a particular suburb or a neighborhood in a large city, including

(Continued)

sexual assaults, thefts, burglaries, and property crimes. They are always ready to lend assistance with identifying and capturing pedophiles. On a larger scale, they can be used to assist with AMBER Alerts and fugitive apprehension. The media also is helpful regarding traffic control for large-scale special events like holiday celebrations, concerts, or professional sporting events.

With respect to criminal detection, the print and broadcast media can give detailed descriptions of wanted suspects, including photos or a sketch artist's rendition. The broadcast media can display security camera video clips from ATMs, gas stations, retail establishments, and even from a standard security system for a public parking garage or private high-rise residence. Likewise, the media can be useful in locating and identifying individuals in missing person cases.

Indeed, the media can be a valuable resource for a police department on many different levels. Law enforcement officers should proactively use the media because, if used properly, the media can be an effective conduit between the police and the public." **Cook County Sheriff (Retired) Michael F. Sheahan**

Michael F. Sheahan is the former sheriff of Cook County, Illinois (1990–2006). During his 16-year tenure, Sheriff Sheahan managed a department that had over 7,000 employees, a police department, an annual budget of well over $400 million, and the largest single-site jail in the United States—the Cook County Jail. Over 100,000 inmates are housed annually in the Cook County Jail. Prior to becoming the Cook County sheriff, Mr. Sheahan was an alderman in the Chicago City Council and was the chairman of the Police and Fire Committee. Prior to becoming an alderman, Sheriff Sheahan was a police officer in both the Patrol and Youth Divisions of the Chicago Police Department.

Relationships with Reporters

"Over the course of one's tenure at a particular agency, one may deal with the same media representatives on a regular basis. It is important that you know with what type of individual you are dealing. It may be a good idea to get to know the reporter as an individual. Just as you may do with coworkers, have conversations with them about family, sports, or other outside interests that you may have in common. Avoid discussing controversial topics such as politics or religion, as those could be used against you in the future. A personal rapport and trust may help ease the sometimes adversarial relationship between law enforcement and media. It may also result in the reporter respecting your wishes when you tell them that you can't release certain information about a particular case or situation, and lets them know that you are being honest and not covering up something. Be advised however, that not all reporters or law enforcement officials are open to this type of relationship, and that is just as important to know." **Chief Paul Rigsby, Nolensville, Tennessee**

Chief Paul Rigsby of the Nolensville, Tennessee, Police Dept. has 10 years in law enforcement and 12 years in the fire service. He started as a patrolman in Chapel Hill, TN, and was soon promoted to sergeant. In 2002, he was named fire chief for the Chapel Hill Fire Dept. For five years, he worked simultaneously for the Chapel Hill Police Dept. and the Nolensville Police Dept., while still serving as fire chief. In 2005, he became police chief of the Nolensville Police Dept. and still holds both chief positions today. He is a graduate of the Northwestern University School of Police Staff and Command.

"The police and the media have a symbiotic relationship. Each entity thrives off the other and, assuming that is recognized, it can be an extremely prosperous relationship. Consider this: the police work with the media and provide it with information regarding an at-large criminal. The media flexes its vast broadcasting muscle and informs its audience of the details, and moments later a viewer contacts the police and provides valuable information that leads to the arrest and prosecution of the criminal. Everyone is happy! On the following day, the media is panicked because of the fact that it is "sweeps week" and they have nothing to report for the ten o'clock news. Joe the reporter contacts

(Continued)

his friends at the police department, and they provide him with juicy details of the local politician and his mistress's murder-suicide. Channel 7 gets the scoop, the newsies and police toast each other over cocktails, and all is well in the world!

I hope you enjoyed the trip to fantasyland. The harsh reality of the climate surrounding the police/media relationship is quite to the contrary of the one depicted above. Generally speaking, police officers do not trust the media and vice versa. Oddly enough, both sides have valid reasons for their respective distrust. The media caters to the interests of the public. Bad news sells. Bad news about police officers sells a lot! As a result, a line has been drawn and the media find themselves pitted against the police. I expect this to be the state of the relationship for the foreseeable future. Regardless of this reality, both sides must coexist. The intelligent approach is to recognize the climate and attempt to establish some sort of rapport. Of course in order for any semblance of a working relationship to exist, there must be trust, which is not earned overnight. The groundwork is being laid in some areas, others are miles apart. Stay tuned." **Daniel Herbert**

Dan Herbert has been an attorney for the Chicago Fraternal Order of Police (FOP) since 2005, where his duties include advising and counseling officers. Dan was a Chicago police officer from 1992 to 2001. He was a tactical officer in both the 23rd and 24th districts, on the North Side of Chicago. Dan was a full-time instructor at the Chicago Police Academy from 1997 until 2001, when he left the police department to become a Cook County assistant state attorney. Dan was an assistant state attorney from 2001 to 2005.

"With respect to media-worthy police incidents, there are several things a young police officer must learn. One of these is control at an incident. In order to provide coordination at an event that requires a significant amount of manpower, officers learn that whatever their assignment is, they must attend to this assignment without fail. Often the news media is present at these events and they are looking for information. The news media is often a respected group of individuals wanting to do the best work possible for their viewers. However, there are members of the news media who do not follow respected protocol regarding police department needs at major incidents. For this reason, all officers must be aware of the press policy of each department.

There are two reasons that this is so important. First, the officer has his or her job to do. If that job is neglected, a major problem may develop from lack of attention. This takes place when the officer pays more attention to the news media and neglects his or her assignment. For example, a house fire may require an officer to take a corner and block traffic from entering. If the officer ignores this assignment and instead gives a reporter an interview, individuals may go into a restricted area and become involved in a dangerous situation.

A second reason that there is a restriction on who may speak to the press is that certain information cannot be released to the media and can possibly jeopardize an investigation. The hard work the members of the investigative team perform can go to waste if any uniformed individual begins to give critical information that might tip off a suspect, causing the suspect to go further underground and avoid detection. The main goal of officers is public safety, not public information. As much as it might seem glamorous to be on television, officers must resist the temptation for the ten minutes of fame the sound bite might provide. Officers must check their egos at the door when they decide to do the tasks of a law enforcement officer.

For any job police officers are given, they must strictly and exactly follow their assignment. The goal is to complete the task with the minimum amount of inconvenience to the general public. As such, officers need to understand why departments develop operation plans for disasters that tax the resources of a community. A good plan includes the designation of a press relations officer who ensures that information is both coordinated and accurate. This minimizes the possibility of erroneous information being given to the press, which might result in public panic. The goal is always public safety, which a good press

(Continued)

relations protocol will provide." **Lieutenant (Retired) Thomas A. Dreffein**

Thomas A. Dreffein was a police officer for 32 years at the LaGrange Park Police Department, retiring as a lieutenant. He is a graduate of Triton College, Governors State University, and Western Illinois University, where he received a master's in law enforcement administration. He is a graduate of the FBI National Academy. He currently teaches as an adjunct instructor of criminal justice at Triton College and is also a site supervisor and instructor for North East Multi-Regional Training (NEMRT), a mobile police training unit in Illinois.

CHAPTER *1*

PUBLIC PERCEPTION OF POLICE AND PORTRAYAL IN THE MEDIA

Public perception and trust of law enforcement has changed over the course of time. In the 1950s, police and the media often shared common viewpoints and backgrounds. The relationship between the two was seldom adversarial and police were viewed by most as the "thin blue wall" that kept the less desirable segments in line.[12] For the most part, the police were the "good guys," who protected the rest of society from dangerous elements in society and those who ran afoul of the law.

The political and social upheaval of the 1960s changed both the media relationship with the police and the perception of policing.[13] Clashes between the police and civil-rights and antiwar protesters led to some of these changes, in addition to the distancing of the media from the police.[14]

Reporting on police matters has changed. Today, newspapers have their own editorial policies that dictate what will be printed in the newspaper and how it will appear. Additional factors that determine what gets printed and how it looks or reads include: finances, the tone of the paper, demands of the reader, political outlook, religious considerations, patriotic considerations, crusades and campaigns, ethnic considerations, business considerations, the role in the community the paper sees for itself, taboo subjects, and even, on occasion, the preferences of the editor or publisher.[15] There are values, referred to as news values, which determine how worthy the information is: timeliness, impact, prominence, proximity, novelty, human interest, conflict, and currency.[16]

Police departments are much different places today than they were 50 years ago. While 50 years ago, police departments were made up of mainly white males, now departments are ethnically, sexually, and racially diverse. Many women and ethnic minorities head up major departments across the country.

Television, movies, and other media portray the police much differently. The good cops, bad cops, female police officers, racially diverse police, super cops, cops who bend the law for the greater good, and the dirty and corrupt cops shown on screen all lend a hand in influencing public opinion and stereotypes of the police.

Throughout time, there has been a consistently swinging pendulum of public opinion on law enforcement. The police are sometimes portrayed as heroes. Then focus will shift to cops whose performance or ethics are less than heroic. The media both helps shape that image and also reports on the acts of law enforcement that help to mold public opinion.

Case Study: Those that Helped Mold the Image of the Modern Police Officer—Part One

Joseph Wambaugh

Former Los Angeles Police detective sergeant and best-selling author Joseph Wambaugh is given much of the credit for developing the modern image of police in the movies and on television. Prior to Wambaugh, police officers were portrayed as heroic and unflappable, but were often one-dimensional and unrealistic. Joseph Wambaugh wrote his first novel, *The New Centurions*, while still in the Los Angeles Police Department.

Wambaugh joined the police department in 1960 and served 14 years. Wambaugh brought real-life experience to his writing and wrote in a gritty, realistic, and sometimes darkly humorous tone. Wambaugh's characters are imperfect and flawed and multi-dimensional. Wambaugh explored topics such as drinking, womanizing, and brutality in his works. Some of his other works of fiction include *The Blue Knight, The Choirboys, Lines and Shadows*, and *Floaters*. Nonfiction works include *The Onion Field*, made into a successful movie, and *Fire Lover: A True Story*.

Wambaugh is one of the creators/developers of *Police Story*, which aired on NBC from 1973 to 1977, a popular show which explored both the on- and off-duty lives of Los Angeles police officers. The show was considered groundbreaking for its time and influenced many other shows. *Police Story* was considered a predecessor to later realistic police shows such as the classic *Hill Street Blues*.

Joseph Wambaugh continues to write, with his latest book, *Hollywood Crow,* having been released in 2008.

Case Study: Those that Helped Mold the Image of the Modern Police Officer—Part Two

Hill Street Blues

Set in a generic unnamed city, the classic *Hill Street Blues* is considered one of the best dramatic television series of all time. Airing from 1981 to 1987 on NBC, the show featured a large ensemble cast and explored the on- and off-duty lives of the police officers assigned to the Hill Street precinct. The show also explored the stress of police work and the effect it has on personal lives, along with a realistic depiction of a gritty urban area with gang and drug problems. The show earned 98 Emmy nominations during its seven-season run.

On the show, the police were portrayed as mainly good people, flawed and imperfect, who struggle with real-life issues. The captain of the precinct, Frank Furillo, played by actor Daniel Travanti, was a complex character—a divorced father, a strong leader who commanded respect, a recovering alcoholic involved in a romantic relationship with public defender Joyce Davenport, played by Veronica Hamel. The show also depicted officers as multidimensional characters, with a wide range of policing styles and philosophies. It helped shaped public perceptions and images of police.

Case Study: Those that Helped Mold the Image of the Modern Police Officer—Part Three

COPS

Since the show's premiere in 1989, *COPS* has been one of America's most popular television shows. The show was originally proposed during a writers' strike. *COPS* has helped make police officers seem more accessible and more human. It has interested many people in police work and is generally regarded as great public relations for police officers and law enforcement.

COPS has aired in over 100 cities across the United States and has also been shot in foreign countries. *COPS* is America's longest running documentary and is shown on FOX on Saturday night and throughout the week in syndication.

WHAT THE PROS SAY

"You are master of the unspoken word, but the spoken word is the master of you." **My mother, many years ago**

"The above is a very true statement regarding what we say, and even more so as a public official. In today's finger-pointing and who-is-to-blame society, what we say can be a very volatile concoction.

Many careers have gone down in flames from just an 'off the cuff' or an 'off the record' remark made to the wrong person. The media wants news and information and if they can garner anything from any one of us, they have accomplished their mission.

The media has no obligation to us in law enforcement and public service, and they have readily displayed this on many occasions.

For many years I have heard news reports on various cases I have been a part of or participated in some fashion, and the media reports bear no resemblance to the actual events. At times I would like to scream and tell them how the event really occurred, but we just cannot allow ourselves that forbidden luxury.

By nature, people in law enforcement are individuals who seek the truth. And seeing things misrepresented or overstated makes us want to scream. At times our profession is taken to task and made to look foolish, inept, and even dishonest, and our only recourse is to swallow hard and take it. At times even our press spokesperson cannot set the record straight for many reasons. And even when the spokesperson tries to express law enforcement's position, it is often taken out of context or even left out of a particular news report.

I believe one way to look at the situation is that reporters tend to look at us as informants, and that is far from flattering. If we let ourselves become information whores, we are headed for trouble. The media in general has no regard for our profession unless they need something or we are central to their story.

(Continued)

Yes, there are some honorable people in the media who do honor their word, but is your career or a particular case worth the risk? An average pension is worth in excess of two million dollars. Are you willing to gamble that just to set the record straight?

Certainly we have the cherished First Amendment right of free speech, but if we speak about anything official, whether directly or indirectly, we can violate an agency regulation or even a law (as with grand jury information). That point aside, we may jeopardize a case or even someone's safety by speaking to the media. Whether our intentions were pure or self-serving does not matter, we have violated a trust, and it is that simple.

If your agency gives you permission to speak to the press, the danger of being misquoted or misrepresented is always lingering. It is the proverbial double-edged sword and it can cut both ways." **Federal Bureau of Investigation Agent (Retired) Francis Marrocco**

Agent Fran Marrocco has had a decorated career in law enforcement. Agent Marrocco is a former Marine Corp sergeant, Glendale Heights, Illinois patrol officer/detective, a U.S. Border Patrol agent, a U.S. Customs patrol officer and special agent, an IRS Internal Security Branch inspector, and an FBI special agent. Agent Marrocco is a certified police instructor with the FBI and the Illinois State Police Training Board. He currently works as a police trainer for North East Multi-Regional Training (NEMRT), as a police instructor and site supervisor, and is an instructor of criminal justice at Triton College and the College of DuPage.

Handling Media Relations as a Law Enforcement Officer

"During my career with the U.S. Marshals Service, I have worked with a myriad of different media outlets, including print, television, and radio. Each outlet reaches out to different factions of the public and provides a beneficial way for law enforcement agencies to convey their message and give the public some insight as to the mission, goals, initiatives, and projects of your agency.

This is why, in my opinion, it is extremely important to establish a relationship with your media contacts prior to an event. I have found that meeting with these individuals in an informal setting (lunch, informal meeting at your office space) gives you an opportunity to give them some background on your agency, lets them meet management officials who they may deal with on a future media event, and puts both parties more at ease.

Law enforcement agencies are typically intimidated, to some degree, by the media. There is a perception that the media are 'out to get them,' when this couldn't be farther from the truth. The media, like law enforcement agencies, have a job to do. Working with them will allow your agency to be portrayed in the best possible light, regardless of the situation. Many public information officers working for law enforcement departments have only worked with the media in a self-promoting capacity. What I mean by this is that they deal with the media via a press release when a felon is captured, when a department has finished renovating their jail facility, or when they have participated in a community service function. This is important and helps to establish the relationship for when a situation arises that requires you, as a representative of your department, to deal with the media on news that may reflect negatively on your agency. In this case, although it is sometimes difficult to believe, the media can act as your friend. It allows you to get the truthful message about the situation out to the public on YOUR terms. Should you choose to say 'no comment' or not return phone calls, rest assured the media will find someone to give them answers—and remember, they still have their job to do. Here are some pointers to get you through a sticky situation:

- Never say 'no comment.' The media will seek out someone who will give them a comment, probably someone who has no business speaking to the issue at hand.
- Feed the media and learn an eloquent way of saying nothing: In some cases, the media realizes that you will not be able

(Continued)

to comment on an ongoing investigation, cannot divulge sensitive material, etc. Then ask them what they are looking for! Explain under what parameters you can comment and what you cannot, and try and help them do their job in the best way possible. For example, if the question regards an employee who is under investigation for misconduct and your department precludes you from commenting on the investigation, give the media a comment such as, 'At this time, we are looking into the allegations of misconduct against our employee. We can assure you that should these allegations prove true, we will follow our guidelines and procedures to ensure that the employee is held accountable and that the conduct is not repeated by anyone within our department.' The media is satisfied, as they got their quote, and you have not divulged any sensitive materials and have actually stated the obvious. However, your agency is not avoiding the media with a no comment statement. You are addressing them, giving them what they want, and allowing them to do their job.

- Specify who will be the spokesperson for your agency: It may seem obvious who the spokesperson for your agency is, but make sure you reiterate this to your employees, especially when the media event is a situation where you are not imparting good news to the public. The media, as we have stated before, will seek out their answers in an effort to do their job effectively. Therefore, consider the above question regarding misconduct. Should you not comment, not return their phone calls, and/or avoid them at all costs, be assured that if they see an employee on his way to lunch with your department insignia on his shirt, jacket, or hat, they will attempt to approach this person to see if they can gain some information. Although you may think, 'My employees know better,' sometimes the lure of getting their name in print, voice on the air, or face on the screen can be too tempting to an untrained media officer. And, if not careful, you could end up working double time to keep up with the media inquiries about the event while also trying to overcome the damage one of your officers has done by 'harmlessly' speaking to the media.

- Control the interview: Remember, the media want something from YOU. With this in mind, you should control the setting, type of questions asked, length of interview, and person who can best speak for your agency given the situation.

- Communicate with the media: For events/situations whose media coverage may be lengthy, make sure you communicate to them when you will provide them information, in what format it will be (press release, press conference, press statement, etc.). If they know that every day at the same time you will be giving them information, it will prevent them from calling incessantly to find out when they can get it.

- Make it easy on yourself: For events that may span a few days, a few weeks, or a few months, create a media operations plan. Consider actions like posting your press releases/statements to your department's website and letting the media know to check there for updates. This will allow you to avoid faxing hundreds of copies all over (especially in national/international events). Also consider dedicating a spare cell phone within your department to the media for inquiries. This way if you are tied up, you can delegate the media inquiries to one person on one phone. Also, after this event is over, you probably do not want hundreds of media outlets having access to your own cell phone number.

- Work with your department management: Consider being proactive and working with your management on mock scenarios. Pose questions to them that they may

(Continued)

encounter during a media event. Let them know that you are there to support them and that your responsibility includes terminating a press conference/interview, etc., should the direction of the interview turn and not allow your agency to convey their message in the best possible light. As many of your department heads may not have had media training, educate them on what your department's media policy is with regards to what can or cannot be released. For example, the techniques that are used by your officers to locate wanted subjects, your internal policies with regard to discipline, etc. These can be agency sensitive and could impact the situation negatively if released to the public.

- Separate for yourself the key information about the situation: Although some may disagree, I have always tried to be informed of the basic information and not detailed particulars about an investigation. This eliminates the potential to slip during an interview, and also to be labeled as a leak should information somehow get released to the press. You don't really need to know all the details, just enough to provide general information to the public.

- Get an understudy: Should you be on vacation, leave, or unable to handle the press inquiries at the time of your event, you need to have someone available to step in and handle the situation. Be proactive and find or provide training to this individual. Make sure your management is comfortable working with this person and that, when discussing press-related matters as they relate to your agency, this person is always included so he or she is prepared in the event of your absence during a critical event.

- Don't forget your foreign language media outlets: Foreign language media outlets can reach a key part of the population that the mainstream media outlets do not. If you have language issues with these media outlets, try to solicit assistance from other law enforcement officers or agencies to aid you as an interpreter. You will find that a lot of foreign language media feel ignored in events that have both a positive and potential negative impact on your agency. By working with them to ensure that that information is put forward to their readers/viewers/listeners, they may become some of your biggest allies.

These tips have helped me successfully navigate the 'media jungle' through good times and bad. I hope that you are able to take some of these tips and use them within your own respective departments. The public's perception of law enforcement is occasionally molded by their personal experiences. In some cases this may be a trooper writing them a traffic ticket, a family member detained by law enforcement on an investigative matter, or what they have seen on television shows. Use the media to convey to the public YOUR department's message. Good luck!" **Supervisory Inspector Shannon M. Robinson, United States Marshals Service**

Supervisory Inspector Robinson is with the U.S. Marshals Service, Investigative Operations Division. She has served with the Marshals Service for 15 years. She is the public affairs officer for the U.S. Marshals Service in both Northern Indiana and Northern Illinois. Inspector Robinson served as National Spokesperson for the U.S. Marshals Service during the murder of the family of Judge Joan Lefkow, which occurred in Chicago in 2005. This was one of the largest media events in U.S. Marshals Service history. She has served as a U.S. Marshals Service instructor in the area of public relations, and has taught classes on the lessons learned during the Lefkow investigation in foreign countries. Inspector Robinson previously worked as a journalist for the State-Journal Register *in Chicago.*

"Throughout my 30-plus year career in law enforcement, I have seen the effects that the media, particularly TV and the movies, have had upon

(*Continued*)

law enforcement and the image officers convey. It never ceased to amaze me how easily the fictional world could influence the actual mannerisms and behaviors of real law enforcement personnel.

I had never heard the term *perps* used except on TV and in movies, and then all of sudden many of the young officers are using the term.

Early on in my career, Clint Eastwood came out with the *Dirty Harry* movies, and the sale of Smith and Wesson .44 magnums went through the roof, with many officers opting to carry the latest hand cannon. Whether it was to intimidate or imitate, I am not sure, but officers were influenced by the image they saw on the screen.

Some of the images we see are very dark and cynical and can tend to influence our behavior. It is believed that what works on TV must work in real life. This is a false assumption made by a few. In the world of TV and movies, the police hunker down and take an 'us against them' mentality, and this has carried over to real life. Both law enforcement and the general public see TV, movies, and the media as actual lifelike representations of how we are to behave.

When working undercover, some of the suspects I encountered had Hollywood ideas as to how a true criminal looked and behaved, and on occasion you had to play the part. Our life was mimicking the art form." **Federal Bureau of Investigation Agent (Retired) Francis Marrocco**

CHAPTER 2

LEGAL GUIDELINES IN LAW ENFORCEMENT/ MEDIA COMMUNICATION

FIRST AMENDMENT

"Congress shall make no law respecting an establishment of religion, or prohibiting the free exercise thereof; or abridging the freedom of speech, or of the press; or the right of the people peaceably to assemble, and to petition the Government for a redress of grievances."[17]

SIXTH AMENDMENT

"In all criminal prosecutions, the accused shall enjoy the right to a speedy and public trial, by an impartial jury of the State and district wherein the crime shall have been committed, which district shall have been previously ascertained by law, and to be informed of the nature and cause of the accusation; to be confronted with the witnesses against him; to have compulsory process for obtaining witnesses in his favor, and to have the Assistance of Counsel for his defense."[18]

THE LANDMARK CASE OF DR. SAM SHEPPARD[19]

The case of Dr. Sam Sheppard is an example of how pretrial publicity can negatively impact a trial. Dr. Sheppard was charged in Ohio with murdering his wife, Marilyn Sheppard, in July of 1954. Dr. Sheppard, represented by F. Lee Bailey, had his conviction overturned. The case provided the foundation for the television show and later the movie *The Fugitive*.

Marilyn Sheppard was bludgeoned to death on July 4, 1954. From the outset officials focused suspicion on Dr. Sheppard, who was arrested on a murder charge on July 30 and indicted August 17. His trial began October 18 and terminated with his conviction on December 21, 1954. During the entire pretrial period, virulent and incriminating publicity about the accused and the murder made the case notorious, and the news media frequently aired charges and countercharges besides those for which the accused was tried.

Three months before trial, he was examined for more than five hours without counsel in a televised three-day inquest conducted before an audience of several hundred spectators in a gymnasium. Over the three weeks before trial, newspapers published the names and addresses of prospective jurors, causing them to receive letters and telephone calls about the case. The trial began two weeks before a hotly contested election in which the chief prosecutor and the trial judge were candidates for judgeships. Newsmen were allowed to take over almost the entire small courtroom, hounding the accused and most of the participants. Twenty reporters were assigned seats by the court within the bar and in close proximity to the jury and counsel, precluding privacy between the accused and his counsel. The movement of the reporters in the courtroom caused frequent confusion and disrupted the trial, and in the corridors and elsewhere in and around the courthouse they were allowed free rein by the trial judge. A broadcasting station was assigned space next to the jury room.

Before the jurors began deliberations, they were not sequestered and had access to all news media, though the court made "suggestions" and "requests" that the jurors not expose themselves to comment about the case. Though they were sequestered during the five days and four nights of their deliberations, the jurors were allowed to make inadequately supervised telephone calls during that period.

Pervasive publicity was given to the case throughout the trial, much of it involving incriminating matter not introduced at the trial, and the jurors were thrust into the role of celebrities. At least some of the publicity deluge reached the jurors. At the very inception of the proceedings, the trial judge announced that neither he nor anyone else could restrict the prejudicial news accounts. Despite his awareness of the excessive pre-trial publicity, the trial judge failed to take effective measures against the massive publicity, which continued throughout the trial, or to take adequate steps to control the conduct of the trial.

The United States Supreme Court later held that the massive, pervasive, and prejudicial publicity attending Sheppard's prosecution prevented him from receiving a fair trial consistent with the due process clause of the 14th Amendment.

The Court also held that though freedom of discussion should be given the widest range compatible with the fair and orderly administration of justice, it must not be allowed to divert a trial from its purpose of adjudicating controversies according to legal procedures based on evidence received only in open court.

The Supreme Court further held that the trial court failed to invoke procedures which would have guaranteed the accused a fair trial, such as adopting stricter rules for use of the courtroom by newsmen as the defense counsel requested, limiting their number, and more closely supervising their courtroom conduct. The court should also have insulated the witnesses; controlled the release of leads, information, and gossip to the press by police officers, witnesses, and counsel; proscribed extrajudicial statements by any lawyer, witness, party, or court official divulging prejudicial matters; and requested the appropriate city and county officials to regulate release of information by their employees.[20]

CHANGE OF VENUE

The trial of a criminal offender will take place in the jurisdiction in which the offense was either wholly or partly committed.[21] While the exact laws vary from jurisdiction to jurisdiction, state to state, the prosecution or the defendant may make a motion for a change of the place of trial on the ground that there exists in the jurisdiction in which the charge is pending such a prejudice against him on the part of the inhabitants that he cannot receive a fair trial in that jurisdiction.[22] The court shall conduct a hearing and determine the merits of the motion.[23] If the court determines that there exists in the jurisdiction where the prosecution is pending such prejudice against the defendant that he cannot receive a fair trial, it shall transfer the cause to a jurisdiction where a fair trial may be had.[24]

The burden is on the defendant to show that the alleged prejudice actually exists and that by reason thereof, there is a reasonable apprehension that he cannot receive a fair trial.[25] The fact that there is potentially harmful publicity within a community does not by itself establish proof of community prejudice, as each case must be judged on its own facts.[26]

Exposure to publicity about a case is not enough to demonstrate prejudice because jurors need not be totally ignorant of the facts and issues involved in a case. Crimes, especially heinous crimes, are of great public interest and are extensively reported. It is unreasonable to expect that individuals of average intelligence and at least average interest in their community would not have heard of any of the cases that they might be called upon to judge in court. A juror must, however, be capable of disregarding his or her impressions or opinions and decide the case based solely upon the evidence presented in court.[27] Total ignorance of the case is exceptional and is not required.[28] What is required is the assurance that a juror will be able to set aside all information he or she has acquired outside the courtroom, along with any opinions formed, and decide the case strictly on the evidence as presented in the courtroom.[29]

RELEASE OF INFORMATION BY LAW ENFORCEMENT AGENCIES

Law enforcement officers and agencies should not exercise their custodial authority over an accused individual in a manner that is likely to result in either: 1) the deliberate exposure of a person in custody for the purpose of photographing or televising by representatives of the news media or 2) the interviewing by representatives of the news media of a person in custody except upon request or consent by that person to an interview after being informed adequately of the right to consult with counsel and of the right to refuse to grant an interview.[30]

EXTRAJUDICIAL STATEMENTS BY ATTORNEYS

Criminal procedure is often divided into two parts. First, there is the investigative stage, which leads up to the arrest and charging of the case. Once the case is brought into the courtroom, there is the adjudicative stage of criminal procedure. In this second part, the investigation still continues, but the media focus often shifts from the police to the attorneys involved in the case. In a police-related matter, involved attorneys may include the defense attorney, the prosecution, and perhaps civil attorneys.

In some instances, the attorneys' interests may coincide with that of the police. In others, they may be in direct contrast. Nonetheless, attorneys are also bound by laws and ethical standards of what information they can and cannot release to media and what they can and cannot talk about. Violations of these rules can lead to challenges on the credibility of evidence, evidence not being admitted, acquittal, mistrial, changes in venue, sanctions against attorneys, and the loss of one's license to practice law.

A lawyer should not make or authorize the making of an extrajudicial statement that a reasonable person would expect to be disseminated by means of public communication if the lawyer knows or reasonably should know that it will have a substantial likelihood of prejudicing a criminal proceeding. Statements relating to the following matters are ordinarily likely to have a substantial likelihood of prejudicing a criminal proceeding: 1) the prior criminal record (including arrests, indictments, or other charges of crime) of a suspect or defendant; 2) the character or reputation of a suspect or defendant; 3) the opinion of the lawyer on the guilt of the defendant, the merits of the case, or the merits of the evidence in the case; 4) the existence or contents of any confession, admission, or statement given by the accused or the refusal or failure of the accused to make a statement; 5) the performance of any examinations or tests, or the accused's refusal or failure to submit to an examination or test, or the identity or nature of physical evidence expected to be presented; 6) the identity, expected testimony, criminal record, or credibility of prospective witnesses; 7) the possibility of a plea of guilty to the offense charged, or other disposition; and 8) information which the lawyer knows or has reason to know would be inadmissible as evidence in a trial.

Statements relating to the following matters may be made: 1) the general nature of the charges against the accused, provided that there is included therein a statement explaining that the charge is merely an accusation and that the defendant is presumed innocent until and unless proven guilty; 2) the general nature of the defense to the charges or to other public accusations against the accused, including that the accused has no prior criminal record; 3) a request for assistance in obtaining evidence; 4) information necessary to aid in the apprehension of the accused or to warn the public of any dangers that may exist; 5) the existence of an investigation in progress, including the general length and scope of the investigation, the charge or defense involved, and the identity of the investigating officer or agency; 6) the facts and circumstances of an arrest, including the time and place and the identity of the arresting officer or agency; 7) the identity of the victim, where the release of that information is not otherwise prohibited by law or would not be harmful to the victim; 8) information contained within a public record, without further comment; and 9) the scheduling or result of any stage in the judicial process.

GAG ORDERS

Gag orders are court orders issued by a judge. In a criminal case, these orders can prohibit anyone with any involvement in the case from speaking with the media. This may include the police and the prosecution, courtroom personnel, witnesses and their agents, attorneys, spokespersons, and also the defense. Those subject to the gag order may be forbidden from commenting or discussing subject matter of a case with agents and employees of the media, including but not limited to newspapers, magazines, television, radio, and Internet media sources.

Such orders are only given in the most extreme cases, where the fair trial rights of the defendant or the government are likely to be unfairly prejudiced by pretrial publicity and cannot be adequately protected by less restrictive alternatives. This is not a form of censorship, such orders do not act as a bar on the media covering the incident, but only prevents the involved parties from speaking about the incident publicly. Absent a clear and present danger to the fairness of a trial or other compelling interest, no rule of court or judicial order should be promulgated that prohibits representatives of the news media from broadcasting or publishing any information in their possession relating to a criminal case.[31]

Gag orders are most often issued by a court in cases that have gained widespread media coverage and publicity. A gag order was granted several days before the 2008 criminal trial of a 24-year-old woman who was charged with running a stop sign and crashing a van into a school bus in Minnesota, killing 4 and injuring 16. The judge stated, "The court is well aware of the extensive publicity that has surrounded this case." The judge cited statements by both the state and defense to the media. The judge further stated, "At this critical juncture, on the eve of the jury trial, the balance between allowing state and defense commentary about the case must necessarily shift to the necessity of selecting a fair and impartial jury required by our constitution." In that case, the judge ordered all "attorneys, parties, witnesses, jurors, employees, and officers of the court" to refrain from making any statements about the case outside of the courtroom.[32]

MEDIA AND SEARCH WARRANTS

The United States Supreme Court has held it is unconstitutional to allow reporters and photographers to come along when police exercise search or arrest warrants in a home, and it has unanimously ruled that the officers may be sued for violating the constitutional protection against unreasonable searches.[33]

In a unanimous opinion, Chief Justice Rehnquist wrote, "We hold that is a violation of the Fourth Amendment for police to bring members of the media or other third parties into a home during the execution of a warrant when the presence of the third parties in the home was not in aid of the execution of the warrant." Thus, ride-alongs are constitutional, but bringing the media onto private property while executing a warrant is unconstitutional and will subject the officers and their department to liabilities.

RELEASING THE NAMES OF JUVENILES

Many states forbid the releasing of names of juveniles, except those who are charged as adults. The charging of a juvenile as an adult for a crime is a rarity, and usually it is only done in violent crimes such as murder or rape. Most states forbid the media and the public to have access to juvenile criminal records. Some states do allow the media and public to access the records for violent offenses or offenses that would be felonies if the offender were an adult.

WHAT THE PROS SAY

"Due process requires that the accused receive a trial by an impartial jury free from outside influences. Given the pervasiveness of modern communications and the difficulty of erasing prejudicial publicity from the minds of the jurors, officers and lawyers need to be very careful when speaking with the press. As flattering as it may be to be sought out by the media and to have your comments quoted in the paper, remember that the story is not about you. Case in point—consider Mike Nifong, the Durham, North Carolina, District Attorney who prosecuted members of the Duke Lacrosse team for a rape that allegedly occurred on March 14, 2006. Mr. Nifong gave approximately 70 interviews in the first two weeks after the allegations were made public. He referred to the lacrosse team as a 'bunch of hooligans,' gave his personal opinion on the case stating, 'I am 100 percent sure that a rape occurred,' and questioned why the accused needed lawyers 'if they are so innocent.' It seemed that Mr. Nifong was more than willing to try the case in the press, a fact that may have been motivated by his contested primary election that was being held on May 2, 2006.

Following the election, numerous inconsistencies in the victim's allegations were revealed, including contradictory comments as to the number of attackers—at times she claimed that up to 20 individuals had assaulted her, and in other accounts, she alleged only 3 attackers. All charges in the rape prosecution were dismissed in April of 2007 for lack of evidence.

(Continued)

While the case was pending, charges were made that Mr. Nifong had conspired to withhold exculpatory DNA evidence in a report to the defense and that he had made misrepresentations to the court. In November of 2006, the North Carolina State Bar accused Mr. Nifong of violating numerous ethical provisions including the making of 'extrajudicial statements that the lawyer knows or reasonably should know will be disseminated by means of public communication and will have a substantial likelihood of materially prejudicing an adjudicative proceeding.' When asked for a comment by a reporter on his way into the ethics hearing, Mr. Nifong stated, 'I'll do my talking inside the courtroom.' If only he had taken that approach from the start.

On June 16, 2007, the North Carolina State Bar Disciplinary Committee voted to disbar Mr. Nifong, and he submitted his resignation as District Attorney two days later. In October of 2007, the three accused players filed federal lawsuits against Mr. Nifong and several members of the Durham Police Department. These suits are still pending as of the date of this publication." **Assistant State Attorney Patrick Coughlin**

Patrick Coughlin is a supervisor in the Cook County State Attorneys' Office. He specializes in long-term narcotic investigations and has worked on numerous local, state, and federal investigations into drug trafficking organizations. Patrick is a frequent lecturer to various law enforcement agencies in the Chicago area, and he is an adjunct instructor for Kaplan University.

CHAPTER 3

DEPARTMENTAL GUIDELINES AND POLICIES

In every police department, a spokesperson should be designated for media events and inquiries. This person should be someone reliable, trustworthy, and trained in media relations.

Reporters have goals, and during an interview there are certain things that they try to achieve.[34] They seek to understand complex issues, find the truth in times of controversy, ensure their story is contextually complete, get specific information, learn quickly all that can be learned on the issue and the topic at hand, and challenge the interviewee.[35] In an interview situation or a press conference, officers should establish certain rules and always abide by them. Press officers should always call a reporter back, even if they are not sure if there is anything they can say.[36] Never wing it, as this increases the chance that something other than your intended message will be read or viewed by the masses.[37] Do not hesitate to say "I do not know."[38] And if you do not know, say, "Let me get back to you," and mean it, and do get back to them.[39]

Always gather as much information as possible about the interview and the interviewer.[40] Find out what the topic is. Write objectives for your interview, and always plan ahead.[41] Prepare for possible questions, and think of answers for them. Practice your answers, including how you will bridge to your main points.[42]

When being interviewed, conduct yourself as a professional. Never say anything to a reporter that you would not feel comfortable having published on the front page of a newspaper or broadcast on the nightly news. Never assume anything is off the record. Keep your responses short and to the point.[43] Maintain eye contact. Dress appropriately—either in uniform, a suit, or business casual. Speak clearly, enunciate, and speak slowly enough to be understood. Speak in simple terms, using plain language. Do not attempt to use big words that are not part of everyday vocabulary. Be friendly, but not overly familiar. Remember that you represent your agency. Make them proud.

The Los Angeles Police Department is one of the largest police departments in the nation. They have a well-written media handbook for officers and members of the media. In it, police/media relations are discussed. Rules and regulations are laid out in depth. "The department views the media as an avenue by which to communicate with and educate the public on matters of importance. To accomplish this, the media must be given as much access as legitimately possible to assist them in their news gathering and reporting duties. When asked for information regarding a police matter, officers should decide if they possess sufficient facts and are qualified to respond, and whether the person asking is appropriately credentialed to receive the information. Officers should avoid representing their own opinions as facts."[44]

The Chicago Police Department's policy is "to cooperate impartially with the news media in providing information on crime and police-related matters while simultaneously conforming to the protections guaranteed to individuals under the U.S. Constitution."[45]

In most circumstances, an incident, crime scene, and accompanying command post will be closed to the media. The purpose of such constraints is to protect the integrity of the investigation and to ensure a safe, coordinated, and unrestricted response by law enforcement and other emergency personnel.[46] Limitations to the incident and crime scenes should be lifted as soon as the situation warrants.[47] News media will be permitted on a crime scene only after medical, forensic, and investigating personnel have completed their examinations of the crime scene, and any other legitimate police purpose is not compromised by the media presence.[48] Media access to a crime scene on private property will only be permitted after the owner or the owner's agent informs the police that the owner authorizes the media's presence.[49]

Do not establish artificial barriers limiting access to crime scenes.[50] Do not prevent the taking of pictures or interviews in public places.[51] News reporters may photograph or report anything or interview anyone they observe when legally present at an emergency scene. This includes officers, victims, and witnesses.[52]

WHAT THE PROS SAY

"In my law enforcement career, my experience with the press was often initially restricted, because the Illinois State Police had designated specific officers to be public informational officers. These were the officers who were authorized to speak to the press about newsworthy matters. As someone who devoted his career to the investigation of outlaw motorcycle gangs, their culture, and activities, I would often be contacted by the press, especially during times of intergang violence.

When I was contacted by the press about outlaw motorcycle gangs and related criminal activities, I would be required (under policy) to refer them to the Springfield, Illinois, State Police public information officer for the press to get their information. However, if the public information officer had no knowledge of outlaw motorcycle gangs and their criminal activities, I would be contacted back by the public information officer, who would request and allow me to give information to the press.

(Continued)

During some of my major criminal investigations, including some motorcycle gang bombing incidents, I found that by making my own press contacts in advance was to my advantage. In the 1980s, in Illinois, there were many federal and state investigations related to the outlaw motorcycle gangs. I found that I was able to identify specific investigative reporters from local newspapers and television who had good reputations and integrity, and I would give them exclusive information regarding breaking cases.

From what I have found, there are some members of the press who want to present valid information to the public and interesting articles and stories for their readers and viewers. However, there are also reporters that will hound the law enforcement community for information, even when it is not in the best interest of the case or the victim.

When I worked for both a Federal Gang Task Force and also for a Major Crimes Task Force, there was only one person from law enforcement that was assigned to brief the press. My experience was that I would still be contacted and questioned by members of the press because of my knowledge of motorcycle gangs, regarding the cases we worked on, because the cases were high profile and in the press daily. What I would do would be to direct the press to the designated officer, only timely and valid information would be released, and there were no sources who 'would not be named and would not be identified for a particular report or case.'

Officers should remember this: the press is NOT the enemy and should not be treated with disrespect. On the contrary, a mutually respectful relationship is beneficial to everyone." **Sergeant (Retired) Joe J. Santercier, Illinois State Police, Motorcycle Gang Investigator**

Sergeant Santercier retired from the Illinois State Police in 1996. He has worked criminal investigations, narcotics, and organized crime. He has worked numerous high-level motorcycle and organized crime investigations. He was an instructor at the Illinois State Police Academy, instructing on motorcycle gangs and narcotics investigations. He has testi-fied as an expert witness in numerous cases in state and federal court as a motorcycle gang expert and is regarded as one of the nation's leading motorcycle gang experts. Sergeant Santercier retired from the Illinois State Police in 1996 and is currently a program manager for special projects at North East Multi-Regional Training (NEMRT), which conducts law enforcement training for police agencies in Northern Illinois.

"Officers must be aware of their departmental policy on talking to the media. Officers should also be aware of state laws regarding media coverage. Certain comments, in a criminal case, when made by the government, may lead to a defense motion for a change of venue. This is a motion in which the defendant alleges that due to the media coverage or comments made, he is unable to get a fair trial in that jurisdiction."
Assistant State Attorney Arunas Buntinas

Arunas Buntinas is a 12-year veteran prosecutor with the Cook County State Attorney's Office who is assigned to the Gang Crimes Unit. He has handled hundreds of murder cases and tried numerous bench and jury trials. He is a graduate of the National District Attorney's Association career prosecutor's course, a member of the Capital Litigation Trial Bar (lead counsel), and a member of the United States Supreme Court Trial Bar.

CHAPTER 4

TO SHARE OR NOT TO SHARE?

A police department needs to have a well-written and clearly defined policy for dealing with the media. It must be clear what information can and cannot be publicly disclosed. For purposes of this chapter, we will focus primarily on and examine the media policies of two departments with long histories of dealings with the media, the Chicago Police Department and the Los Angeles Police Department.

The Los Angeles Police Department's Media Relations Handbook states that:

> When an event being investigated is so spectacular or unusual in nature as to stimulate general community interest, the news media may be notified. An Area commanding officer may make such notifications, however, Media Relations Section personnel may assume responsibility for releasing information regarding events of major proportions.[53]

Los Angeles allows the following information to be provided upon request, unless the information would endanger the successful completion of an investigation or a related investigation, or would endanger the safety of a person involved in the incident:

- Arrestee's full name (except juveniles)
- Area of residence and occupation

- Physical description, age, sex, and descent
- Time, date, location of arrest
- Factual circumstances, such as time and location; resistance by subject; pursuit necessary to arrest; use of weapons by subject; use of force by officers; identity of arresting/investigating officer; limited description of evidence; the nature, substance, and text of charge; and any request for assistance from the public
- Amount of bail and location held
- All charges including warrants
- Parole or probation holds[54]

The Los Angeles Police Department's policy is that "the name of a victim of any crime . . . may be withheld at the victim's request, or at the request of the victim's parent(s) or guardian if the victim is a minor."[55]

The following is nonreleasable information; according to the Los Angeles Police:

- The identity of the suspect prior to arrest
- The results of the investigation prior to arrest, unless release of the information will:
    ◦ Aid in the investigation
    ◦ Assist in the apprehension of the suspect(s)
    ◦ Warn the public of danger
- Employee/personnel matters
- Prior criminal record, reputation, or character of suspect
- Confession or existence of a confession
- Any photograph or mug shots unless:
    ◦ The release will aid in arrest
    ◦ The release will aid in investigation

- The release will warn public of danger
- The arrestee has been booked for a particular crime
- Identity or any personal information regarding a juvenile arrestee or suspect without permission from a juvenile court
- The identity, credibility, or testimony of prospective witnesses
  - Any personal opinion as to the suspect's guilt, innocence, or merits of the case
  - Any information known to be inadmissible in court
  - Results of investigative procedures (e.g., fingerprints, polygraph tests, or ballistic tests)[56]

The Chicago Police Department allows the following information to be disseminated for an accused adult who is in custody and has been charged on a signed complaint or is wanted on an arrest warrant issued by a judge:

- The accused's name, age, address, and occupation
- The time, place, and reason for the arrest
- The nature, substance, and text of the charge
- The scheduling or result of any step in the judicial proceedings
- Any information to aid in the apprehension of the accused or to warn the public of any dangers that the accused may present
- Requests by the department for assistance in obtaining witnesses or evidence
- Convictions that were part of criminal histories
- A request for an arrestee identification photograph
- General crime and news information[57] (except that which is prohibited or limited by their departmental orders and policies)

The Chicago Police Department may release the following information:

- The identity of a crime victim will be released . . . except when the release of such information may endanger the victim's life or physical safety.
- The name of the deceased person may be given to the news media only after the next of kin has been notified and their consent obtained.
- Information concerning physical evidence will be released only with the approval of the detective division commander in charge of the investigation. If necessary, the state attorney's office may be contacted for further guidance.
- No photo of an officer under investigation shall be made available to the media prior to a conviction for a criminal offense or prior to a decision being rendered by the Police Board.[58]

The following information may be released in any incident where the accused adult or victim is incapacitated or refuses to have any personal information released:

- General description of the incident
- Gender of the injured
- Age of the injured
- Hospital where the injured has been transported
- General medical condition of the injured, e.g., conscious, unconscious[59]

The Chicago Police Department disallows the following information from being released to the news media:

- The identity or addresses of witnesses or cooperating individuals, or specific information from their oral or written statements that could reasonably be used to identify them or endanger their lives or physical safety

- The names or addresses of sex-crime victims

- Juvenile records or information that will identify juvenile victims, offenders, or arrestees, including those charged as adults

- The content of any confession, statement, or admission[60]

Staging the movement of an arrestee for the sole purpose of allowing the arrestee to be photographed or videotaped by the news media is prohibited.[61] Medical information of victims, witnesses, and offenders should be treated as confidential. Disclosure of such confidential medical information may result in legal sanctions and disciplinary action by the department.[62]

In short, most departments with well-written and clearly defined policies allow the factual circumstances of an incident to be released. Court and bond information and criminal charges can be released to the media. Officers are prohibited from speaking about their personal opinions as to guilt, innocence, or the merits of the case.

Occasionally, police will be called on to comment on unfavorable or negative press. In order to maintain a reputation for openness, credibility, and accessibility, even in the face of an uncomfortable situation, here are certain guidelines to follow:

- Do not change press policy in mid-incident.

- Tell the truth, and then move on.

- Do not make bad news bigger than it really is.

- Attempt to convey an attitude of "business as usual."

- Stay calm and collected in your responses.

- Emphasize the silver lining.[63]

Departments should never use the following responses:

- Refuse to talk to the press at all (While there may be many details that you should not and cannot talk about, a refusal to talk is a very bad idea.)
- Lie
- Get mad
- Plead ignorance
- Dribble out as little information as you can, and as slowly as you can
- Pass the buck to someone else[64]

Many departments, such as the Chicago Police Department, have restrictions on their members participating in media interviews when acting as a nonrepresentatives of the department. Such restrictions can include participation during off-duty hours and not conducting the interview at a police facility. Department members should preface any comments with a clear prelude that the statement about to be made is a personal viewpoint and is not representative of the department's position. The member should not appear in uniform or wear any department insignia or item.[65] Examples of a police department member acting as a nonrepresentative of the department when engaging in media activities can include political activities, hobbies, and work associated with off-duty jobs.

Case Study: "Born to Raise Hell": Richard Speck and Change of Venue

Convicted mass-murderer Richard Speck was born on December 6, 1941, in Monmouth, Illinois.[66] He was raised in Texas by his mother and stepfather.[67] He was a poor student and began to suffer from alcoholism at an early age. His early life was marked by dropping out of school, sporadic employment, and frequent arrests. When he was 19, he had "Born to Raise Hell" tattooed on his arm.[68]

Speck had led a criminal lifestyle, having been arrested for stabbing, drunkenness, trespassing, and as a suspect in rape and murder before the fatal dates of July 13–14 of 1966.[69] On that horrific occasion, Speck murdered eight student nurses, a crime for which he would be convicted and sentenced to death.

The crime generated enormous media attention. It stunned the police, the public, and the news media. The crime was dubbed "The Crime of the Century,"[70] as other crimes have been both before and after. The sheer savagery and randomness of the crime, combined with the innocence of the victims, shocked not only Chicagoans, but people across the country. "Before July 14 of 1966, none of us comprehended the possibilities of random violence of this magnitude," said William "Bill" Martin, a legendary attorney who prosecuted the case. "And it shattered a lot of illusions we had about safety and security. No one would have believed before we heard about this mass murder that one man could be capable of taking helpless victims one by one and stabbing and strangling them. Sadly, after that night of horror, we have become accustomed to it."[71]

Speck was even later referred to as the "Adam" of the phenomenon of making killers media icons for considerable profit. Other such killers included as John Wayne Gacy, Ted Bundy, Charles Manson, David "Son of Sam" Berkowitz, and Jeffrey Dahmer. One writer explained that what made Speck "the groundbreaking Adam" of this new form of human industry was his timing. In 1966, TV was on the rise and news magazines were in full flower, ready and able to take local crimes to a national audience. Speck, with his haunted pock-marked face, was the talk of the country.[72]

While the crime was committed in Chicago, it generated so much publicity that the defense attorneys who represented Speck requested, and were granted, a motion for a change of venue. In other words, the case would be tried in a different jurisdiction than where it occurred. Such motions by defense counsel are somewhat uncommon, and they are rarely granted. Speck's trial was eventually heard in Peoria.

At trial, the facts of the case came out through the evidence. In the summer of 1966, Speck was working as merchant marine. Unemployed, but looking for work,[73] he had been drinking heavily that night and was in the middle of a drinking binge. At 11:00 P.M. on the night of July 13, 1966, Speck broke into a townhouse at 2319 East 100th Street, on the Southeast Side of Chicago, which was being used as a dormitory for student nurses. Armed with a knife, Speck proceeded to terrorize, rape, torture, and kill eight women. The victims died of strangulation and stab wounds.[74] The victims of Speck's mass murder were Pamela Wilkening, Gloria Jean Davy, Suzanne Bridget Farris, Mary Ann Jordan, Nina Jo Schmale, Patricia Matusek, Valentina Pasion, and Merlita Gargullo.[75] Speck also sexually assaulted one of his victims.[76] There was one survivor to Speck's terror. That woman, Cora (Corazon) Amurao, escaped, hiding under a bed while Speck was out of the room with one of his victims.

Local residents were awakened by the screams of Corazon Amurao, who hid under the bed until 6:00 A.M., and then screamed from the second floor window, "Help me! Help me! Everyone is dead . . . Oh God . . . He's killed them all!"[77]

The police were able to match a smudged fingerprint that was found at the murder scene to another provided by the FBI, which belonged to Richard Speck. Another Speck fingerprint was found on the door at the scene.[78] By 11:00 A.M. on July 14, police had his name and a photograph from the Coast Guard. Newspapers named Speck, ran his photo, and described his tattoos.[79] Corazon Amurao, the surviving witness, had been able to provide a key piece of evidence to the police, telling them that the offender had a tattoo reading "Born to Raise Hell" on his arm.

Two days after the murders, Speck was identified by a one-eyed drifter named Claude Lunsford. Speck, Lunsford, and another man had been drinking the evening of July 15 on the fire escape of the Starr Hotel at 617 W. Madison, in Chicago.[80] On July 16, Lunsford recognized a sketch of the murderer in the evening paper and phoned the police at 9:30 P.M. after finding Speck in his (Lunsford's) room at the Starr Hotel. The police, however, did not respond to the call, even though their records showed it had been made.

On July 16, Speck attempted suicide,[81] and the Starr Hotel desk clerk phoned in the emergency around midnight. Speck, who was not recognized by the police, was taken to Cook County Hospital at 2:30 A.M. on July 17. At the hospital, Speck was recognized by Dr. LeRoy Smith, a 25-year-old surgical resident physician, who had read about the "Born to Raise Hell" tattoo in a newspaper story.[82] The police were called and Speck was arrested.[83]

Then Chicago Police Superintendent O. W. Wilson held a press conference without the knowledge of the state attorney's office and announced that Speck was the killer, based on fingerprint evidence recovered at the scene.[84] Wilson insisted that only Speck could have done the crime and was criticized by some legal authorities as "hanging the suspect" without a fair trial.[85] Because of this pretrial statement, Gerald W. Getty, Richard Speck's public defender, asked for a change of venue and put on a three-day hearing to support his request. The request was granted without objection from the prosecution.[86]

Speck's jury trial began April 3, 1967, in Peoria, Illinois, a city three hours southwest of Chicago, with a gag order on the press. At trial, Speck was dramatically identified in court by the sole surviving student nurse, Cora Amurao. When Amurao was asked if she could identify the killer of her fellow students, Amurao rose from her seat in the witness box, walked directly in front of Speck and pointed her finger at him, nearly touching him, and said, "This is the man."[87]

Lieutenant Emil Giese of the Chicago Police Department testified regarding the fingerprints which were matched, providing scientific evidence for conviction. Along with Amurao's testimony, the evidence against Speck proved his guilt beyond a reasonable doubt.

On April 15, 1967, after deliberating only 49 minutes, the jury found Richard Speck guilty of eight counts of murder.[88] The jury recommended the death penalty. When later asked if Richard Speck had got a fair trial, Speck defense attorney, then the Cook County Public Defender Gerald W. Getty replied, "Absolutely."[89]

On June 5, Richard Speck was sentenced to death by Judge Herbert J. Paschen.[90] Speck was sentenced to die in the electric chair.[91] The Illinois Supreme Court affirmed Speck's death sentence in November of 1968.[92] In June of 1971, the United States Supreme Court reversed the affirmation, ruling potential jurors opposed to capital punishment in both Richard Speck's case and 41 other death penalty cases had been improperly excluded.[93] On September 20, 1972, the Illinois Supreme Court, following the U.S. Supreme Court's ruling, voided Richard Speck's death sentence.[94] On November 22, 1972, Richard Speck was sentenced to eight consecutive sentences of 50–150 years (400 to 1,200 years altogether).[95]

Speck's first opportunity for parole came up in 1976. He was denied parole.[96] In September of 1978, the Illinois Parole Board denied parole again and decided to review his case every three years rather than annually.[97] Subsequently, the board denied parole to Speck in 1981, 1984, 1987, and 1990.[98]

A change of venue for a jury trial is very rare. It usually only occurs in high publicity trials. The legal standard for a change of venue is that there can be extreme situations in which pretrial publicity is so pervasive that it is not curable by the most careful voir dire, which is also known as jury selection, so that a change of venue is a necessary remedy.[99]

Examples of high-profile cases with a change of venue include the 1992 trial of the four Los Angeles police officers in the Rodney King incident. This trial was moved outside Los Angeles County to Simi Valley in neighboring Ventura County. The defendants were found not guilty.

In the trial of Oklahoma City bomber Timothy McVeigh, the court granted a change of venue and ordered the case transferred from Oklahoma City to the U.S. District Court in Denver, Colorado, presided over by U.S. District Judge Richard Matsch. McVeigh was convicted by a jury and later sentenced to death. He was executed in Terre Haute, Indiana, in 2001.

In 1999, there was a change of venue in the murder case of Amadou Diallo, a case in which the defendants were members of the New York City Police Department. That trial was moved to Albany, and the defendants were found not guilty.

In the murder trial of serial killer John Wayne Gacy, a jury pool from outside of Cook County was brought in to decide the fate of Gacy.[100] The crimes for which Gacy was prosecuted occurred in Cook County. The trial, however, was heard in Chicago, Cook County, Illinois.

In the aftermath of his trial and sentencing, Speck took up painting, and to the shock of many, he was actually able to make money from his paintings. The families of his victims later sued and were successful in their attempts to stop Speck from making money on his prison paintings.[101] He was also known for making homemade hootch, or moonshine, alcohol fermented and distilled from old fruit.[102] In a 1978 interview from prison with columnist Bob Greene, Speck said, speaking on prison life: "I like hooch [moonshine] and I like speed. I don't like marijuana. I used to stay high on reds [barbiturates], but no more.

It's all right to get high on that stuff when you're young, but I'm 36 now. That's too old for reds."[103]

When interviewed by Greene, Speck spoke of letters received from women who wanted to visit him and develop romantic relationships with him. Speck also talked about refusing a prison job and being disciplined for the refusal: "They wanted me to work in the vegetable room. I wouldn't do it. A man's got to get up at 4:30 in the morning to work in the vegetable room. I don't like to get up that early."[104]

He showed little remorse about the murders: "If I had to do it over again, it would be a simple house burglary." He took pride in the prison code of silence: "You could kill a man in front of me, and I didn't see it. My back was turned." He said he did not consider himself to be a celebrity criminal like John Dillinger: "I'm not like Dillinger or anybody else. I'm freakish."[105]

He said he had a message for the American people: "Just tell 'em to keep up their hatred for me. I know it keeps up their morale. And I don't know what I'd do without it."[106]

Greene asked him if he was afraid he'd get in trouble with prison authorities for telling him that he had committed the murders, that he took drugs and drank liquor in his cell, that he had mail-ordered pornography and had it sent to Stateville. Speck laughed and said, "How am I going to get in trouble? I'm in here for 1,200 years."[107]

Due to the infamy of his crimes, Richard Speck always remained in the public eye, even when incarcerated. He became the subject of nightly news lead stories, an A&E network special, and meetings by Illinois lawmakers when home videos made in prison of Speck and other inmates surfaced.[108] Illinois corrections officials were called before a state legislative panel to answer questions about how closely they watched one of the nation's most notorious and infamous multiple killers.[109] The videos were made in an area and with equipment that was supposed to be used for Illinois Department of Corrections staff training.[110] The prison video showed Speck wearing women's underwear with female breasts due to hormone use. Speck engaged in oral sex with another inmate on tape and ingested what appeared to be powder cocaine.[111] Speck also flashed a roll of 100 dollar bills.[112]

When asked what it was like to kill and strangle someone, Speck remarked, "Strangle a person? It's not like what you see on TV . . . about three seconds and they're dead. You gotta go at it for about three and a half minutes . . . takes a lot of strength."

When asked how he felt about "killing all those ladies," Speck shrugged and said, "Like I always felt. Have no feeling. If you're asking if I felt sorry . . . no."[113] In admitting the killing, Speck broke his claim of drug-induced amnesia which made him unable to remember the murders.[114] When asked why he had killed the young nurses, he said, "It just wasn't their night," and then laughed.[115]

People were shocked at the way Speck, once sentenced to death and serving up to 1,200 years in prison, was living while incarcerated. Commenting on prison life, Speck said, "If they only knew how much fun I was having, they'd turn me loose."[116]

Richard Speck died of a heart attack in prison on December 5, 1991, the day before his 50th birthday.[117] But the case will forever be remembered. "The Speck case marked an end of innocence in the 20th century as far as the possibility of random, unprovoked mass murder," prosecutor Bill Martin said. "It was the first . . . Speck didn't know these women. There was no getting even. So it was totally unprovoked. I think people weren't that cautious about locking their doors and did not have a fear that a stranger would break into your home in the middle of the night and essentially for no reason at all."[118]

WHAT THE PROS SAY

"When a crime is committed that will be reported on by the media, descriptions of the offender(s) should be given, their crimes and offenses, along with their modus operandi, or MO. The MO is released so that someone with information might recognize the crime or the offenders and pass that information along to the police. Specific information about the crime should not be given out by the police, especially in a pre-arrest situation." **Assistant State Attorney Arunas Buntinas**

Off the Record

"When giving information to the media, particularly when dealing with an individual reporter, it is important to make sure you are in agreement as to what certain terms mean. In other words, be clear on definitions. For example, the phrase 'off the record' may mean one thing to you but another to the reporter. To some, 'off the record' means that nothing that is about to be said can be used in the story. To the reporter, it may mean the information can be used, but they may not reveal the source by using such phrases as 'a source close to the investigation' or 'a police department official who wished not to be identified.' However, be careful because one is treading on dangerous ground anytime the phrase 'off the record' is involved." **Chief Paul Rigsby, Nolensville, Tennessee**

"Officers should not be afraid to speak to the media. Know what the status of the investigation is. Prepare in advance before speaking. Understand what is off-limits to discuss. Know what you can talk about. Know what you cannot talk about. If you have questions about information that perhaps should not be disclosed, consult with prosecutors before speaking to the media. If you are speaking about a criminal case in the media, know the facts of the case. Statements that you make about the case can be used against you in court if there are any inconsistencies." **Assistant State Attorney Arunas Buntinas**

Relationships with the Media

"When dealing with members of the media, it is best to trust no one.

In law enforcement, there will always be conflicting relationships. Sometimes, when multiple law enforcement agencies are involved in a single investigation or multiple connected investigations, the agencies will have perspectives that are not identical to one another. That may even be true between police agencies and prosecutors. But, generally, these law enforcement agencies will have identical or similar goals. It is impossible for the media to share the perspective of the law enforcement officer. More importantly, the goals of the media are entirely inconsistent with the goals of law enforcement. The sole concern of the media is to broadcast or publicize a story; they are never concerned about the effect upon a criminal investigation or upon a criminal case.

Members of the media will seek out and cultivate relationships with members of law enforcement. The reason for this is obvious: to be able to gather information about an investigation before it is revealed publicly. They will gain the trust of the law enforcement officers by keeping promises to not publish information. Once that trust is established, the media will then make assurances in future incidents to publish information learned from the law enforcement officer without revealing the source of the information. In keeping such promises, the media again gains the trust of the law enforcement officer. This becomes a dangerous slippery slope. The goal, ultimately, is to strengthen the relationship to the point where the media can rely upon the law enforcement officer to reveal anything and everything about an investigation, without thinking twice. While this may seem relatively harmless, experienced law enforcement officers will be able to foresee a myriad of problems that could arise from information being publicized prematurely.

For example, if police have a suspect in custody, his identity should never be released to the media before charging. The media has access to resources that will enable them to learn personal information about the

(Continued)

suspect, even if they are only told of his name. The media is then liable to publicize the suspect's identity. If the suspect's identity, be it by name or appearance or otherwise, is publicized, potential witnesses may learn of his identity from the media. Any subsequent identification by such witnesses of that offender will be deemed as questionable, based upon those witnesses learning of the suspect's identity through the media, rather than from the incident itself.

The media will always make the argument that it is somehow fueling the right of the general public to have access to information. This, of course, is a silly, self-serving argument. No one in the general public would make the argument that he or she needs to *immediately* know all information regarding a criminal investigation, as it is learned by law enforcement. Any reasonable person would agree that the general public could wait to learn of details of a criminal investigation until such details can be released without potentially damaging the investigation. Only the media, in its desire to be the first to report a story, would make a contrary argument. For that reason, when dealing with members of the media, it is best to trust no one." **Assistant State Attorney Fabio Valentini**

Mr. Valentini is the supervisor of the Cook County State Attorney's Office Felony Review Unit. The Felony Review Unit is responsible for evaluating potential cases to be prosecuted in Cook County. Mr. Valentini has been a Cook County Assistant State Attorney for 17 years. He has tried hundreds of criminal trials, including nearly 100 jury trials and approximately 60 murder jury trials. He is an adjunct instructor for Kaplan University, where he teaches Criminal Law and procedure-related classes.

"When dealing with the press you have to keep in mind that the reporter sometimes has an interest in making the story as controversial as possible. It must be kept in mind that the reporter is competing to get his story in a profile spot. The more high-profile stories the reporter gets, the better assignments he receives in the future. I had one reporter during an interview tell me if I could come up with a better quote, he could get the story on the front page. With this in mind, some reporters are willing to take your words out of context to make the story more interesting. The simplest response could be switched out of context to mean something completely unintended." **Assistant State Attorney Joe Cataldo**

Assistant State Attorney Joe Cataldo is a first chair in the Felony Trial Division of the Cook County State Attorney's Office. He has tried over 50 jury trials, and over 25 murder trials. He is a member of the Capital Litigation Trial Bar. He is currently the chairman of the Chicago Bar Association Criminal Law Committee and serves on the Board of Directors for the John Marshall Law School Alumni Association.

"The media can be a blessing to the law enforcement community. They can provide real-time assistance in missing person cases, and they can provide invaluable aid in hunting for a fugitive. The media also can play a pivotal role in assisting the police during civil emergencies (e.g., riots, floods, fires, or other natural disasters). However, the goals of the media and the police are not always aligned. Sometimes, when dealing with the media, it is prudent to take the 'less is more' approach.

If it becomes necessary to deal with the media during a criminal investigation, I suggest the following approach: tread lightly, only discuss known facts, avoid hyperbole, and never discuss your opinions. It is a reporter's job to poke and prod in an effort to get as much information from you as possible. They are trained to do that and their editors expect it. However, the information a reporter seeks is often information that should not be in the public domain at that point in time. You should avoid feeling compelled to divulge too much. After all, there is a time and a place to publicly discuss all the steps that were taken in a particular investigation—the trial.

Well-crafted statements to the media serve two purposes. First, they can protect the integrity of an investigation. You never want your bad choice of words to undermine a criminal investigation or prosecution. Second, some prosecutions result in an acquittal. Others ultimately

(Continued)

lead to exoneration. When this occurs, civil lawsuits for defamation, false arrest, and malicious prosecution usually follow. If you end up as a defendant in a civil lawsuit, any statements that you made to the media certainly will be used against you in that proceeding. Therefore, curt, factual statements about an investigation can also insulate you from potential civil liability.

I want to share one more observation regarding how the police should view the media. A few years ago, I had a candid conversation with a well-respected reporter for one of the major Chicago daily newspapers. I asked him why the media is so critical of law enforcement. I also asked why his newspaper never prints human-interest stories about how hard police officers work and the good they bring to the communities they protect. His response was interesting and insightful. He said that every day, airplanes safely take off from and land at O'Hare Airport. The fact that this occurs is not newsworthy—it is expected. However, if a plane crashes, well . . . that is newsworthy!

I took his response to mean that the hard work police officers do every day is *expected* by the media, and thus, it is not newsworthy. But when a police officer is accused of abusing his/her authority or otherwise stepping out of line, well . . . that is newsworthy! So do what is expected, but try not to make yourself 'newsworthy.'" **Terrence J. "T. J." Sheahan**

Terrence J. Sheahan is a former prosecutor with the Cook County State Attorney's Office. He currently is a litigation partner at the Chicago law firm Freeborn & Peters LLP. In addition to working on a wide range of commercial litigation matters, Mr. Sheahan focuses his practice on class action litigation and civil rights defense. His experience includes cases relating to false arrest, malicious prosecution, wrongful conviction, defamation, conspiracy, municipal liability, and constitutional law.

CHAPTER 5

INTERACTING WITH THE MEDIA IN SEX CASES

For the purposes of this book, we will define rape as sexual penetration or touching and fondling for the sexual arousal of either the victim or the offender. This would include situations where the offender may touch the victim in a sexual way, but he is unable to become sexually aroused.[119]

Sex offenders are among the most dangerous and violent of criminals. Often, the crimes of rapists are serial in nature. That is, where there is one rape, there may be many. Investigation of rapes, especially stranger rapes, can sometimes focus on MO, or modus operandi. A rapist may select targets that are similar in age, appearance, location, or sex. Reaching out to the media in sex cases can help publicize not only the fact that there has been a sexual assault, but it also serves to alert the public and allows them to take safety precautions.

A description of the offender should be released to the media, including the sex of the offender, the race, the approximate age, the approximate height and weight, hair color, hairstyle, clothing, if a weapon was used, along with any other unusual physical characteristics. Depending on the circumstances, officers may want to release details about the type of car that the offender is driving. Keep in mind that the vehicle may be a crime scene, containing evidence of the sexual assault.

Officers should not release any information to the media that may cause the offender to destroy evidence of a crime, unless the good in releasing the information outweighs the benefits of keeping those aspects of the investigation secret.

Investigators should always keep certain pre-arrest and pre-charging details of the sexual assault and the investigation private. This is to ensure that the goals of the investigation are met. The police should not release information about the crime that victims, witnesses, or offenders could read in the newspaper or hear on television before they have spoken with the police. When that happens, and information is brought to the attention of police by someone with involvement in the case, then that information may be called into question and the defense can claim it is unreliable. The police should always withhold details of any criminal incident from the public so that when the police speak to victims, witnesses, and offenders, they can verify and corroborate that information.

Under no circumstances should the name, address, or any contact information of the victim be released to the media.

Case Study: Registered Sex Offenders and the Internet

The United States Supreme Court, in *Smith v. Doe*, 538 U.S. 84 (2003), stated that the posting of sex offenders' names and information on the Internet is constitutional. The Court held:

> [T]he stigma of Alaska's Megan's Law results not from public display for ridicule and shaming but from the dissemination of accurate information about a criminal record, most of which is already public. Our system does not treat dissemination of truthful information in furtherance of a legitimate governmental objective as punishment. On the contrary, our criminal law tradition insists on public indictment, public trial, and public imposition of sentence. Transparency is essential to maintaining public respect for the criminal justice system, ensuring its integrity, and protecting the rights of the accused. The publicity may cause adverse consequences for the convicted defendant, running from mild personal embarrassment to social ostracism. In contrast to the colonial shaming punishments, however, the State does not make the publicity and the resulting stigma an integral part of the objective of the regulatory scheme.
>
> The fact that Alaska posts the information on the Internet does not alter our conclusion. It must be acknowledged that notice of a criminal conviction subjects the offender to public shame, the humiliation increasing in proportion to the extent of the publicity. And the geographic reach of the Internet is greater than anything which could have been designed in colonial times. These facts do not render Internet notification punitive. The purpose and the principal effect of notification are to inform the public for its own safety, not to humiliate the offender. Widespread public access is necessary for the efficacy of the scheme, and the attendant humiliation is but a collateral consequence of a valid regulation.

> The State's website does not provide the public with means
> to shame the offender by, say, posting comments underneath
> his record. An individual seeking the information must take
> the initial step of going to the Department of Public Safety's
> website, proceed to the sex offender registry, and then look
> up the desired information. The process is more analogous
> to a visit to an official archive of criminal records than it
> is to a scheme forcing an offender to appear in public with
> some visible badge of past criminality. The Internet makes
> the document search more efficient, cost effective, and con-
> venient for Alaska's citizenry.[120]

Every one of the 50 states and the District of Columbia have sex
offender registration laws. Most jurisdictions currently publish lists of
registered sex offenders residing in that jurisdiction. As more police
departments make use of the Internet as a tool, there is easier public
access to this public information.

In Sapulpa, Oklahoma, Detective Sergeant Mike Heafner stated that
the online sex offender registry was the most visited area of the department's website.[121] Detective Sergeant Heafner told a newspaper, "I think
because of the situations with these types of crimes, where there are a lot
of child victims, a person ought to have the right to know where these
criminals live. They may have paid their debt to society, but good people
have the right to know where they are."[122] In Oklahoma, all convicted
sex offenders residing, working, or attending school in Oklahoma are
required to report their whereabouts. The Oklahoma Sex Offenders Registration Act requires that an offender report his full name, alias, date of
birth, sex, race, height, weight, eye color, Social Security number, driver's
license number, and home address. Police departments also keep public
records such as descriptions of the offenses, dates of the convictions, and
sentences imposed, along with where the offender is residing.[123]

In Bangor, Maine, Police Chief Ron Gastia told a public gathering, "We
can't protect everybody every minute of the day . . . So we encourage
people to get on the website. That's how you stay informed."[124] At the

same public forum, a Bangor detective also issued a public plea for assistance if they are aware of persons in violation of the sex offender registration laws and to see if new offenders have moved into their neighborhood, stating, "I encourage people to check the registry as frequently as possible because it's literally changing constantly."[125]

When interviewed about his department's registry, Washington, D.C., Police Chief Charles Ramsey stated, "The Sex Offender Registry is an important tool for keeping residents and other members of the community informed about the presence of sex offenders in their neighborhood." Chief Ramsey further stated that the registry "is not a cure-all to preventing sex offenses against children," but stated that he hoped that parents and guardians use the registry as an opportunity to talk with their children about sexual predators.[126]

Case Study: The Kobe Bryant Rape Case

In the summer of 2003, the future appeared very bright for National Basketball Association (NBA) superstar Kobe Bryant. He was 24, considered one of the best players in the world, and the new face of the NBA—the heir apparent to Michael Jordan as the most marketable and sought-after endorser of products. He had already played seven NBA seasons and was coming off of a season where he averaged a sensational 30 points per game. Playing for the Los Angeles Lakers, he teamed up with veteran star Shaquille O'Neal to form a seemingly unstoppable duo. He had huge contracts to act as a spokesman for Nike, McDonald's, and Sprite.[127] The Nike contract alone was for $40 million.[128]

On June 30, 2003, the day before he was scheduled to have what was expected to be a routine knee surgery in Vail, Colorado, Kobe Bryant checked into the Lodge & Spa at Cordillera near Edwards, Colorado.[129] The next day, a 19-year-old employee of the Lodge & Spa made a report to local sheriff's deputies that she had been sexually assaulted by Bryant and indicated that she wanted criminal charges brought against him.[130] The case quickly turned into a he said/she said scenario. The married Bryant initially denied having sex with the woman. He eventually admitted to adultery, but not to a rape. Bryant claimed the sex was consensual.

Bryant was later arrested and charged with rape. The criminal charges were eventually dismissed. Bryant settled a civil lawsuit with his accuser shortly thereafter.

When an offender is arrested in a rape case and goes to trial, he will often have one of two defenses. The first is that sex occurred between the two parties, but it was consensual sex. The second is that the victim was raped, but the offender was not the person that raped the victim. The first defense, consensual sex, will most often be used in cases where the offender and the victim know each other, where they have dated, where they have had previous sexual relationships, where there is a history of communication between the parties, where the offender may be well-known or a celebrity, where the victim is a prostitute, where there is DNA evidence, and where the victim has no injuries or did not resist. The second defense, someone else did it, will be the defense where the rape is a stranger rape, where there is no physical or DNA evidence, and where there is nothing to tie the offender to the victim.[131]

To many, it seemed impossible that Kobe Bryant, who had an all-American image, was good looking, had a beautiful wife, and was a multimillionaire many times over could have committed such a crime. *Newsweek* magazine printed: "It seemed impossible that the 24-year-old Los Angeles Laker, best known for his signature dunks and his mega-watt smile, could commit such a crime."[132]

Some of Bryant's own teammates indicated that Bryant was somewhat of an enigma. Rick Fox, a teammate, who was married to former Miss America and actor/singer Vanessa Williams, stated, "I think a lot of people never really got to know Kobe at all," and added that Bryant was hard to connect with and "kept to himself."[133] Teammates noted that Bryant preferred to dress and undress by himself and stay in his hotel room by himself after games instead of going out with his teammates. Bryant had married his wife, Vanessa, when she was an 18-year-old high school student, and they did not have any prenuptial agreement.[134] One teammate stated Bryant was "too goody-two-shoes to [stray from his wife] . . . but obviously we didn't know him as well as we thought."[135]

After the crime was reported to the police on July 1, the victim went to the hospital to get an exam on July 2. On July 4, 2003, the sheriff got the judge to issue an arrest warrant for Kobe Bryant.[136] Bryant flew from California, surrendered, and was released after posting a $25,000 bond.[137]

The detective who initially interviewed the accuser in the case later testified that he was told by her that Bryant "forced her to turn around, bent her over a chair, pulled her panties down and entered her from the rear." The encounter took five minutes, and the accuser stated she was crying as Bryant moaned, "I like Vail, Colorado."[138] When first confronted by the police, Kobe Bryant denied that he had sex with the woman. He told the media that he knew better than that. Within three weeks, however, Bryant admitted to being guilty of adultery, but innocent of rape.[139] Before the incident, Bryant had reportedly consulted with a divorce attorney, but after he admitted to adultery, Bryant gave his wife, who he had met when she was 16 and he was 21 and already an NBA star, a $4 million diamond ring.[140]

Investigators obtained a warrant for Bryant several days after the incident, after they had talked to the accuser and Bryant, but before any test results had been returned. Many critics feel this was a huge mistake in the investigation. The test results should have been examined before such a crucial decision was made; the results would play a key role in the decision of how to proceed with the case.

Jeralyn Merrit, a criminal defense attorney who was not involved in the Bryant case, but who was one of Timothy McVeigh's attorneys in the Oklahoma City Bombing case, later wrote online:

> If fault lays anywhere with the case, it is with the sheriff's department. The sheriff went behind the DA's back and got an arrest warrant for Kobe within days of the incident. The DA was forced to make a rushed decision to charge with the glare of the spotlight on him. He did so before he had sufficient time to investigate the allegation. The sheriff's office failed to preserve crucial evidence in Kobe's room . . . They look like keystone cops.[141]

After getting the warrant, the Eagle County, Colorado, sheriff who supervised the investigation and obtained the warrant stated that "he would not agree" if the local district attorney's office chose not to file a felony sexual assault charge against Kobe Bryant.[142] "We would not have done what we did unless we thought charges should be filed," stated the sheriff. "Based on what I know of the evidence, I would expect [the prosecutor's office] to file charges."[143]

In the meantime, the prosecutor stated that he was proceeding with a review of the case and that a decision to file or decline charges was expected soon.[144]

Noticeable tension was created between the sheriff's office and the prosecution as a result of the sheriff's actions. A source in the district attorney's office stated that the sheriff made a misstep in protocol in obtaining the arrest warrant by going to the judge first instead of the prosecutor's office.[145] A sheriff's investigator assigned to the case stated, "If there wasn't probable cause, we would not have arrested him [Kobe Bryant]."[146]

The prosecutor's office had initially raised questions about Kobe Bryant's arrest and the methods of the sheriff's office. The prosecutor stated that the sheriff's office had not followed the standard procedure of asking the district attorney's office for a warrant. Instead, they went to a judge. Later, however, the prosecutor's office backed off and stated, "What's done is done."[147]

The sheriff continued to back the decisions his office made, stating, "I'm convinced our investigators did an excellent job."[148] But in news reports, a former Denver prosecutor stated that the sheriff's office made numerous mistakes. Prosecutor Norm Early said that the office made the first of a series of mistakes with the unusual arrest of Kobe Bryant, stating that the sheriff "jumped the gun" with the arrest, and "whenever someone in this case did something they wouldn't normally do, it was a problem."[149]

Another criminal defense attorney and legal analyst points to the securing of the arrest warrant by the sheriff early in this high-publicity media case as a key point in the downfall of the case:

> The [Eagle County] Sheriff's Department had an obliga- tion to find the facts, whether they were good or bad, and it's clear they put the blinders on . . . There was a rush to arrest him [Bryant], vilify the guy, then sit back and gripe when all of the facts turned out against them. The woman was not asked the tough questions. They [the prosecution] didn't want to test the scientific evidence—why? Because they wouldn't like the results.[150]

The high-profile nature of the case and the fame of the accused offender had nothing to do with the quickness with which the investigation moved, according to the sheriff's office. "When they told me that the case involved Kobe Bryant, I had a blank look on my face. The name didn't mean any- thing to me . . . This case had nothing to do with his celebrity status."[151]

On July 18, 2003, the prosecutor's office filed a single count of fel- ony sexual assault.[152] Bryant assembled an experienced legal team for his defense that included Pamela Mackey and Hal Haddon. Pamela Mackey had previously represented Colorado Avalanche goalie Pat- rick Roy in a domestic violence case where charges were dismissed.[153] Haddon had previously represented JonBenet Ramsey's father, John Ramsey, along with writer Hunter Thompson. Haddon had also ran the 1988 presidential campaign of Gary Hart.[154]

During the prosecutor's news conference detailing the charges, Kobe Bryant released a statement saying he had committed adultery. His wife, Vanessa, issued her own statement saying she would stand by her husband. Two hours later, the couple joined their attorneys at a nationally televised news conference from the Staples Center, where the Lakers play. There, Bryant declared his innocence and tearfully apologized to his wife.[155]

On October 9, 2003, a preliminary hearing began in which evidence was heard against Kobe Bryant. The hearing ended on October 15. On October 20, 2003, the judge who heard the preliminary hearing ruled that Bryant must stand trial.[156]

Shortly after Bryant's arrest, it quickly became apparent that the defense was consensual sex, and both sides, the defense and the prosecution, began to work on their strategies for the case. Since there were two sides to the actual incident, Bryant's and the accuser's, both sides worked on the circumstances and evidence that would corroborate their versions of events. The accuser had a bruise on her jawline and vaginal tearing.[157] The defense examined other aspects of the accuser's behavior that could have led to the injuries besides nonconsensual sex with Bryant.

On March 2, 2004, defense attorneys stated the accuser had engaged in sex with someone else less than 15 hours after her alleged assault. The accuser's attorney denied that claim.[158] On June 10, 2004, the judge rejected a defense bid to overturn the state's rape shield law. The judge later rejected the defense's request to give the instruction to any possible jury that investigators failed to gather evidence that could have suggested that Bryant was innocent.[159] On July 23, 2004, the judge held that information about the accuser's sexual activities in the three days before her hospital exam could be admitted into evidence.[160] After losing a First Amendment fight with the media, on August 10, 2004, the judge released closed-door hearing transcripts in which a defense expert says she believed the accuser had sex with someone else after her encounter with Bryant and before her hospital exam. The defense also said that the accuser had received nearly $20,000 from the state's victim's compensation fund.[161]

The defense in the Kobe Bryant case had long implied that the accuser's injuries might have been the result of "sleeping around with three men in three days."[162] The defense highlighted the fact that the accuser herself told the investigating detective that she and Bryant were flirting and then kissing before their sexual encounter.[163] While many speculated the defense would waive a preliminary hearing, for fear that testimony heard at that hearing would be devastating to Bryant and taint the jury pool,[164] the defense was very aggressive and began to advance their theory from the initial stages of the case.

The detective that testified at the preliminary hearing against Bryant stated the accuser initially was excited that he was staying at the hotel where she worked, that she eagerly showed him around the premises on a private tour, and that she flirted with him.[165] The detective testified the accuser told him that Bryant complimented her on her clothes and her height and asked her if she had a boyfriend. Bryant invited the woman to his room, and at his urging, the accuser showed him a tattoo on her ankle and revealed a second one on her back by lifting up a one-piece black dress.[166] She exchanged kisses with him for five minutes; Bryant initiated the kissing by kissing her mouth and neck.[167] The accuser said she was fine with the kissing and was excited that Kobe Bryant was showing interest in her.[168] The detective testified that during the five minutes she was sexually penetrated, Bryant never let go of her neck, and he moaned and told her during sex that "he liked Vail, Colorado."[169] The detective stated he was told that the woman cried throughout the rape and was forced to kiss Bryant's penis when the rape had concluded.[170] Authorities seized clothing worn by Bryant and the woman that night, and a laboratory analysis discovered streaks of her blood on the inside front of his shirt and on her panties.[171]

The defense team attacked the story of the accuser and brought to the attention of the media that she had reportedly attempted suicide twice to get the attention of an ex-boyfriend earlier in the year[172] and that the underwear that she wore to the rape exam contained sperm and pubic hair that did not belong to Bryant.[173]

The media began to focus on the accuser as well, with one man garnering considerable air time with his claims that the woman bragged about the sexual assault at a party and gave a graphic description of the NBA star's anatomy.[174]

Commenting on the case, after the dismissal and the defense strategy of going after the accuser's version of events, defense attorney Jeralyn Merrit stated online:

> I think Colorado's rape shield law worked in this case. The accuser's prior sexual history was ruled inadmissible. Only her contemporaneous sexual history, that she may have engaged in sex within 72 hours of her rape exam, would come into evidence. The People chose to charge Kobe with a more serious form of sexual assault, alleging that he applied physical force and injured her. The Sixth Amendment justly requires that he be allowed to introduce evidence to refute the charge . . . There was a revelation in the court transcript that a defense expert held the opinion that the accuser engaged in sex within 15 hours of her encounter with Kobe. If believed by the jury, they would not find such behavior consistent with that of a true rape victim.

> The defense in this case was nothing less than outstanding. They left no stone unturned. Law students should be required to study the pleadings and transcripts to lean how to defend a sexual assault charge. This case sets a great example of how to conduct trial preparation and how to provide effective assistance of counsel.

> Any woman can be raped. A woman can say 'no' at any time, provided she effectively communicates that 'no' to her partner. That's not the message of this case. The defense did not attack

her character. They attacked her story. The defense was that Kobe was not the cause of any physical injuries she suffered, but rather, such injuries resulted from repetitive sexual activity over a three-day period. Since the prosecutor upped the charge by alleging Kobe caused her injuries, this was not only fair game, but required to allow him to present a defense.[175]

With the defense attacking the accuser's story, the media attention, and the feuding between the prosecution and the police, the case began to unravel. Infighting between the prosecutors, infighting between the accuser's own attorneys, the large amount of money Kobe Bryant possessed to advance his defense, and the accuser changing her own story led to the downfall of the criminal case.

Shortly after the onset of the case, the accuser's family hired former Eagle County, Colorado, prosecutor John Clune as an attorney to guide her through the legal system and protect her privacy. Clune, the former chief deputy in the district attorney's office, had prosecuted numerous acquaintance-rape cases.[176] To handle any potential civil lawsuit against Kobe Bryant, high-profile attorney Lin Wood was retained. Lin Wood was renowned as an attorney who specialized in defamation lawsuits and had gained national acclaim by securing large settlements for Richard Jewell, the security guard who had been named by several news organizations as a suspect in the 1996 Atlanta Olympic Bombing case. Wood also represented John Ramsey, father of JonBenet Ramsey, and former United States Representative Gary Condit, who was questioned in the disappearance of Chandra Levy.[177] The civil litigator Wood, 52, was known for his confrontational style and penchant for grabbing headlines, while the then 33-year-old Clune was known for his low-key style.[178] Wood saw the case as one that belonged in civil court and saw criminal court as a disadvantageous venue for acquaintance-rape cases; the former prosecutor Clune disagreed.[179]

Early on in the case, the judge had imposed a gag order, which barred all parties from discussing the case.[180] At the request of Kobe Bryant's attorneys, a later gag order was issued, a sweeping gag order which stated that Lin Wood and John Clune had commented improperly on the merits of the case and on Kobe Bryant's character.[181] A gag order based on the comments of a civil attorney who represents an accuser in a lawsuit that has yet to be filed is somewhat unusual. Gag orders are most often imposed either due to the high-profile nature of a case or the specific actions of the police, prosecution, or defense.

The prosecution was also involved in infighting. The two prosecutors who were assigned by Eagle County District Attorney Mark Hurlbert to handle the case argued over who would handle the direct examination of the victim. The prosecutors stopped talking to each other. It was even suggested that a mediator be brought in to assist with their differences, which was rejected by one of the attorneys.[182] Regarding the difficulties with the prosecutors, Lin Wood commented, "Every case and every witness has its problems, and this case and this witness were no different. . . but skilled lawyers handle them, not add to them."[183]

The accuser herself had wavered for months about testifying, overwhelmed by death threats, media scrutiny, repeated court gaffes that revealed her name, and also potentially damaging sealed testimony of a defense expert that the accuser had sex with someone other than Kobe Bryant after the alleged rape and before her medical examination the next day.[184] This would naturally raise many questions as to the nature and origin of the injuries that were attributed to the sexual contact with Bryant.

Additionally, prosecution witnesses began to fall by the wayside. A pathologist was dropped as a prosecution witness on July 15, 2004, after he examined the accuser's injuries and could not establish whether or not her sex with Bryant was consensual.[185]

The prosecutors also argued over whether the defense should be notified in writing that the accuser had changed her version of events. She changed her story about how long she had kissed Bryant, saying it was less than five minutes.[186] Less than a month earlier, she had admitted to the prosecution that she had been dishonest with prosecutors about two other details. The accuser indicated that she had not been honest about why she had been late for work on the date of the rape—she stated that it was because of car trouble, when in fact she had overslept after attending a concert the night before.[187] The other point that she had not been honest about with investigators was that Bryant had made her wash her face before she left his room. The accuser said that she made this part up because she did not think the detective believed the rape allegation.[188] While both prosecutors did not see the lie as central as to whether the rape occurred and knew that Kobe Bryant had initially lied to the police as well, the prosecutor who supported notifying the defense stated, "The first one was a white lie . . . The second lie was certainly of more concern because it was about one of the events that occurred during her contact with Bryant."[189]

Fourteen months after accusing Kobe Bryant of raping her, the accuser was put on the witness stand by prosecutors in a mock trial to see how she would hold up under hostile cross-examination, and the answer was that she did disastrously.[190] An angry Lin Wood stated, "They tore down her confidence in an exercise that should be designed to build up her confidence."[191] The defense team, in the meantime, had conducted several mock trials, including one where Bryant did testify and was cross-examined.[192]

As the family of the accuser lost faith in the prosecution, they shifted from a shielding policy to a more aggressive one. Her civil attorneys wanted her out of the criminal case and began to engage in secret talks with Bryant's attorney to withdraw from the criminal case. A big part of negotiations was an apology from Bryant.[193] A civil suit was also planned.

On August 10, several weeks before the criminal case was set for jury trial, the accuser filed a civil lawsuit. A prosecutor commented, "The timing certainly wasn't ideal. But we didn't have any say over that decision." When one files a civil suit while the criminal case is still pending, it creates a defense that the accuser is motivated by money, by winning the lawsuit. This can damage the credibility of the accuser.[194]

On September 1, 2004, prosecutors reluctantly dropped the sexual assault criminal case against Kobe Bryant and cited the accuser's unwillingness to proceed with the trial against him. The district attorney stated he "reluctantly made the difficult decision to dismiss" the sexual assault after several meetings with the woman, her family, and her civil attorney.[195]

As the criminal case was dropped, Kobe Bryant's criminal attorney Pamela Mackey read an apology from Bryant:

> First, I want to apologize directly to the young woman involved in this incident. I want to apologize to her for my behavior that night and for the consequences she has suffered in the past year. Although this year has been incredibly difficult for me personally, I can only imagine the pain she has had to endure. I also want to apologize to her parents and family members, and to my family and friends and supporters, and to the citizens of Eagle, Colo.
>
> I also want to make it clear that I do not question the motives of this young woman. No money has been paid to this woman. She has agreed that this statement will not be used against me in the civil case. Although I truly believe this encounter between us was consensual, I recognize now that she did not and does not view this incident the same way I did. After months of reviewing discovery, listening to her attorney, and even her testimony in person, I now understand how she feels that she did not consent to this encounter.
>
> I issue this statement today fully aware that while one part of this case ends today, another remains. I understand that the civil case against me will go forward. That part of this case

will be decided by and between the parties directly involved in the incident and will no longer be a financial or emotional drain on the citizens of the state of Colorado.[196]

In the aftermath of the Kobe Bryant rape case, the civil case was settled in March of 2005. Bryant spent over $12 million in legal fees on the criminal case, even before the civil suit was settled.[197] Sponsors such as McDonald's dropped Bryant from endorsing their product.[198]

Legal analysts said the case against Bryant was never particularly strong, and in some cases, they reacted with disdain to the announcement that the charges were being dropped. One defense attorney stated, "The prosecution has always said somebody's name was being dragged through the mud—it turns out that it was Kobe Bryant's . . . This dismissal comes a year late."[199] One legal analyst called the case "an unmitigated disaster for true victims of sexual assault."

The judge extended his sympathy to Bryant's accuser, apologizing to mistakes that led to the release by the Colorado Judicial Department of the victim's name at least four times and the transcript of a closed rape shield hearing that emphasized the defense's point of view: "This court has made mistakes. I take full responsibility for all errors."[200] Three men were arrested in separate incidents for harassing the accuser, two of them eventually going to prison for their threats.[201]

Kobe Bryant continues to star for the Los Angeles Lakers. His jersey, a good indicator of player popularity, was the second top-selling jersey in the last ten years, behind Michael Jordan[202] and was the second top seller behind Kevin Garnett for the 2007–2008 NBA season.[203] He was the NBA's Most Valuable player for the 2007–2008 season, which was the first time he had won the award. He represented the United States and starred on the gold medal winning 2008 Olympic team that competed in Beijing, China.

WHAT THE PROS SAY

"I prosecuted a sex case where the defendant was a serial rapist. His MO was that he would commit a home invasion and then rape the female occupants inside. Years ago, he had been convicted of a criminal sexual assault and was released from prison on that offense. Within weeks of his release, he had begun to offend again. The new rape committed by the defendant was reported in the news due to its extremely brutal and shocking nature.

A police officer who was involved in the original arrest and conviction learned through media reports about the new rape. This effective news reporting helped the officer recognize the MO as very similar to that of the rapist who he had helped put in the penitentiary years ago. In a textbook example of good police work, this officer called the detectives who were investigating the recent rape. Investigation revealed that the offender was recently paroled. After talking to the detectives and sharing information, it was learned that both the offender in the old incident and the new incident had made the victims say some unique and distinctive vulgarities during the sex act.

Further investigation revealed that this offender had been paroled to a location three blocks away from this new offense. The offender was arrested, and evidence led to his prosecution. He was convicted and is now serving three life sentences plus a sentence of 60 years in the penitentiary." **Assistant State Attorney Arunas Buntinas**

"In police investigations it is important to keep in mind what the public has a right to know balanced with the right to be safe. The Chicago Police Department uses a number of tools to meet these goals. Community Alerts, Sex Offender Registration, AMBER Alerts, Crime Stopper wanted posters, and email alerts are some of the ways that a police department can keep the public informed. In Chicago, officers from the Community Policing Office contribute by keeping businesses, schools, and churches informed.

Community Alerts are helpful in that they notify the community at large about a particular crime or crime pattern. They give the public further information as to what they can do and whom to contact if they have information in relation to that particular crime. The Chicago Police Department has an email notification system that is accessible to all residents. This system is designed to distribute Community Alerts more widely. Obviously, in sex investigations, the victims are not named publicly. It may be important in certain situations to hold back some elements of the crime that only the real perpetrator would know. In creating Community Alerts, the Chicago Police Department uses a tool called FACES to create an image of the wanted offender if he is unknown. A Community Alert can be made with a general description of the wanted offender and later amended to include photographs or FACES images.

Sex offenders are required to reregister every year in person with the police department in the jurisdiction they reside for the rest of their lifetimes. The period when a person is required to register used to be ten years from their conviction or release from a penal institution, hospital, or other facility, whichever is later, but this law has been changed. The Chicago Police Department keeps the public informed and notifies a list of schools and child-care facilities of the listing of sex offenders in the city of Chicago. A sex offender as defined in the Sex Offender Registration Act is any person who was charged with a sex offense as defined by law and is convicted of such offense or an attempt to commit such an offense. It further includes someone who is found not guilty by reason of insanity or someone who is certified as a sexually dangerous person as defined by law. Kidnappers and offenders of murders involving a victim who was under 18 years of age are required to register. The offender has to sign a form stating that he is aware of his duty to register and that the procedures have been explained to him. The offender has ten days after establishing residency to register in person.

The AMBER Alert Notification Plan is an emergency alert plan, coordinated through the Illinois State Police, which makes information

(Continued)

regarding abducted and endangered children immediately available to the citizens of Illinois. The plan has two basic criteria that must be met. First, the child must either be under 16 or have a proven mental or physical disability. Second, the police must believe that the child is in danger of serious bodily harm or death. The plan is not to be used for runaways, and it is not to be used in most child custody situations, but each case is judged individually. A photograph of the child is to be used in each request. The AMBER Alert is entered into LEADS notification to on-duty officers and is made through the police radio for a period of four to eight hours.

Crime Stopper wanted posters encourage citizens to become involved in the apprehension of offenders by supplying information on offenders who are currently wanted for investigation by the Chicago Police Department. The program provides a cash reward of up to $1,000 to citizens who supply the department with information leading to the arrest and charging of the wanted offenders. Naturally, Chicago Police Department members are exempt from receiving any cash rewards. Email alerts are sent out to Chicago-area businesses, community organizations, and schools. Officers from the Community Policing Office are responsible for physically distributing flyers and posters in the businesses, schools, and churches. Individuals can subscribe for email alerts on the department's CLEARPath website. In the event that the offender is arrested or the case is closed, a follow-up alert will be sent to inform citizens that the poster has been 'deactivated.'" **Detective Mark DiMeo**

Detective Mark DiMeo is a 21-year veteran of the Chicago Police Department. He has been a detective for ten years. The last seven of those years have involved his working exclusively with the sexual assault/abuse of minor children at the Chicago Children's Advocacy Center. Detective DiMeo has investigated hundreds of cases involving offenders having sexual contact with children.

CHAPTER 6

INTERACTING WITH THE MEDIA IN ROBBERY CASES

The Model Penal Code defines robbery as: "A person is guilty of robbery, if during the course of a theft, he or she: a) inflicts serious bodily harm upon another, or b) threatens another with or purposely puts him in fear of a serious bodily injury, or c) commits or threatens to commit any felony of the first or second degree."[204] It is often said that a robbery is often one bad move away from becoming a beating, a hostage situation, or even a homicide.[205]

There are as many different types of robberies as there are different types of robbers. Most robberies are a risk assessment by the offender in that they either involve low risk and low reward or a higher risk but higher reward. Targets are usually selected based upon their appearance of being weak or vulnerable or having something of great value.[206]

Most robberies are serial in nature. Where there is one robbery, there are often many. Investigation of robbery often focuses on MO, especially with younger robbers who are not yet career criminals. Some robbers may just rob a particular type of victim (females, people they perceive as being intoxicated, illegal immigrants, persons of a different race or ethnic background than the offenders) or a particular location (convenience stores, liquor stores, stores staffed by one person, stores staffed by women, people or stores in wealthy areas, stores without cameras).[207]

Reaching out to the media is a step that should be taken in serial robberies, high-profile robberies, or robberies in which a victim was hurt. This serves to alert the public and allows them to take safety precautions.

As with a sexual assault, a description of the offender should be released to the media, and the same consideration should be given to what information should and should not be released to the public.

The goal of the investigation is to find the truth. In order that information given by the victim, witnesses, and the offender can be verified and corroborated, certain information should not be released to the public before arrest and charging.

Under no circumstances should the name, address, or any contact information of the victim or the witnesses be released to the media.

Case Study: North Hollywood Shootout

Anyone who worked in law enforcement during the time remembers when they first saw the haunting news footage of the shootout on February 28, 1997, in North Hollywood, Los Angeles. Heavily armed men robbing a bank engaged in a wild gun battle with Los Angeles police who responded to the scene. At the end of the incident, 12 officers and 8 civilians were injured. Remarkably, all survived.[208] Both offenders were killed.[209] The shootout was captured on camera, much of it by news helicopters. It was every officer's worst nightmare of heavily armed offenders, drugged on the sedative Phenobarbital[210] to calm their nerves and kill their pain, with seemingly unlimited supplies of ammunition.

When the 44-minute episode was over, the robbers, armed with seven firearms, including automatic weapons and armor-piercing bullets, over 3,300 rounds of ammunition, wearing body armor and metal trauma plates, had fired over 1,200 rounds.[211] This included several hundred rounds fired at police and television cameras. Sixty-two cars were hit by bullets.[212] Bank robber Larry Phillips, Jr., was shot 11 times, including a self-inflicted gunshot wound to the head.[213] His accomplice Emil Matasareanu was hit 29 times by police[214] and managed to live for 40 minutes after being hit. Over 100 police officers responded to the scene.[215]

The robbers choose the Bank of America branch in Laurel Canyon.[216] The well-planned effort, which included months of preparation and surveillance, netted the robbers $303,305.[217] As they had walked into the bank, however, they were observed by police, who radioed for backup after hearing the more than 100 rounds that were fired inside by the offenders in this takeover-style bank robbery.

When the offenders exited the bank, there were already dozens of police cars on the scene. The offenders shot at the officers. News helicopters and SWAT helicopters arrived at the scene. The SWAT helicopters passed on crucial information about the offenders to the officers on the ground. The media helicopters, like the police helicopters, got shot at, but they broadcast the entire incident from their time of arrival. Los Angeles Police helicopter pilot Charles Perriguey not only had to dodge 150 rounds fired at him by the gunmen as he surveyed the scene from above, but he also had to maneuver around several media helicopters that were competing for the best camera angles.[218]

Both offenders were ultimately killed. Phillips, walking on foot, was shot numerous times by police. He then shot himself under the chin while a police officer's bullet simultaneously severed his spine. Matasareanu died engaging Los Angeles SWAT officers in a shootout after commandeering a truck from its owner, but he was unable to start it because the owner had managed to escape with the keys.

Seventeen of the officers who were part of the shootout were awarded the department's highest honor, the Medal of Valor, by Los Angeles Police Chief Bernard C. Parks, who called the officers the "bravest of the brave."[219] This was the largest number of officers that had ever been awarded the Medal of Valor in one single incident.[220] "We pay tribute to these officers for their courage in that instance when the circumstances became dangerous and deadly; where with the next breath their valiant efforts were above and beyond the call of duty," said Chief Parks. "Their actions clearly display the dedication behind our motto, 'to protect and to serve,' and the bravery and valor of our Los Angeles police officers."[221]

Los Angeles Mayor Richard Riordan said the gun battle with the two heavily armed bank robbers showed the world a model of courage under fire. "The North Hollywood shootout showed graphically to all Angelenos that our police officers are putting their lives on the line every day," Riordan said.[222] Television broadcaster Paul Moyer, who read the commendation reports for all of the officers, stated, "On that day, the world literally watched heroes save a community."[223]

In the aftermath of the shootout, the estate of Emil Matasareanu filed a lawsuit against Los Angeles police officers and paramedics, claiming that they conspired to kill him, as he lay on the ground for more than 30 minutes without being given medical attention.[224] The thought of these violent offenders profiting in a lawsuit from this incident shocked many. "I think these guys were as wrong and as wicked and as evil as anybody we've ever encountered. For them to even stand a chance of recouping some money from the taxpayers makes me angry," said LAPD Captain Richard Wahler.[225] "The officers' behavior was exemplary," said Assistant City Attorney Don Vincent, who defended the city against the suit. "An officer who Matasareanu had tried to kill called an ambulance for Matasareanu within a minute."[226]

Police and fire department officials have said that rescuers in the first ambulance to reach the scene, about ten minutes after Matasareanu surrendered, opted to take a wounded citizen to the hospital because his injuries were severe but treatable. Matasareanu, the rescuers decided, appeared to have little chance of survival. Authorities said they could not send in a second ambulance because the area was not safe and other suspects were believed to be at large.[227]

The *Los Angeles Times* also did an investigative report in which they alleged mistakes had been made by the police during the shootout.[228] The police chief defended his officers, stating to the media at a news conference, "I wish [*Times* reporters] were there when it happened . . . I think it's great they can make these kinds of allegations from the quietness of their office a year later, but we have to realize the scope of an unprecedented attack on police officers where over 2,000 rounds were fired within 45 minutes."[229]

A Los Angeles Police Board ruled that the 29 officers who fired their weapons during the incident acted "within policy" and were justified in their shooting.[230] "I don't think anyone in their lifetime has seen, in a domestic situation, that kind of firepower and that kind of blatant disregard for the law," Chief Parks said about the two suspects. "It brought an overwhelming amount of support for field officers . . . I think citizens saw for the first time what they [officers] may be confronted with."[231]

CHAPTER 7

INTERACTING WITH THE MEDIA IN HOMICIDE CASES

Homicide is the most serious of crimes. It is the taking of the life of a person by another person. It is the most serious of investigations. Those who are assigned to homicide investigations are often among the most experienced and qualified investigators. Homicide convictions frequently carry with them the most serious penalties. Those investigating any aspect of a homicide owe it to the victim, owe it to the suspected offender, and owe it to society to conduct a complete and thorough investigation.

There is no statute of limitations on murder. The next lead on a murder may arise from the next street stop, domestic call, or narcotics arrest the officer participates in. One never knows where the next piece of information on a homicide will come from. A homicide investigation may be a never-ending process. It is important to keep the public safe, protected, and informed.

Likewise, it is important that many details of the homicide be kept from the public and the media. This ensures that witnesses that may come forward could not have researched the case or read or heard about this information from the media.

Before an arrest is made in a homicide case, police have the duty to protect the public and to make them aware of any danger they may be in. They also owe the victim and the family of the victim the right to justice. They owe the witnesses the right to be safe after they may have cooperated with law enforcement. They owe the possible offender or suspect a thorough, unbiased, and complete investigation, and if the case is charged, a fair trial.

In a homicide, before charging, police may give the media a general description of the incident, the gender and age of the injured, along with information as to whether the victim is deceased.

Investigators should disclose the identity of a homicide victim only after the next of kin has been notified. Neither the identities nor the addresses of witnesses should be disclosed, nor any information that could be used to identify them or endanger their lives or physical safety.

The Chicago Police Department, for one, prohibits results of the investigation from being released to the media prior to arrest unless release of the information will aid in the investigation, assist in the apprehension of the suspect(s), or warn the public of danger. The department prohibits the release of any photograph or mug shots unless the release will aid in arrest, aid in investigation, or warn the public of danger.

Case Study: Richard Jewell Olympic Bombing Case

In July of 1996, Atlanta, Georgia, was hosting the Olympic Games. Centennial Olympic Park, located in downtown Atlanta, is a venue that had been specifically designed and built as a central gathering place for Olympic Games visitors and athletes. On July 27, 1996, shortly after midnight, there was a concert in the park.[232] Richard Jewell, working a temporary job as a security guard, discovered a suspicious package, an abandoned green knapsack.[233] Jewell alerted Georgia Bureau of Investigation officers.[234] Minutes later, the bomber called 911 to deliver a warning. Jewell was among those who helped evacuate the park of its many occupants. At 1:20 A.M., the suspicious package, which contained three pipe bombs, exploded.[235] Two people died in the explosion. A woman was killed when a nail struck her in the head. A cameraman died of a heart attack when he ran over to the area of the bombing to cover the attack. One hundred and eleven persons were injured.[236]

The explosion occurred ten days after the explosion of TWA Flight 800, in which 230 persons were killed over the Atlantic Ocean after the plane took off from John F. Kennedy Airport in New York, New York.[237] Law enforcement was under tremendous pressure to solve the case almost instantaneously so that the Olympic athletes and visitors would not be crippled by fear.[238]

Richard Jewell, the security guard who found the bomb, was hailed as a hero for his work. Jewell was praised for the quick thinking that presumably saved lives.[239] He gave interviews to the print media and appeared on CNN's *Talk Back Live* program and on NBC's *The Today Show*.[240]

In the days that followed, however, he would go from hero to villain, and ultimately he would be exonerated and praised as a hero again. He would be portrayed as a failed law enforcement candidate, a wannabe cop who had manufactured and planted the bomb so that he could find it and gain attention.[241]

Three days after the bombing, he was identified in an article in the *Atlanta Journal-Constitution* as the focus of police attention.[242]

The *Atlanta Journal-Constitution* was the first newspaper to report on Jewel's status as a suspect.[243] The Federal Bureau of Investigation, which was investigating the blast, came up with a profile of the offender—a lone bomber. That profile was leaked to the media.

In a July 30 article, the *Atlanta Journal-Constitution* reported, "Richard Jewell, then 33, a former law enforcement officer, fits the profile of the lone bomber. This profile generally includes a frustrated white man who is a former police officer, member of the military or police wannabe who wants to become a hero."[244] The newspaper reported that after the bombing, Jewell "approached newspapers, including the *Atlanta Journal-Constitution*, seeking publicity for his actions."[245]

A July 31 *Atlanta Journal-Constitution* article reported that Jewell had "a history of overzealous policing in Habersham County." The newspaper also reported that "[I]nvestigators now say Jewell fits the profile of a lone bomber and they believe he placed the 911 call."[246]

The *Atlanta Journal-Constitution* offered the following analogy in an August 1 column, comparing Jewell to the "Atlanta Child Murderer," convicted killer Wayne Williams, who was convicted in two deaths and a suspect in more than 20 more murders[247]:

> Once upon a terrible time, federal agents came to this town to deal with another suspect who lived with his mother. Like this one, that suspect was drawn to the blue lights and sirens of police work. Like this one, he became famous in the aftermath of murder. His name was Wayne Williams. This one is Richard Jewell.[248]

It was perfectly proper for FBI agents to have looked at Richard Jewell. The person who reports a crime is almost always investigated.[249] The FBI also remembered an incident at the 1984 Olympics in Los Angeles in which the cop who "found" a bomb on a bus for Turkish athletes turned out to have planted it.[250] This "modified Munchausen syndrome," in FBI terminology, occurs in someone who wants to be a hero so badly that he creates emergencies so he can rescue people.[251] Jewell fit this profile and also had the characteristics of people who use pipe bombs—"white single men in their 30s or 40s with a martial bent."[252] The FBI also had tips from the president of Piedmont College, where Jewell had previously worked. The president described Jewell as "a little erratic," "almost too excitable," and too gung ho about "energetic police work."[253]

The government received many tips and allegations about Jewell, including that he had wondered aloud whether the tower he was guarding could withstand a bomb blast. A neighbor at his country cabin said he had heard a loud explosion, seen a large cloud of smoke rising from the woods, and then seen Jewell at the edge of the woods, looking "very nervous." Jewell had also told coworkers, "You better take a picture of me now because I'm going to be famous." As a deputy sheriff in Habersham County, Jewell owned an olive-drab military-style knapsack very much like the one that contained the bomb, yet he denied this to the FBI; also, as a Habersham County deputy he had received some training about bombs, particularly pipe bombs. Furthermore, Jewell was known as someone who never took breaks, and he had left his post between 10:00 and 10:15 on the night of the bombing.[254]

NBC Nightly News reported on the day that suspicions about Jewell were publicly revealed and that his arrest was imminent.[255] *NBC News*, however, also went on to say that Jewell was not even an official suspect.[256]

The police searched Jewell's home, where he lived with his mother.[257] His background was investigated. The public persona of Jewell became that of a stooge, an idiot seeking attention. Jay Leno referred to Jewell as the "Una-doofus,"[258] a takeoff on the Unabomber, convicted killer Ted Kaczynski. Jewell later described the surveillance by reporters who set upon him as "like piranha on a bleeding cow."[259]

As the investigation progressed, a *Newsweek* magazine author wrote:

> If there's anyone who would seem to have the right to sue the living daylights out of the media and government, it's Richard

Jewell. He's the soft-spoken security guard who was fingered as a suspect in the pipe-bombing at the Olympics—just days after he was hailed as a hero for discovering the bomb sack. Ever since, his life has been hell. FBI agents and reporters follow him everywhere and he's been stigmatized as a daffy wanna-be cop. Problem is, federal law-enforcement authorities haven't charged him with anything, and Justice Department sources tell *Newsweek* they are growing less confident he's their man—even while stating publicly he remains a suspect.[260]

It should be noted that *Newsweek* is a competitor to *Time* magazine, whom Jewell had a claim against.

No evidence led to the arrest or prosecution of Richard Jewell. He subsequently filed lawsuits for libel against several media organizations, including NBC, CNN, the *New York Post*, several radio stations, and the *Atlanta Journal-Constitution*.[261] Jewell also filed suit against Piedmont College, his former employer. Jewell's lawsuit claimed that the defendants in the lawsuit portrayed him as a person with a "bizarre employment history and aberrant personality who was guilty of criminal involvement in the Centennial Olympic Park bombing."[262] Jewell's attorney, Lin Wood, referred to the *Atlanta Journal-Constitution* as the "real culprit" of the lawsuit.[263]

In looking at the Jewell case, it is clear that law enforcement authorities investigate many suspects or "persons of interest" who are never charged with any crime. Chasing down all leads, no matter how unpromising, is part of the responsibility that comes with investigating crimes. In other words, this is what is known as good police work. Seldom, however, are the names of uncharged suspects publicized.[264] Richard Jewell would have remained the hero of the case had that general rule held true.[265] As *Time* magazine later recounted: "The entire weight of federal law enforcement and the global media bore down on one very ordinary man, convinced that he's guilty—and it turns out he's innocent."[266]

Because he was never charged, any defamation suit that he could bring against the media presumably would be a stronger case than that which could be brought by a wrongfully accused person who was formally charged with a crime.[267] It was generally felt that if the case were to go to trial, Jewell would have had a hard time winning a libel suit, because he would have to prove that something written or broadcast was false.[268] If a court decided that Jewell was a public figure, he would also have to prove that the falsehood was intentional or made in reckless disregard of the truth. This issue of whether he was a public figure is "a tough borderline case," said one First Amendment expert.[269] Absent serious inaccuracies, Jewell had "a grievance but not a case." Even invasion of privacy claims could have been countered by the public's legitimate interest in whether FBI investigators had found the right person, said the expert.[270]

A U.S. District Court judge ordered the public disclosure of the affidavits filed by the FBI to conduct searches of Jewell and his property on October 23. On October 26, the U.S. Attorney's Office issued a public statement announcing: "Mr. Jewell is not a target of the Centennial Olympic Park bombing investigation.[271] Barring any newly discovered evidence," it continued, "this status will not change."[272]

The director of the FBI initiated an investigation into the cause of the media leak. It was policy that media leaks were prohibited and could result in dismissal.[273] Jewell's lawsuits were not against the government, which did properly investigate a crime, but rather confined to the media.

Jewell reached monetary settlements with CNN and NBC over their coverage of the bombing and with an Atlanta radio station that used his picture in a billboard campaign. The settlement with NBC was said to be $500,000.[274] *Time* magazine agreed to print a clarification about its coverage.[275] Even in their clarification, *Time* reported:

> Richard Jewell seems like the most hapless individual you
> could find for a contest against such powerful antagonists
> as the FBI and the media. An overweight, single man in his

30s, he hasn't amounted to much in life. He belongs to the one demographic group—working-class, Southern white males—about whom society still seems to allow slurs, like "bubbas." He also seems to be one of those ineffectual men who take things too far when they are given a little power. In the movies, when an ordinary person faces great, malign forces, that person is played by Gary Cooper or Harrison Ford. Jewell seems to be a pudgy version of Barney Fife. In this mismatch, he wouldn't appear to have a chance.[276]

In 2006, Georgia Governor Sonny Perdue publicly thanked and awarded Jewell on behalf of the state for saving lives at the Olympics.[277] The award read: "Mr. Jewell deserves to be remembered as a hero for the actions he performed during the Centennial Olympic Games. He is a model citizen, and the state of Georgia thanks him for his long-standing commitment to law enforcement." The award said, "Many lives were spared due to the efforts of Richard Jewell."[278]

Ultimately, Eric Rudolph, a radical former army rifleman was arrested and charged with the Olympic Park Bombing.[279] Rudolph had launched a campaign against abortion clinics, homosexuality, and the intermingling of cultures.[280] He was a survivalist and the subject of a manhunt that lasted five years.[281] Rudolph was on the FBI Ten Most Wanted List and was arrested in May 2003.[282] In April of 2005, he pled guilty to the Olympic Park Bombing. Rudolph's written statement for his guilty plea revealed that his plan was to embarrass the United States government in the eyes of the world at the Olympic Games for their sanctioning of abortions. Rudolph hoped his actions would either cancel the Olympic Games or create a "state of insecurity" that would cause people not to attend the games and hurt the Olympic Games' profits.[283] These plans were unsuccessful. Rudolph also pled guilty to the bombings of two abortion clinics and a gay bar.[284] He is serving a life sentence in prison.[285]

Richard Jewell was found dead in his home on August 29, 2007. The cause of death was severe heart disease.[286]

WHAT THE PROS SAY

"In a homicide case that I prosecuted, a sketch had been made of the offender. That sketch of the offender was put on television. A clothing description of the offender was also broadcast by the television news. The offender's family realized that both the clothing description and the appearance of the person in the sketch matched that of their relative. The family called the police. Through the sketch being publicized and the help of the family, the police were eventually able to arrest both this defendant and his co-offender." **Assistant State Attorney Arunas Buntinas**

CHAPTER 8

INTERACTING WITH THE MEDIA IN SERIAL MURDER CASES

> Serial murder occurs when one or more individuals ... commits a second murder and/or subsequent murder; is relationshipless (victim and attacker are strangers); occurs at a different time and has no connection to the initial (or subsequent) murder; and is frequently committed in a different geographical location. Further, the motive is generally not for material gain but is usually a compulsive act specifically for gratification based on fantasies. The key element is that the series of murders do not share in the events surrounding one another. Victims share in common characteristics of what are perceived to be prestigeless, powerless, and/or lower socioeconomic groups (that is, vagrants, prostitutes, migrant workers, homosexuals, missing children, and single and often elderly women).[287]

Perhaps no crime captures the attention of the media and the public like serial killings. Serial killers gain headlines and are labeled with nicknames that sell newspapers and gain television ratings. The Nightstalker, Jack the Ripper, The Torture Doctor, Killer Clown, D.C. Snipers, BTK Killer (Bind, Torture, and Kill), and The Atlanta Child Killer are names that are etched in our consciousness. The public is fascinated and terrified of serial killers. The media play on the public demand for information on the serial killer.

The public has an interest in being safe and feeling secure. Public anxieties demand quick apprehension of a serial offender; however, conducting investigations requires an enormous amount of resources and agency coordination.[288] Major issues in managing a case such as a serial murderer investigation include the media impact,[289] public pressure, and the adversarial tone of the news media.[290] Long-term media coverage creates immense pressure on law enforcement efforts.[291] Police must establish an acceptable working relationship with the press during the course of a serial killer investigation.[292]

The content and tone of the stories related to the killer can contribute to the hysteria surrounding the murders. Content analysis of newspaper crime coverage has demonstrated that the vast majority of crime coverage by newspapers relates to violent and sensational crime.[293] Newspaper reporting overemphasizes violent crime and does not address either personal risk or prevention techniques, and thus the public's fears become exaggerated.[294] It has been said that serial murderer headlines in newspapers or lead-ins to television shows are designed to attract readers and viewers and do not inform.[295]

Competition among the media for press and television coverage can be disruptive to the investigation.[296] It is the job of the reporter to find out as much information as he or she can about the subject being reported.[297] The more information the reporter has, the better the story. In an investigation, some information should be withheld from the public, protecting the integrity of the investigation, protecting witnesses, victims, and victims' families.[298] This is also done to protect the offender's constitutional right to a fair trial.[299]

The serial killer himself is often egotistical, self-centered, and sociopathic. He often craves attention for himself. In *The Killers Among Us:*

An Examination of Serial Murder and Its Investigations, author Steven Egger explains this phenomena:

> Serial Killers often long for recognition . . . In many instances, a serial killer who is caught and who has confessed has rarely been given attention prior to his apprehension. Most serial killers who have been caught and who have confessed to the police thoroughly enjoy the attention they receive from the police, and especially the news media, now clamoring to interview them and write their story. This is why so many of the killers are willing to grant interviews to the press . . . And since society hungers for insight into a serial killer's life—a description of his handiwork and the splatter of blood—true-crime books continue to enjoy a strong market in our society.[300]

In every law enforcement criminal investigation, the number one goal should be to find the truth. There must be pieces of information that are withheld from the public and not released to the media. As the investigation develops, these would be pieces of information that only the police and the killer would know. A proper balance must be found between informing the public and the media, keeping them aware of the investigative efforts and progress that is being made, and not compromising the investigation.

Case Study: The Green River Killer

In the early 1980s, Gary Ridgway became one of America's most prolific serial killers. Under the nickname the Green River Killer, he also became one of the most infamous. Most of his victims were prostitutes and were killed in and around Seattle and the King County, Washington area. Ridgway was arrested on November 30, 2001,[301] when DNA evidence connected him to the body of four murder victims that had been found in 1982.[302] Ridgway pled guilty in November of 2003 to 48 counts of first-degree murder.[303] The murders for which Ridgway was convicted occurred between 1982 and 1984. Ridgway claimed to have killed 71 women[304] and killed until 1998.[305] Ridgway, a married housepainter who would sometimes lure his victims into his car and into a sense of comfort by displaying his son's photo, was sentenced to life without parole.[306]

Ridgway had held down a job with the same company for 32 years.[307] Neighbors recalled him as a good man, who often worked on the yard[308] and studied the bible.[309] People who knew him initially expressed disbelief that he would be involved in serial killings.[310] But for nearly two decades, he was also a prime suspect in the killings of almost 50 women.[311] Ridgway had been arrested for soliciting prostitutes on two occasions.[312] He was known by acquaintances as someone who picked up and used the services of prostitutes.[313] He had been interviewed twice in connection with the killings.[314] Police in connection with the investigation had searched his home and car.[315] He passed a polygraph test.[316] King County Sheriff Dave Reichert, who was on the initial task force investigating the Green River deaths in the 1980s, said that Ridgway had been one of his "top five suspects" from the beginning.[317]

In 1984, young *Seattle Post-Intelligencer* reporter Mike Barber received a letter in the mail from the Green River Killer.[318] The letter read, "what you need to know about the green river man."[319] Barber later wrote:

> The letter that morning already had been handled by several copy aides, opened and paper-clipped to the envelope. The typing was illegible, and the writer hadn't bothered to put

spaces between his words. You had to decipher it by drawing lines between words.

As I perused it, however, the letter immediately took on the aura of something important. I remember stopping suddenly and thinking "fingerprints," and making a copy so I could write on it. I looked for a clear plastic lunch bag in which to put the letter. I called together a couple of my editors to consider what we had.

A source had told me that one of the psychological profiles of the Green River Killer indicated that he might try to contact the media or police. The *P-I* ran a classified ad asking "callmefred" to contact us again.

He never did.[320]

The *Seattle Post-Intelligencer* shared the letter with the Green River Task Force, made up primarily of local police investigating the case.[321] Forensic tests on the letter were negative for fingerprint evidence.[322] The Green River Task Force then sent it to the FBI's Behavioral Science Unit for analysis.[323] "Some of the information contained in the letter has not been made public, which leads us to believe the person writing it may somehow be involved," Tonya Yzaguirre, a latent-print examiner for King County, wrote to the FBI.[324]

A supervisor in the FBI criminal profiling program reviewed the two-page letter and decided the letter's author "has no connection with the Green River homicides," according to his letter to a detective on the Green River Task Force. The profiler said the author had access to the task force and that the letter was a "feeble and amateurish attempt to gain some personal importance by manipulating the investigation."[325] The killer never again attempted to contact the media.[326] It is not believed that this conclusion by the profiler delayed the investigation.[327]

Gary Ridgway later confessed to writing the letter, bringing it up himself during the interview process with police, and explained what each comment in the letter meant. Court documents stated that Ridgway's letter contained "myriad references to the killings and a number of false-hoods."[328] The letter also described real evidence and details not pub-licly known, such as necrophilia and the fact that some of the victims' fingernails had been cut off.[329] The letter also includes what was later learned to be false evidence planted at crime scenes by Ridgway to con-fuse investigators. "He chews gum, he smokes," the letter reads. Ridgway did neither, but he planted cigarette butts and gum at crime scenes.[330]

The *Seattle Post-Intelligencer* and reporter Mike Barber never wrote about the letter until after Ridgway's confession and conviction 19 years later, as the paper was unable to prove who wrote the letter at the time of the writing.[331]

Case Study: Son of Sam Letters and the Son of Sam Laws

It was one of New York City's biggest crime stories ever, in a city that is famous for just that. In the summer of 1977, the Son of Sam killer was on the loose. The murders and stories written about them caused a panic in a particularly frenzied summer in New York City. The Son of Sam killer quickly developed a reputation for haunting "lover's lanes"[332] and shooting young victims parked in cars in the early hours of the morning. Defiantly, he wrote letters to police and to the media.

The summer of 1977 in New York was marked by the infamous black-outs in July, which led to widespread looting and riots. Over 1,000 stores were damaged during the blackouts, over 1,000 fires were reported, and over 3,000 persons were arrested. All the while, baseball's New York Yankees were in a particularly tough battle in a legendary season, win-ning their division, the American League Championship Series, and the World Series in the season that earned Hall of Fame slugger Reggie Jackson the nickname Mr. October.

The Son of Sam shootings began on July 29, 1976,[333] with the killing of Donna Lauria, 18, and wounding of her friend, Jody Valenti, 30, in the

Bronx. It was not until after the fifth attack and the third homicide— the killing of Virginia Voskerichian, 19, in Forest Hills on March 8, 1977—that police publicly linked all the shootings to the same gun.[334]

Many of the victims were female, attractive, and had long dark brown hair. The killing spree ended when David Berkowitz was arrested on August 10, 1977. Berkowitz had killed six persons—Donna Lauria, Christine Freund, Virginia Voskerichian, Alexander Esau, Valentina Suriani, and Stacy Moskowitz.

After his arrest, the public learned about the Son of Sam. David Berkowitz was born in 1953. He was initially known as the 44-Caliber Killer. He subsequently claimed that he had received his orders to kill from his neighbor's dog, whose name was Sam. David Berkowitz was an Air Force veteran who did not see combat and who was given an honorable discharge. At the time of his arrest, he was working for the United States Postal Service.

Berkowitz had apparently read about the investigation prior to his arrest. His attack on April 17, 1977, led to the deaths of victims Alexander Esau and Valentina Suriani, who had been kissing in the front seat of a car.[335] David Berkowitz first dropped a note on the ground, prior to his killings, addressed to New York City Police Captain of Detectives Joseph Borelli, one of the leaders of the investigation.[336] Berkowitz then fired four shots through the windshield of the car and later recalled, "It was my best job, because it resulted in two deaths."[337] The contents of that letter were not released at that time to the public or to the press.

Police Commissioner Michael Codd launched a massive police investigation. The commissioner announced the formation of a task force that eventually swelled to 100 detectives and 200 uniformed officers. The squad handled more than 200 telephone calls a day, compiled a file of more than 10,000 suspects and interviewed 3,167 of the leading candidates.[338] Four detectives spent four weeks locating all 56 Charter Arms Bulldog .44-caliber revolvers registered to owners in the New York area and contacted about 2,000 gun dealers around the nation, to no avail.[339]

David Berkowitz also wrote a letter to New York *Daily News* columnist Jimmy Breslin. Breslin and the newspaper notified the police. One week later, the letter was published. Widespread panic resulted. Publicity from the letter also led to thousands of tips. The story about the Son of Sam killer and his letter to Breslin sold millions of newspapers.

Breslin published excerpts of the letter he received from the Son of Sam and wrote frequently about the case. Breslin received widespread criticism for printing the letters from the Son of Sam. It turned out, however, that Breslin had first brought the letter to police investigators and then written about it—at their request—in hopes of establishing some communication with the killer that might provide more clues to his identity.

Breslin noted, "Every cell in your body tells you that this letter was news."[340] When New York *Daily News* ran the letter, two million copies[341] of the paper were sold. Jimmy Breslin later disclosed that the New York police wanted the letter released to the public to induce the killer to write again and reveal more clues to his identity. Breslin also consulted with top police officials and a criminal psychiatrist recommended by them before carefully framing a response to the letter in a published column.[342] Three fingerprint experts also spent six weeks analyzing and testing the letter.[343]

David Berkowitz was later arrested after he had been issued a ticket on his car near the murder scene of Stacy Moskowitz. Subsequent investigation linked him to the crimes. A woman who lived nearby remembered seeing an officer ticket a cream-colored car parked near a fire hydrant about a block from the murder scene. The ticket had been placed on a Ford Galaxie owned by postal worker David Berkowitz. On August 10, 1977, the police arrested Berkowitz. He was carrying a manila envelope. In it was a revolver.[344] "You got me," Berkowitz said, smiling. "How come it took you so long?"[345] He confessed to the police upon arrest. His fingerprints also matched print fragments on the letter that was left for Captain Borelli on April 17, 1977.[346] When Captain Borelli came face to face with David Berkowitz, he asked him, "Do you know me?" Berkowitz replied, "Sure, I wrote you a letter."[347]

Due to the sheer volume of news relating to the case and the race by reporters to top their media competitors, it is generally felt by many that the media crossed the line in reporting the Son of Sam case. It has been said that this was a case of the media at its best and its worst.

There were big questions as well over whether the news media—particularly in New York—had gone beyond the bounds of good journalism and good taste. "It was one of the more nauseating, disgusting displays I've ever seen in my life," said one editor. A local anchorman disagreed. "It was not disproportionate to the human reaction to tragedy," said Dave Marash of WCBS TV. "From Shakespeare through history, it's always been the gory stories that have fascinated people most."[348] The coverage raised questions about the personal involvement of journalists in the case and the impact their stories may have had on the killer, on the yearlong hunt for him, on other homicidal personalities, and on the fears of the public. "Just about everything done by the press here . . . has made a bad situation worse for the residents of New York," said an article in *The New Yorker* magazine. But Police Deputy Inspector Timothy Dowd, one of the police who led the search for Son of Sam, judged that "on balance, the press was very helpful."[349]

All three United States television networks dominated their evening newscasts one night with the story of the arrest—NBC and CBS for about 8 minutes and ABC for nearly 20. The *Daily News* sold 2.2 million copies, 350,000 more than usual, and the *New York Post* went over 1 million, which was its biggest sale since the shooting of presidential candidate Robert Kennedy nine years before.[350]

In New York City, newsstands reported the greatest demand for papers since the assassination of President John F. Kennedy in 1963. Enlarged press runs of the city's three dailies were quickly snapped up. The *New York Post* Thursday edition sold more than 1 million copies—about 500,000 more than usual—with editions that blared the one-word headline "Caught!" in two and a half-inch crimson type over a picture of Berkowitz. The *Daily News*, the country's largest circulation daily newspaper, increased its 1.9 million press run by 400,000 copies only to find this was inadequate. And copies of the *New York Times*, which increased its run by about 50,000, also quickly disappeared.

Three cameramen and a reporter were arrested in Yonkers after sneaking into David Berkowitz's cluttered studio apartment. But according to many from both the police and the media, the more serious excesses were those that found their way into print in the weeks and months leading up to the arrest.[351]

Police, however, later thanked the *News*—and the *Times*—for not printing information about partial fingerprints they had found on Breslin's Son of Sam letter. Indeed, throughout the manhunt, the press generally went along with police recommendations about releasing information. A week before 20-year-old Stacy Moskowitz was murdered on a street in Brooklyn, the *News* learned that the cops thought the killer might strike in that borough, but it did not print the information. On the other hand, the police said they were hampered by reports of some of their stakeouts and by one interview with an eyewitness.

Throughout New York City, young women cut and dyed their hair so as not to have the long brown hair thought to attract the killer.[352] Police put decoy couples in cars along lovers' lanes hoping to lure him.[353]

David Berkowitz later pled guilty to six murders and to wounding seven other people.[354] On June 12, 1978, he was sentenced to six life sentences in prison for the murders.[355]

The case has been widely publicized since then. The story of David Berkowitz and the Son of Sam has been publicized in numerous television documentaries, shows, and movies. The *Summer of Sam* was a hit movie directed by Academy Award–nominated director Spike Lee. It starred John Leguizamo along with Academy Award–winners Mira Sorvino and Adrien Brody. The movie highlights the media coverage, the panic, and sensationalism of the case.

In the aftermath of this case, and because of the intense media attention paid to David Berkowitz and the Son of Sam, New York enacted a law which prevented criminals from benefiting financially from their misdeeds, and earmarked any profits from the offender's books, notes, letters, interviews, along with other media communication to the victims and their families.[356] The law was nicknamed the Son of Sam law.

The first Son of Sam law was passed in 1977, after reports that publishers were offering David Berkowitz huge sums of money for the rights to his story.[357] While that particular law was held to be unconstitutional by the United States Supreme Court in 1991, the law was amended, and the overwhelming majority of states have Son of Sam laws in place which prohibit criminals from profiting financially from selling or telling their stories to the media.[358]

Case Study: Washington, D.C., Sniper, Chief Moose, and Media Communications

In October of 2002, the area of Washington, D.C., and the surrounding states of Maryland and Virginia were terrorized by sniper killings. John Allen Muhammad and Lee Boyd Malvo's shooting rampage, which began on October 3, 2002, left ten dead and three wounded.[359]

During the investigation, a multi-jurisdictional task force was set up. The FBI, the ATF, numerous state and local police departments, along with other law enforcement agencies were involved in the investigation. When the police decided to begin communicating through the media with the person whom they believed was a lone sniper, it was decided that Montgomery County, Maryland, Police Chief Charles Moose would head up the investigation.[360]

As the killings went on, the killer left notes to the police. Near one murder scene, the killer left a Tarot "Death" card with the words "Dear Mr. Policeman, I am God."[361] On multiple occasions, the killer attempted to talk to the police, but was dismissed as a possible prank call. In a letter to police, the writer complained that at least six failed attempts to phone authorities since the killing spree began were "ignored" by "incompetent" people taking the calls.[362] The sniper complained in one angry note that he had been hung up on when trying to call the police.[363]

In this case, unlike many, Chief Moose headed up the investigation and also acted as the media spokesman. One veteran police official stated that was not standard protocol and in fact was not advisable. "You don't let the top guy be your spokesman," he said. "You do want someone who knows all of the details speaking to the press. If there is something that cannot be answered, and the top guy is speaking to the media, it looks like you are hiding something from the media and the public. And, if you have a spokesman, and they get it wrong, you can always claim that they were not in know and correct it—that cannot be done when you use the top guy as the spokesman."

But this situation was different. The panic caused by the sniper attacks was compared to a hostage situation. "This is a hostage situation, but it's a hostage of cities . . . Chief Moose is acting as the negotiator and this is the first time that the media is not an observer, but a participant in the hostage negotiation . . . That's what makes this case unique," stated Dr. Tod Burke, a Radford University expert on serial murder.[364]

"All of these things are designed to maximize the killer's feeling of power, superiority, relative to the community and the police," said Jack Levin, the Director of the Brudnick Center on Violence and Conflict at Northeastern University, as he alluded to the calling cards, messages, and notes that both this killer and others have left behind.[365] "The serial killer may take pleasure in taunting the cops, stating, 'See, I'm better than you,'" said Robert Castelli, a professor at John Jay College of Criminal Justice in New York and a former investigator with the New York State Police.[366]

In the Washington Sniper case, the killers sought out Chief Charles Moose, who was the "top guy," and who to the killer may have symbolized the investigation. "It could be that the killer perceive[d] Moose as the head guy and anyone else as a lackey. He may want to talk to the top man, not an underling," said Dr. Tod Burke.[367] "A lot of times, perpetrators will want to establish communications with that [visible] person," noted criminal profiler Reid Maloy.[368] In the Son of Sam case (discussed above), the killer reached out with letters to one of the police officials heading the investigation and also to New York City journalist Jimmy Breslin.[369]

Several days before the sniper was apprehended, Chief Moose said police had received a fresh communication from a person believed to be the sniper. But for the second time in recent days, Moose said a technical snafu had impeded their efforts to talk to each other.[370] Moose looked into the television cameras, spoke to the gunman, and stated that the method of communication suggested by the sniper was not possible, but that he did want to keep talking. "It is important that we do this without anyone else getting hurt," he said, hours after the sniper had shot his 13th victim, a bus driver standing in the doorway of his vehicle before 6:00 A.M.[371] Hours before, Moose had publicly pled with the sniper to call back because his call was partially inaudible, stating, "The person you called could not hear everything that you said. The audio was unclear and we want to get it right. Call us back so we can clearly understand."[372] Instead, the bus driver was shot.

At a press conference the next day, Moose reverted back into his role as guardian of public safety and stated, "We have not been able to assure anyone their safety with regards to this situation . . . We realize that the person or the people involved in this have shown a clear willingness and ability to kill people of all ages, all races, all genders, all professions. Different times, different days, and different locations."[373]

Moose had previously spoken to the killer through the media, after the shooting of a 13-year-old boy who was about to enter school. Moose asked the sniper to call a toll-free number, use a private post office box, or "another secure method." Moose stated, "You indicated that this is about more than violence . . . we are waiting to hear from you."[374]

The media noted that as Moose held his daily sniper briefings, it seemed as if his sentences were crafted with surgical precision. And they were, as FBI experts helped the chief write much of what he said—even when it appeared that Chief Moose was losing his temper, his words were guided by those who understood, or were attempting to understand, the sniper and his motivations.[375] If Moose or the police "misspeak and enrage the person, [they could] inspire the person to kill more,"[376] another criminologist noted. "What's unusual is the two-way communications. Both the cops and the killer are using the media to get messages back and forth. And of course, it's extremely unusual to be using the telephone . . . But, then again, what about this case is not unusual?"[377] One law enforcement official working on the investigation stated, "It's a coordinated response . . . There's a huge desire not to do things that will provoke the shooter."[378]

Professor Eric Hickey of California State University at Fresno and the author of *Serial Murderers and Their Victims* stated:

> It does appear to me that he is trying to mitigate this situation to some extent, trying to keep this guy at bay, trying to extract him a little bit and make him feel omnipotent. . . He is truly a mediator here. He is trying to keep people from being killed . . . The chief is definitely playing to this guy because he has to. Anything he can do to stop the sniper from shooting more people, he has to do.[379]

As the killings went on, the killers grew more confident and perhaps sought new ways of achieving the intoxicating highs that the killing produced; they began to make bizarre requests of Chief Moose. They apparently wanted to operate him like a puppet. In a press conference shortly before the arrest of the offenders, Chief Moose stated, "You have indicated that you want us to do and say certain things . . . you asked us to say 'we have caught the sniper like a duck in a noose.'"[380]

On Oct 24, 2002, John Allen Muhammad and Lee Boyd Malvo were arrested. They were found sleeping in their car, a blue Chevy Caprice at a rest step near Myersville, Maryland. At that time, police had been tipped off that Muhammad and Malvo were the snipers by a former army friend of Muhammad, Robert Edward Holmes, and police corroborated that information. The description of the car had been released to the public and the media. A truck driver noticed the car and used his truck to block the sniper's car while police were alerted. A weapon was recovered from the car that was linked to most of the sniper shootings. The car had been transformed into a killing machine by cutting a hole in the trunk to help create a hidden sniper's perch.[381]

Both Muhammad and Malvo were subsequently convicted of the murders in both Virginia and Maryland. Muhammad was sentenced to death in Virginia and to six life sentences in Maryland. Malvo was given life sentences in both Virginia and Maryland.

Case Study: The Letters of the BTK Killer

Dennis Rader was an Air Force veteran and president of a church council. He had worked 14 years installing alarms for ADT Security Systems,[382] and later worked as a compliance officer for Park City, Kansas. He was married, a father of three, and a former volunteer troop leader for the Boy Scouts.[383] Dennis Rader was also someone known by a far more sinister name, the BTK Killer. This self-coined nickname was used when he wrote to newspapers in the 1970s.[384] BTK stood for "Bind, Torture, and Kill."[385] Rader killed ten persons around the Wichita, Kansas, area between 1974 and 1991. He taunted police with letters that boasted of his murders, but he yielded few clues to his identity.[386]

By 2004, the case had long grown cold. BTK resurfaced in March of 2004 with a letter to a local newspaper, the *Wichita Eagle*, in which he sent photographs of the crime scene of a 1986 victim, Vickie Wegerle, along with her driver's license.[387] This let police and the media know that he was responsible for a killing that the BTK serial killer had never been credited for. He also hinted that he might be plotting more murders.[388]

Over the next 11 months, he led police on a very public chase, sending them letters and leaving packages in libraries and shopping malls.[389]

What police did now know, which is evidence that they did not have in the 1970s, was that the BTK Killer had left DNA, including semen, at three of his murder scenes.[390] Police had been communicating with BTK regularly and corresponded with BTK in a *Wichita Eagle* classified ad. In the ad, Wichita detectives falsely assured Rader that they could not trace a computer disk.[391]

Rader then sent another communication. In February 2005, Wichita television station KSAS received a translucent, purple floppy disk accompanied by a 3×5 index card with a message from BTK: "Any Communications will have a # assigned from now on, encase [sic] one is lost or not found."[392]

The BTK task force enlisted the expertise of Randy Stone, a 39-year-old Desert Storm vet who started in the Wichita Police Department's Forensic Computer Crime Unit in 1998. When Stone checked the disk, it contained only one file, named "Test A.rtf." The text of the file instructed investigators to read the index card, which did not provide clues. Stone checked the disk properties to see the previous user: someone named Dennis. Then he checked to see where the disk was last used: Wichita's Christ Lutheran Church. There was one Dennis on the church website's list of officers, a man named Dennis Rader.[393] After more than 31 years of investigation and over 100,000 man-hours, through the use of Guidance Software's EnCase Forensic program, the police had retrieved deleted files that contained Rader's name as the author. Other digital data indicated that the computer on which the disk was used was owned by Rader's church, where he was president of the council.[394]

"On a scale of one to ten, it was about a three in terms of computer forensics," Stone says. "As simple as that was, the sad thing is 95 percent of law enforcement in the U.S. could not have done something like that."[395]

With the name of a known suspect and DNA evidence left on crime scenes, police executed a search warrant and obtained a DNA sample from his daughter's medical records in order to establish a familial match.[396] The DNA tests showed that there was a great statistical likelihood that Dennis Rader was the BTK Killer who had left his DNA on the earlier crime scenes. That told police that "BTK was the father of Mr. Rader's daughter," said Lieutenant Kenneth Landwehr, who led the investigation.[397]

Rader was arrested for his crimes on February 25, 2005, and pled guilty with detailed, chilling courtroom confessions on June 27, 2005. Rader was sentenced to ten life sentences in the state of Kansas.[398]

CHAPTER 9

POLICE USE OF FORCE CASES AND POLICE SHOOTINGS

Police use of force cases and, more frequently, officer-involved shootings are cases that attract media attention. They are serious incidents. Departments should demonstrate the willingness to investigate these matters thoroughly and effectively. The vast majority of these incidents are later proven to be justifiable, meaning that the conduct of the officer was both legal and proper. Departments should also be willing to be upfront, honest, and willing to speak with the media about these incidents. This avoids the appearance of any type of cover-up.

In officer-involved shootings, a supervisor should ensure that the involved officer's weapon is not handled by anyone prior to the time that it is taken to the crime lab. All witnesses and anyone else who may have relevant information should be interviewed.

The goal of any investigation should be to find the truth, and police use of force and officer-involved shooting cases should be no different. An officer other than the involved member should be assigned to conduct the investigation. Often, outside agencies may play a role in the investigation, such as a prosecutor's office or the state police. Larger departments should have some type of internal affairs division, which handles matters of this type and acts and operates separately from the rest of the department.

One officer wrote in a Greensboro, North Carolina, newspaper about media and public attention concerning officer-involved shootings:

> When a police officer is involved in a shooting, public interest is high—and justified. After all, a public servant has either inflicted serious injury or taken the life of a member of the very community he or she is there to serve . . . Almost immediately after the situation plays out in real time, it plays out in the media. Bold headlines, newscast teasers, video footage of flashing police lights and a necessarily limited release of information, when used together, tend to sensationalize the events that have unfolded.
>
> Contrary to what movies and television portray, officers do not take satisfaction, pride or joy in shooting a suspect. Indeed, they may feel only the gratitude of survival or the relief of knowing that they prevented the death of another human being.
>
> The after-effects of an officer-involved shooting continue long after the incident has ended. Immediately after the shooting, the officer is placed on administrative leave, a normal course of action that indicates no wrongdoing by the officer . . . One of the most difficult things for many officers to accept is the negative public opinion that often appears in the local media. Some individuals verbally attack the police officers, blaming them for using deadly force or calling them killers for doing so . . . In recent years this country has seen a growing problem with school, church, and mall shootings where gunmen execute helpless victims. When police officers respond to these situations with deadly force, they are declared heroes. Officers who must use deadly force to protect their own lives deserve that same respect.[399]

The media is justified in its role in reporting facts of use of force and officer-involved shootings, based on the public's right to know the details and also in its role as a watchdog for the public.[400]

If the police use of force or shooting is justified, make that finding known to the media. Likewise, if the use of force or shooting is not justified, make that finding known to the media as well, along with any punishment or disciplinary actions taken.

Case Study: Demetrius DuBose Police Shooting

On July 24, 1999, in San Diego, California, police responded to a call of a burglary. The occupant of an apartment in the Mission Bay area had come home to find a man sleeping on the couch in his living room. Police were called and responded. A confrontation occurred between the offender and the police. The incident ended with former National Football League (NFL) linebacker and Notre Dame University captain Demetrius DuBose dead, shot multiple times and killed by police. That began a controversy that would end up in newspapers, protests, and courts for years.

Demetrius DuBose was born in 1971. He graduated from private Catholic grade and high schools. He was a basketball, track, and football star in high school, as well as a student body officer.[401] He was awarded a scholarship for football to Notre Dame University, traditionally one of the best football programs in the nation and one of the country's finest academic institutions. He was a captain on the team, and he made several All-American teams.[402] DuBose was a nominee for the Butkus award, given to the top college linebacker in the nation.[403] He graduated from the university in three and a half years with a double major in government and international relations.[404] He was a second round draft pick in the NFL, drafted by the Tampa Bay Buccaneers football team, the 34th player overall.[405] He signed a contract worth over one million dollars with the Buccaneers[406] and played for four years with them, before signing with and being cut from the New York Jets.[407] At the time of his death, he was aspiring to become a professional beach volleyball player.[408]

His football days were not without off-the-field incidents, and Demetrius DuBose's life appeared to spiral out of control after his NFL career ended. While at Notre Dame University, DuBose was suspended for two games, and the university penalized him by taking away two scholarships, after DuBose accepted a loan from a couple who were university graduates and backers.[409] As a junior, DuBose was arrested at a party along with Notre Dame star quarterback Rick Mirer, and they were charged with public intoxication and disorderly conduct.[410]

After being cut by the Jets, DuBose's life began to fall into a pattern of drug abuse and bizarre incidents. In September of 1998, he was arrested at a downtown club in South Bend, Indiana, the city where Notre Dame is located. He was asked to leave the club by a security guard, an off-duty police officer. He was being escorted out when he jumped, ripping a 20-foot pipe from the ceiling and causing the club to flood with over 1,600 gallons of water. DuBose then fought with several police officers and spit on the original officer with whom he had a confrontation. DuBose also had marijuana in his possession.[411]

There were rumors among his former teammates that DuBose was destitute, and it appeared that he was living out of his car.[412] In February 1999, he was arrested for trespassing and resisting arrest after fighting police when he was asked to leave a restaurant he had been ejected from the night before.[413] In June of 1999, California Highway Patrol officers came across DuBose's Land Rover parked on the side of the highway. Inside was DuBose, under the influence and possessing nearly an ounce of ketamine, an animal tranquilizer and club drug known as "special K." When asked to perform field sobriety tests by police officers, DuBose was unable to recite the alphabet.[414]

On the night of his death, Demetrius DuBose was staying with a roommate. He went to the home of a neighbor, slid open the glass door, and went to sleep inside. The occupant came home and found DuBose. He called police about a break-in. The neighbor was filling out a burglary report with police when DuBose was observed outside and pointed out to the police.[415]

Police went over to detain DuBose. The 6'1", 235-pound DuBose stopped, grabbed an officer, and flipped the officer over his shoulder, dropping him in a concrete plant box. Officers sprayed DuBose with mace, but that was unsuccessful. He then fled on foot. Officers chased him. He turned around when he was unsuccessful in his attempts to hide behind a building. He assumed a fighting stance. At that time, San Diego police officers were equipped with nunchakus, plastic fighting sticks that are martial arts weapons. An officer used the nunchakus on DuBose. They had no effect. DuBose then disarmed the officer and took possession of the officer's nunchakus. DuBose was able to disarm a second officer of nunchakus. He walked away.[416] He then turned and charged the officers. Officers fired their guns. DuBose was hit 9 to 11 times with bullets and was killed.[417] An autopsy later determined that DuBose had cocaine, ecstasy, and alcohol in his bloodstream at the time of his death.[418]

A San Diego police spokesman stated that DuBose had "tossed around one of [the] officers like he was a rag doll."[419] Initial police investigations ruled that it was a justifiable use of deadly force by police.

Yet many persons were not satisfied with that finding. The family of Demetrius DuBose filed a federal lawsuit against the police and the city of San Diego.[420] Some civic leaders in the African American community stated that police provoked the violent response by mishandling the initial contact.[421] Some said that it was unnecessary to handcuff DuBose and that he may have been handcuffed only because he was black.[422] A member of the executive committee of San Diego's NAACP chapter stated, "The way that the police handled the investigation is what escalated the tension and let things get out of control." Another civic leader likened the shooting to "lynching under the color of authority."[423] A former teammate and Notre Dame counselor asked, "Why did they have to shoot him in the chest? Couldn't they have shot him in the leg? He didn't have a gun. So why? Was this called for?"[424]

After the initial police investigation, the county prosecutor's office conducted an investigation. Their investigation found that police officers were justified in their use of force against Demetrius DuBose.[425] District Attorney Paul Pfingst ordered the 368-page report of the investigation, including sworn statements by witnesses and the involved police officers, posted on the county government's website. The district attorney said, "This won't convince people who don't want to be convinced, but I think it's going to be very hard for someone to say there's been a cover-up when they can dial up the case and get all the witness statements on the Internet."[426] San Diego Police Chief David Bejarano indicated that he agreed with the finding that the shooting was justified, but planned private meetings with African American leaders and attended a community meeting.[427]

After the release of the report, several hundred protesters staged a march in downtown San Diego to demand a special session of the city council to discuss the shooting.[428]

Both the Federal Bureau of Investigation and the U.S. Attorney reviewed reports and witness accounts, and they found both that the shooting of Demetrius DuBose was justified and that there was no evidence that his civil rights were violated.[429] The FBI special agent in charge of the San Diego office stated to the media, "It's my opinion that a thorough investigation was done and there is nothing left to do; we saw no violation of civil rights statutes."[430]

A citizen's review board in San Diego also heard the case and found that the officers were acting within police policy. The review board did say that the officers could have used better judgment and questioned why the officers tried to handcuff DuBose during the initial questioning.[431] In response to the report, San Diego Police Chief David Bejarano stated that he felt police acted properly.[432] Chief Bejarano also attended a settlement conference in the civil case, where he argued that the case should go to trial so a jury could vindicate the two officers.[433]

In February 2003, a racially diverse federal jury unanimously concluded that San Diego police officers were justified in their use of deadly force on Demetrius DuBose and that the department was not liable.[434] Police Chief Bejarano held a press conference for the media and stated, "The police department is gratified by the jury's findings, but remains mindful that a man lost his life in this encounter . . . We reviewed this shooting as we do with every other involving one of our officers. We try to learn from each incident in the hope that new knowledge might prevent another officer-involved shooting."[435]

The next month, Chief Bejarano wrote a letter to the *San Diego Union-Tribune*, the city's largest newspaper. In the letter, he stated, "Two of the most difficult challenges the San Diego Police Department and other law enforcement agencies have faced are 'racial profiling' and officer-involved shootings. Shortly after my appointment as chief of police in 1999, the [shooting] of Demetrius DuBose . . . sparked public debate over the use of force. [The shooting was] tragic to all involved. Officers involved in fatal shootings must make a split-second decision that in many cases leaves emotional scars that last a lifetime. A federal jury recently returned verdicts in favor of the city in the DuBose case. Although it was unfortunate, a life was lost; the verdicts vindicated the officers and the department's use-of-force procedures, policies, and training."[436]

WHAT THE PROS SAY

Limitations of Video-Documented Police Use of Force Encounters

"As an experienced law enforcement consultant in the field of police misconduct and use of force, I would like to share my experiences regarding video documented incidents and some of the limitations that I have encountered when analyzing them. Law enforcement being videotaped is occurring with increasing frequency, as witnessed on the news. Therefore, this information is designed to assist the officer, the supervisor, the investigator, or the trier of fact in evaluating a use of force incident. Remember that it can happen to you! Video is everywhere in our daily lives. There are video capabilities everywhere, except for public washrooms (I hope). It is important for a patrol officer working the streets to understand the limitations this medium has and its ability to accurately capture a use of force incident.

(Continued)

Technology has made it possible to videotape someone almost everywhere, through digital recording devices in police cars, police stations, public areas, cell phones, and personal handheld video cameras, just to mention a few. This makes an officer subject to video documentation 24/7 in real time as to what transpired at any given point in time. Surprise! It is like candid camera. Unfortunately, officers may not be aware that an incident may have been videotaped until days or weeks later, often when a videotape surfaces from a third party. To assist your written documentation, I would suggest a review on 'Guidelines for Documentation of a Use-of-Force Encounter.'[437]

We would all agree that experience, in most cases, is the best teacher. So I would like to share some details that happened to two officers on a case I worked on as a consultant, who were unaware they were being videotaped. The case involved a large retail department store's security video documenting a young female shoplifting. The district security supervisor reviewed the video-documented incident in their security office. It involved local police officers, who first questioned and then arrested the juvenile shoplifter.

The store's security supervisor had no police experience, yet he believed what he saw was excessive force. He presented a copy of the video to authorities, who initiated an investigation over a month after the incident. Think, from your own personal experience, how difficult it sometimes is to remember what you had for breakfast four days ago. Imagine without good written documentation how difficult it would be to refresh your memory. What would the accuracy of your recall from an incident several months ago be? Your recall may be documented and measured against someone who has a copy of the video of the incident and the opportunity to review, analyze, and then compare the video to your statement. Unable to review the video documentation before questioning, the officers were ordered to give separate statements, which were not completely supported by the video.[438]

At the conclusion of the investigation, unfortunately, one officer was suspended for 30 days, and the other, a female officer, faced criminal charges and was terminated from her department. Be aware that all documented footage is subject to review by 'Monday morning quarterbacks.'

If one of your fellow officers has had to respond to this type of investigation, involving allegations of misconduct or excessive use of force on video, then ask him to share his experiences and learn from them. Experience may be the best teacher, but this type of situation is better learned from other officers as opposed to personal experience. Remember Murphy's Law: 'Whatever can go wrong, will go wrong,' and prepare for it. It you use physical force to arrest a suspect, then assume that you have been videotaped, and document accordingly. It is smart to think 'what if,' and retain a copy of the case report, the arrest report, and any additional reports and notes for at least a year. This will allow you to refresh your memory, if needed. If in doubt as to what could happen, just remember the Rodney King incident, which led to global publicity for the officers. Officers were indicted, several served prison time, riots ensued, and King was awarded $3.8 million in a civil suit he filed against the officers and the City of Los Angeles.

Over the past 20 years, I have evaluated numerous use of force incidents that were captured on video. Many have had similar limitations. Know that these limitations may help confirm or refute allegations of excessive force.

I would like to discuss one additional videotaped incident which I did consulting work on. Initially, my review led me to believe that the officer may have acted inappropriately in his use of force. This incident involved an off-duty uniformed officer who was working security on a riverboat casino. The casino had video cameras located throughout the facility. The video cameras documented the arrest. There were, however, no audio recordings. The security office was small and congested, filled with furniture and equipment, and had no interview area. As a result, the suspect had to stand. I later learned that the arrestee had threatened to fight with the casino security officers, as well as the accused officer.

(Continued)

It appeared from his behavior that he was intoxicated. This was later supported by other documentation, including police reports, witness statements, and the personal observation of the arresting officers.

The booking area where the alleged acts of excessive force took place had a single ceiling-mounted video camera. The arrestee's lawyer got a copy of the video and presented it to the Attorney General's Office and federal authorities. A civil rights investigation was conducted into the incident. A civil lawsuit was then filed against the officer. As a result, an internal departmental investigation was initiated against the officer. The force which was at issue involved a handcuffed subject, seen slightly moving towards the officer, as the officer stood an arm's length away and directly in front of the arrestee. The subject's verbal threats and his forward movement prompted the officer to react by grabbing the arrestee with both hands on his outer biceps, and he turned and placed the offender on the floor. During the takedown procedure, the arrestee's head struck the corner of a padded office chair. There were no visible injuries. Then the arrestee went out of the range of the video behind a tall file cabinet. The officer was seen as he turned, looking down at the suspect, and then he performed a stomping motion with his right leg. It at first appeared to be a retaliatory kick from the camera angle, which supported the plaintiff's allegations.

After I interviewed the officers, the witnesses, read the police reports, and did an in-house reenactment, it clarified what had happened in the video. I was then able to better understand the totality of the circumstances at the moment the force was applied, by putting myself in the same circumstances as that of the accused officer. The camera had limitations and did not capture the arrestee as he attempted to kick the officer in the groin before the leg stomping motion, nor did the video camera accurately illustrate the room dimensions by documenting how small and congested it was. The size of the room limited the officer's mobility and options to avoid possible injury, which made the force 'objectively reasonable' under the circumstances.

One of the problems with most video footage is that the video is without audio recording. A notable exception is the video which is sometimes mounted inside of a police squad car. In the aforementioned case, the video, without audio recording, was one-dimensional and therefore unable to document important facts, such as the verbal threats made towards the officer to physically harm him, and the movement by the offender was perceived by the officer to be the start of a knee lift at the officer's groin.

I have listed some points that I would like to share with the reader. The information has helped me to better understand that video documentation is good, but also that it has limited capabilities and that it does not tell the whole story. It must therefore be reviewed as a tool, as a piece of the puzzle, but not as the absolute and final determining piece of physical evidence. To keep it in proper perspective, captured video footage always needs clarification and complete follow-up investigations to support and/or dispel what the eye sees. Consider the following in any video-documented incident:

- The video may not document verbal conversations due to no audio capabilities or too much background noise.
- The video may only capture a portion of the entire incident due to dynamic movement, obstructions, and weather conditions.
- Video is normally seen from only one prospective angle.
- At night, poor lighting conditions may cast shadows obstructing clarity.
- The presence of multiple officers standing around may obstruct portions of the video.
- At night there may be little or no illuminated artificial light source to increase clarity.
- If there is audio capability, the distance between the officer and the video unit may affect transmission reception range.

(Continued)

- Unknown equipment malfunctions can affect clarity.
- Video equipment can be damaged during physical conflicts.
- There may be a failure of an officer to turn a body microphone on.
- Video time stamps and counters often do not match real time.
- A video camera cannot automatically zoom in as needed to increase clarity.
- Black and white video footage has more shadows than color.
- Weather conditions may affect clarity, for example, rain, snow, or fog.
- Extremely fast movement may be difficult to see.
- Spit or clear fluids are difficult to see on video replay.

There may be more things to consider based on the particular circumstances at issue. Remember, do not jump to conclusions based on an initial viewing of a particular video-documented use of force incident. Wait until you have reviewed, researched, and analyzed all the pertinent evidence. There is an old adage in police work, passed down from the veteran cops to the rookies: 'Kid, believe half of what you see and nothing of what you hear.'" **Chicago Police Officer (Retired) James Marsh**

Officer James Marsh is a retired 25-year veteran of the Chicago Police Department. He taught physical training and self-defense at the Chicago Police Academy. He is one of the nation's leading use of force consultants and runs his own company, Marsh and Associates. His website may be viewed at www.jmarshassoc.com, and he may be emailed at jmarsh7618@aol.com.

CHAPTER 10

POLICE CORRUPTION CASES

There may be no bigger betrayal of the public trust by law enforcement than corruption cases. The breaking of laws by those entrusted to uphold them is also highly offensive to the vast majority of honest men and women in police work.

As with any investigation, in a corruption case, the goal should be to find out the truth. The investigation should be thorough and complete. Illegitimate claims of corruption or of excessive force should be weeded out. These false claims may perhaps be made by someone with a financial motive, someone seeking leverage in a criminal case, someone with an agenda against law enforcement. But when the claims of police corruption are substantiated, then the department should take action swiftly and without delay.

Police corruption gives the whole system the appearance of being tainted and illegitimate. It undermines legitimate efforts and builds mistrust within the community. It discourages people from coming forward with information about crimes and from cooperating with law enforcement.

In corruption cases, law enforcement needs to reach out to the media to let the public know steps are being taken to investigate accusations of corruption. Law enforcement officials should also notify the public about what steps are being taken with officers against whom claims have been substantiated, and if any prosecution will take place.

Often, corrupt officers will pick and choose their victims carefully, in much the same way any other savvy criminal would do. They will choose their victims based on them being high reward and low risk. Part of the low risk means that the victim will likely not come forward to complain of any police wrongdoing. The media can be a helpful tool to reach out to possible victims who may have not been aware of an ongoing investigation.

Case Study: Technology and Police Radios and Computers

Police should operate as if they are always being monitored and watched by some type of technology. Many police cars are monitored by video and audio surveillance. Increasing numbers of police cars are equipped with global positioning devices. Many stations are filled with cameras. Officers should be aware of this and should always conduct themselves as professionals, as they would when they believe their actions are not being recorded. Failure to do so can expose them to embarrassment, bring discredit upon their department, and lead in some cases to civil and criminal liability.

Law enforcement should be unbiased and able to put aside any knowledge, experience, and preconceived notions they have in order to work and be able to decide every case on a fact-by-fact basis. Much like a good juror, a police officer should be able to be fair and impartial. Police must be able to conduct an investigation, determine in an investigation whether there is enough evidence to charge, figure out if there is enough evidence to arrest, and work toward establishing the truth.

Officers should also be aware that in virtually every case, the prosecution and the defense attorneys will subpoena relevant videotapes, audiotapes, 911 tapes, and police computer transmissions. What is on these tapes may impact a criminal or civil case.

Jeffrey Dahmer is one of the world's most infamous serial killers. He was convicted in 1992 of the murder of 15 men. Dahmer was arrested on July 22, 1991, when Tracy Edwards, a would-be victim who Dahmer had lured into his Milwaukee, Wisconsin, apartment, escaped, with one handcuff dangling from his wrist, and flagged down the police. The police returned to the apartment of Dahmer, where they spoke to him, searched the apartment, and arrested him. Inside the apartment, police found torsos soaking in acid, severed heads in the refrigerator and freezer, skulls in boxes, a hand and a genital organ in an 80-quart kettle pot, and photos of victims in various stages of dismemberment. Two human hearts and a bicep muscle Dahmer said he planned to eat were in the freezer. A sickening stench permeated the whole scene.[439]

Dahmer had a close call with police in which he was almost arrested on May 30, 1991. In that case, police returned an underage naked male who had run into the street and who had already been disoriented due to an attack to Dahmer's custody.[440] Dahmer killed 14-year-old Konerak Sinthasomphone moments after the police left.[441] Dahmer then killed four more victims between the time of the killing of Sinthasomphone and the time he was arrested when presumably about to kill Tracy Edwards. In that time period, Dahmer killed victims Matt Turner, Jeremiah Weinberger, Oliver Lacy, and Joseph Brandehoft.

In the May 30, 1991, incident, a citizen called the Milwaukee police after her daughter and niece told her of a naked boy wandering on the street. The citizen is reported to have repeatedly asked an officer if he was certain Sinthasomphone was an adult, as he was being returned to the custody of Dahmer.[442] "As positive as I can be," the officer said.[443]

Dahmer, in a display of quick thinking which reflected much about his mental state, told the police officers that the boy was his homosexual lover and had drunkenly wandered out of his apartment.[444] "The story I used was he was a houseguest, a friend who sometimes drinks too much and runs out in the street naked,"[445] Dahmer later testified in a deposition for civil lawsuits filed by the family of the victim against Milwaukee police. Dahmer also testified that he had already injected diluted acid into the boy's skull once when police found the teenager wandering dazed and naked in the street.[446] Dahmer admitted that he would drill a tiny hole into the skulls of his victims "just enough to open a passageway to the brain," and then inject hydrochloric acid to induce a "zombie-like state."[447] Dahmer's testimony at the deposition indicated that police had failed to spot the hole he had drilled in the youth's skull. After the officers left, Dahmer testified that he gave the boy another injection that killed him.[448]

After releasing Sinthasomphone to the custody of Jeffrey Dahmer, police joked about the incident on the police radio; the tape of this was a key part of the victim's family's civil suit against the police officers and the city of Milwaukee. The tape revealed an officer, laughing as he reported finishing his investigation:

> "Intoxicated Asian, naked male," one officer said, "was returned to his sober boyfriend . . . My partner is going to get deloused at the station."[449]

The Dahmer case and the police tapes outraged many in both the gay community and the minority community. Dahmer was gay. Most of his victims were gay, and he had met most of them at malls, gay bars, and bathhouses.[450]

The day before the civil case against the police officers was to go to trial, the city settled for $850,000 with the family of the victim.[451] The two policemen were fired; one later regained his job.[452]

Perhaps no trial in the 20th century attracted more publicity and media attention than the O. J. Simpson murder trial. O. J. Simpson was charged, tried, and acquitted in the murder of his ex-wife, Nicole Brown Simpson, and her friend, Ronald Goldman. O. J. Simpson is a National Football League Hall of Fame member, a former Heisman trophy winner, which is an award given to college football's best player, and an actor who had starred in numerous successful movies and endorsed many products. Despite a great deal of evidence against Simpson, he was acquitted in a case where the defense put the Los Angeles Police Department and its tactics on trial. Public opinion was split along racial lines on whether they felt that Simpson was guilty or innocent. O. J. Simpson is African American; his victims were Caucasian.

In September of 2007, O. J. Simpson again found himself in legal trouble, charged with robbery and other charges stemming from an incident at a Las Vegas hotel. The case went to trial in September of 2008. Part of the defense strategy was to claim that law enforcement had a vendetta against Simpson and were out to get him due to a belief that he had gotten away with murder in the highly publicized earlier case.

In the Las Vegas hotel robbery case, jurors heard as evidence a recording of a police employee exulting on tape, "This is great . . . California can't get him . . . Now we'll be able to."[453]

A police detective conceded during his testimony that the statement, which referred to Simpson's 1995 acquittal for the murder of his ex-wife and Ronald Goldman, was made as a team of officers examined a Las Vegas casino hotel room and that the comment came from a civilian employee of the police department, not a sworn officer.[454]

The defense sought to exploit this as evidence that the police in Las Vegas were out for retribution against Simpson. Simpson's defense lawyer questioned the police detective on the recorded statement made by the civilian employee that referred to getting Simpson. He asked if police were conducting "what's supposed to be an unbiased investigation." The detective indicated that the police were. The defense attorney asked the detective, "And they're prejudging him; they want to get Mr. Simpson?" The detective correctly responded, "I can't say what someone else is thinking,"[455] but the insinuation was clear.

In the O. J. Simpson case, a tape was played of a statement by someone who did not even have anything to do with the investigation of the incident. This is a clear example of why law enforcement personnel must always conduct themselves as if they are on tape. In this case, this statement did not negatively impact the case, as the defendant was found guilty on October 3, 2008. On December 5, 2008, he was sentenced to 9 to 30 years in prison.[456]

Perhaps no event involving the police has shocked the American public more than the Rodney King beating case. In that case, on March

3, 1991, Rodney King, a convicted felon, led police on a high-speed chase. At the end of the chase, four Los Angeles police officers beat Rodney King in an incident that was captured on a home video made by a man from a nearby apartment. The four officers were tried for using excessive force on King, but acquitted in state court. The acquittal sparked days of rioting in Los Angeles. The four officers were then tried in federal court for violating King's civil rights, a move which angered many police officers who claimed that this was a violation of the laws against double jeopardy, or trying a person twice for the same incident. Two of the officers were convicted in the federal trial and two were acquitted. Rodney King was later awarded $3.8 million in his civil suit against the city of Los Angeles and the Los Angeles police.

Evidence of racism by the officers was admitted in the trial, as two of the officers had used their police computers to communicate with each other before the beating of Rodney King and had described a quarrel that had reportedly involved African Americans as something out of *Gorillas in the Mist*, a popular movie at the time starring Sigourney Weaver as a scientist who devoted her life to the study of gorillas. The transcript of that computer transmission is as follows:

> THE STAKEOUT TEAM REPLIES: "Hahahaha . . . let me guess who be the parties."

> 12:47 A.M. THE POLICE RADIO DISPATCHER ALERTS NEARBY SQUAD CARS THAT THE CALIFORNIA HIGHWAY PATROL IS PURSUING A WHITE HYUNDAI AT HIGH SPEED. MINUTES LATER POWELL AND WIND HELP APPREHEND THE DRIVER AND TWO PASSENGERS.

> 12:56 A.M. LAPD SERGEANT STACEY C. KOON NOTIFIES THE NIGHT WATCH COMMANDER AT THE FOOTHILL POLICE HEADQUARTERS THAT ONE SUSPECT HAS BEEN BEATEN BY THE

ARRESTING OFFICERS: "You just had a big-time use of force . . ."

THE WATCH COMMANDER REPLIES: "Oh well . . . I'm sure the lizard didn't deserve it . . . haha."

1:12 A.M. POWELL AND WIND HAVE ANOTHER COMPUTER CHAT WITH THEIR FRIENDS ON THE BURGLARY STAKEOUT: "Ooops."

"Ooops, what?"

"I haven't beaten anyone this bad in a long time."

"Oh not again . . . Why for you do that . . . I thought you agreed to chill out for a while . . ."[457]

In the Rodney King criminal trial against the four police officers in state court, the judge allowed the prosecution to ask questions about race, denying the defense's motion. "To say that those comments aren't racially biased is like sticking your head in the sand," the judge said. "This is probably the first trial in which I will allow racial questions. I feel it's a significant and relevant thought in the case."[458]

The defense attorneys for one of the police officers, Laurence Powell, had sought to exclude the statements from his trial and the trial of three other police officers. Attorneys argued that the comments, made by either Powell or his partner, Timothy Wind, over a police computer system, did not belong in the case because they occurred before Rodney King was beaten. The judge, however, allowed the comments made via the computer to come in as evidence in the criminal case. The judge said race "could be part of the motive here," and the comments were relevant.[459]

Such shocking examples of the use of police communications, police radio, and police computers should be reminders to all of those in law enforcement to conduct themselves as professionals at all times. All actions taken today may be scrutinized tomorrow.

Case Study: 1980s Miami Police Hiring and Corruption

Miami's 1980s image of cocaine and corruption, depicted in movies and television, was shaped by both the lucrative drug trade and also by two events in 1980. That year, a jury acquitted two white policemen for the shooting of an African American male they had stopped, which led to violent rioting in the Liberty City section of the city.[460] At the time, the riots were described by some as "the worst race riots America had seen."[461] Additionally, 125,000 Cuban residents had arrived in Miami as part of the Mariel boatlift. Many of these people were seeking refuge from the communist government in Cuba run by Fidel Castro. The people arriving in Miami also included many inmates of prisons and mental hospitals.[462]

The Mariel boatlift was depicted in the movie *Scarface*, with Al Pacino as Tony Montana, a drug-lord who arrives in the United States in the boatlift.

The number of hard-core criminals arriving from Cuba helped send Miami's murder rate soaring.[463] Dr. Geoffrey Alpert, a criminal sociologist at the University of Miami, estimated that 12 to 15 percent of the Cubans that arrived from Mariel were active criminals, and about 6 to 8 percent were extremely hardened.[464] "They didn't care . . . They would do anything," said Dr. Alpert.[465] In time, however, most of the worst offenders killed each other, went to prison, or awaited deportation.[466] "The Mariel boatlift brought some fairly bad people to our community," stated Alpert.[467]

At least 70 to 75 percent of the cocaine in the United States in the 1980s entered the country through Miami.[468]

One Miami homicide investigator, Lieutenant Mike Gonzalez, called 1980 the year "the world went crazy."[469]

Those in charge of the city decided to hire more police and to hire a more racially diverse group of police. In 1980, in the aftermath of the acquittal of the white police officers who had been charged with the fatal shooting of a black man, Mayor Maurice Ferre stated:

The Fraternal Order of Police in the city of Miami has traditionally been the bastion of a racist group. They are mostly Southern whites, and they don't like Jews, they don't like foreigners, they don't like blacks, and until recently, they have maintained an all-white operation. The reason this city is changing now is because I'm the guy who blew the whistle on the city.[470]

Two years after a hiring freeze on police during the late 1970s,[471] the size of the Miami Police Department nearly doubled in size to combat Miami's soaring crime rate, much of it drug-related.[472] At the time, the city was under a federal order to hire more minorities to the police department.[473] Mayor Ferre persuaded the City Commission to accept a decree under which 50 percent of all future hirings would come from ethnic minorities.[474]

The City Commission then decided that 80 percent of the recruits to the overwhelmingly white Miami Police Department should henceforth be Hispanic or black.[475] In the rush for the affirmative action hiring, the standards to become a Miami police officer fell.[476] Some termed the written test that recruits had to pass in order get hired as a Miami police officer a sham. This test was created by an outside consulting agency that soon afterwards went bankrupt, and the police department was not allowed to see individual results of the tests.[477]

Miami was also left with an unusually young department. In addition to the fact that the new hiring policy resulted in an influx of young officers, the Miami police department also adopted an affirmative action policy of promoting blacks and Hispanics ahead of more senior officers.[478] This caused many Caucasian officers to leave and go to other departments. It also caused a great deal of racial and ethnic strife within the department.[479] There were remedial reading and writing classes for Miami police officers. Police Chief Clarence Dickson himself had previously failed his captain's exams.[480]

"These young officers hit the ground running . . . we had rookies training rookies," later stated Miami Police Spokeswoman Cori Zywotow.[481]

Numerous Miami police officers were charged with roles in drug trafficking, three with murder. In 1988, Chief Dickson asked the United States Department of Justice to examine how the Miami department handled its corruption problem and to "help measure the effects cocaine and other drugs are having on officers."[482] Chief Dickson stated, "We have made a lot of changes—surface changes—to correct problems, based mostly on our in-house critiquing. I want someone on the outside to tell me if we have done enough . . . This will give us the good, the bad, and the ugly—hanging the old linen out . . . like it or not, it's got to be done."[483]

Over 100 current and former Miami police officers had been implicated as being involved in criminal behavior in the three years before the study.[484] The Miami police badge became known to some within the force as the "Master Badge," after the Master Card credit card, because "you could get anything with it."[485]

Fourteen police officers received prison sentences for their connection with the notorious "river cops" case, a cocaine theft ring of police officers which was uncovered in July 1985 when three drug smugglers drowned after jumping into the water.[486] The officers then sold millions of dollars of cocaine for resale.[487] Many of the "river cops," including ringleaders Rodolfo Arias and Carlos Pedrera, were among a large group of officers that the Miami Police Department was forced to hire quickly after the Mariel boatlift and the Liberty City riots.[488] These officers, mainly young officers in their 20s and 30s, appeared to have emulated the lavish television lifestyles of fictional *Miami Vice* detectives Sonny Crockett and Ricardo Tubbs, and favored flashy cars, clothes, and jewelry.[489]

Rodolfo Arias testified that his increasingly corrupt group turned Miami's streets into "its own private crime kingdom." The officers started out by routinely stealing small quantities of drugs and cash from suspects they had detained, and then they expanded to stealing drugs directly from dealers.[490] Arias also testified that he had taken part in the theft of hundreds of pounds of cocaine and had become a millionaire.[491]

One former officer, Omar Manzanilla, when pleading guilty, stated, "I want to apologize for being unable to resist the pressures and temptations that faced me. I have disgraced my badge and my uniform."[492]

Spokeswoman Cori Zywotow stated, "I think police corruption is as old as the hills." According to Zywotow, what was new was the lure that drugs offered to the police, particularly in the Miami area, where so much cocaine passed through when entering the United States.[493] Then Dade County State Attorney and future U.S. Attorney General Janet Reno commented to *Newsweek* that drugs and drug money are a "tremendously corruptive force, not only for the police, but for everybody."[494]

Spokeswoman Zywotow indicated that internal discussions produced several explanations for the corruption in the Miami Police Department—going back to the Mariel boatlift and the Liberty City Race Riots of 1980.[495] Zywotow said that hiring after the riots was often indiscriminate, and many of the new recruits were poorly screened and inadequately trained.[496] The successor of Mayor Ferre as mayor of Miami, Mayor Xavier Suarez, stated he felt that the police department failed to screen the recruits properly.[497] Many of the recruits had criminal records.

At the time, a Federal Bureau of Investigation spokesman, who was heading the Miami police corruption probe, stated, "Miami has the most significant police corruption problem in the nation."[498]

The Miami of today has a very different police department and is a very different city. Yet the lessons learned in the 1980s were painful for the city and reminders to the rest of the nation of the dangers of rapid and reactionary hiring, lowering standards, and the lure of corruption that comes with drugs, money, and illegal enterprise.

WHAT THE PROS SAY

"Police prosecutions are backwards in many ways. The individuals who would normally be a prosecutor's witnesses are now the defendants, and the individuals who we would be cross-examining are now our witnesses. Police officers have an incredibly difficult job. The overwhelming majority of the officers out there do that job with honor and dignity. There are some, however, who cross the line and become criminals. These are the officers who steal money from citizens, be they drug dealers or law-abiding citizens. These are the officers who use excessive force on individuals they encounter on the street.

No one relishes the idea of prosecuting the police, but the public needs to have confidence in the men and women who serve and protect them. Police have incredible power and responsibility. Among those powers, the police have the power to arrest, the ability to carry a firearm on their person, which in most states would otherwise be prohibited, and they have the authority to use that firearm in the course of their duties.

With such powers come certain responsibilities and obligations. A police officer's conduct is held, in many ways, to a higher standard. When an officer engages in misconduct, the public has a right to know about that misconduct. Bringing that information to the public is always balanced with the officer/defendant's right to a fair trial.

Many prosecutors will tell you that criminals will look for the most vulnerable individuals to victimize: the young, the elderly, undocumented aliens, the mentally ill, those who are more unlikely to report a crime and, when they do, to be taken seriously. For every one individual who comes forward to report a crime committed against him, you can bet there are several others out there who did not come forward. Police defendants are no different than other criminals in this respect. They will choose their victims, looking for those that will not report them or will not be believed when they do attempt to report police misconduct.

It is helpful then in these instances, where you have one victim, to let the public know that police officers who cross the line will be prosecuted. Getting that information out to the public then serves a purpose, in that it can bring forward leads on other victims of crimes. Getting that information out to the local press can give a victim, who might otherwise never come forward for fear of retribution, the courage to report police misconduct.

In this digital age, so much of our daily life is recorded on security surveillance tapes. These tapes can prove invaluable in criminal prosecutions, and police prosecutions are no different in this respect. Before, if a citizen claimed to have been beaten without justification by an officer, that citizen would have little recourse without witnesses or some other kind of corroboration. Now, with video surveillance cameras in more and more places, these kinds of allegations can often be supported or disproved." **Assistant State Attorney David R. Navarro**

David Navarro has been an assistant state attorney in the Cook County State Attorney's Office since 1994. He is currently the supervisor of the Professional Standards Unit of the office, which investigates any allegations of excessive force and reviews all officer-involved shootings in Cook County. He has worked on many police corruption investigations and in 2007 was appointed as a special assistant United States attorney to work on an investigation involving the Chicago Police Department Special Operations Section.

CHAPTER 11

WANTED PERSONS AND FUGITIVES

There is perhaps no area where law enforcement and the media have worked together with greater success and cooperation than in the area of tracking down wanted persons and fugitives. There have been many high-profile and celebrated examples of police working hand in hand with the media.

The media is able to publicize the identities and cases of wanted offenders and reach out to an audience beyond that which law enforcement would be able to reach. The media can reach out to persons who may recognize the offender. Media attention also puts pressure on the offender and anyone who may be assisting him in his flight from the law, as it lets the offender know of police investigative efforts to track them down.

While there may be areas where the media and law enforcement may be at odds, journalists have made significant contributions in capturing fugitives.[499] One journalist stated:

> The notion among journalists that we shouldn't be merely a tool of law enforcement does not preclude an appropriate role where we should be colleagues . . . The dividing line is this: our loyalty as journalists always is to the public. If you use that as your guiding star, it will tell you whether it's appropriate to be in a partnership with the police.[500]

The partnership between the police and the media has been strong and long-lived in these types of cases. Police/media cooperation in tracking down wanted fugitives gained impetus in the 1930s, when the Federal Bureau of Investigation and the United States Department of Justice began to use the media savvy term "public enemy" to describe fugitives from the law.[501] In 1950, the FBI, in association with the news media, founded the Top Ten Most Wanted Fugitives list. In 1965, the American Broadcasting Company (ABC), in association with FBI director J. Edgar Hoover, launched the television series *The F.B.I.*, which often included photographs and descriptions of real-life fugitives sought by the FBI.[502] By far the biggest and most successful example of law enforcement and media cooperation began in 1988, with the premiere of *America's Most Wanted*, the television show devoted to the profiling and capturing of fugitives.[503]

Case Study: Rick Church: The All-American Murderer's Manhunt

Woodstock, Illinois, in McHenry County, is a sleepy town of about 20,000 people, right off of the Wisconsin border. The city's website advertises Woodstock as "the kind of city that people fall in love with."[504] The website further touts Woodstock as "a true Midwestern city where community and quality of life are values that are revealed in every street and sidewalk. Beginning in the center of its historic Square and moving out to its farm-cushioned edge, Woodstock is unique—a place that its citizens are proud to call home. So whether you come because of the culture, entertainment, countryside, business opportunities, or just to be a part of its Victorian charm, Woodstock offers a million reasons to stay."[505]

With a low crime rate and a family atmosphere, Woodstock appears to be a wholesome town, a slice of small-town America. But the morning of August 21, 1988, is one that Woodstock would like to forget.

And one-time Northern Illinois College student Rick Church, an all-American boy and former high school football player, is a resident that they would also like to forget.

On August 20, right before he was to leave for his sophomore year at Northern Illinois University, Richard Church sat in his mother's apartment watching movies, drinking whiskey and beer, and taking pills.[506] And his 17-year-old former girlfriend Colleen Ritter was on his mind. Church was despondent and embittered over the end of his relationship with Colleen, a pairing that Colleen's parents did not approve of.[507] The couple had met at Marian Central Catholic High School,[508] when they both were students there. He had played football there, starting at center, and he graduated in 1987.[509]

At 5:00 A.M. on August 21, 1988, Church went to the home where his ex-girlfriend lived with her parents.[510] With a hammer he found in the tool shed, a knife, and a piece of wood with a nail in it, he beat, bludgeoned, and stabbed her parents, Raymond and Ruth Ann Ritter, to death. Church blamed the parents for the breakup of his relationship with Colleen. He then chased Colleen into the street and repeatedly stabbed her.[511] Church came into the bedroom, pressed a towel over Colleen's ten-year-old brother's face, and stabbed him in the right side of the abdomen, apparently with a piece of wood with a nail in one end.[512] He then scrawled an obscenity about Raymond Ritter on the refrigerator door and fled.[513]

He was later identified by Colleen and her brother Matthew as Colleen's spurned boyfriend, Rick Church.[514] Two friends who had spent the night at the Ritter home also identified Church.[515] A neighbor heard Raymond Ritter saying, "What are you doing here? You got no business here. Get the hell out of here."[516] Minutes later, another neighbor heard a female scream.[517] Raymond's bloody body was found at the foot of his bed on the first floor; his wife's body was on her back in bed with a pillow over her face.[518] A great deal of physical evidence was left on the scene, much of which tied Church to the crime.[519]

Following the attack, Church then went home to his mother and believing that he had killed his ex-girlfriend, told his mother, "I killed Colleen."[520] Church took off that morning in his mother's 1981 dark blue Dodge pickup truck.[521]

According to police, he checked into a hotel in Mauston, Wisconsin, that night as Ronnie Quinlan and a few weeks later gave his name as Randy Hunt at a motel in Santa Monica, California. The truck was found that September 13 in West Hollywood, California.[522]

While Church was on the run, the families of both the victims and suspect continued to reside in Woodstock.[523] Law enforcement agencies received "a couple of thousand leads" in the years that Church was a fugitive,[524] from nearly every state in the United States.[525]

The case was the subject of numerous television programs, including *A Current Affair* and *Unsolved Mysteries*. *America's Most Wanted* featured the Church case five times.[526] It was also discussed on *Donahue*, *Oprah*, and *Geraldo*.[527] Both the FBI and the U.S. Marshals were involved in the hunt for Church. McHenry County Sheriff George Hendel indicated that he had contacted some 30,000 law enforcement agencies across the U.S. and "every coroner's office."[528] The search for Church involved local, state, and national agencies.[529] Church's picture was plastered on billboards in California, Arizona, and New Mexico.[530] While on the run, Church was named in a local Woodstock (McHenry County, Illinois) murder warrant as well as an FBI warrant for unlawful flight to avoid prosecution.[531]

The 39 month search for Church ended on November 20, 1991, when Salt Lake City Detective Gary Park was eating at Bennett's BBQ Pit, where Church was an assistant manager.[532] Church was working the cash register when Park stepped up to pay. Park recognized Church as someone whose picture he had seen.[533] Detective Park had recently been flipping through some FBI wanted posters in search of a burglary suspect, and one of the images stuck with him.[534] "When I saw him, I realized he looked like somebody we'd been looking for before," Park said.[535]

In a textbook example of truly outstanding police work, after eating lunch, Park returned to his office and began looking through wanted posters. Park looked at the poster issued by the Illinois State Police for Church's arrest. He then returned to the restaurant with a photograph of Church. The Salt Lake City FBI chief later indicated that Park had seen Church's photo in a Salt Lake City newspaper or on one of the TV programs that portrayed the crime, in addition to the wanted posters.[536] Park sat down at a table and quietly began comparing Church's face with the photograph. He was convinced that Church and the man on the poster were the same. Park privately asked a restaurant employee to identify the cashier. He was told the employee was named Danny Lee Carson.[537]

Park then checked the name through a Utah state computer at the police station that lists all people who have registered for a personal state identification card, and the Carson name with Church's photo turned up on a card issued October 25. Park then called Woodstock police to alert them that he would be sending a photo to them for verification that the man in the picture was Church. Woodstock police indicated that the photo sent to them was Church. A plan was set up with the FBI to arrest Church at the restaurant the next day, Thursday, November 21. Church, however, had that Thursday off. Law enforcement then went to arrest Church at his residence, which was two blocks away from the restaurant.[538] Church resided at the Brigham Apartments, a 150-year-old building once occupied by Mormon founder Brigham Young and his wives.[539] Church gave up peacefully after police showed up at the building just after 8:30 A.M. He had been living there for just a few months and was described by the building manager as a model tenant who paid his $255 monthly rent early, never gave her problems, and was a likeable person.[540]

During his time on the run, Church successfully eluded authorities. He grew a beard, although he later shaved it, and assumed at least two false names, police said. When he reached Salt Lake City, he settled on Danny Lee Carson, but was Ronnie Quinlan before that, police said. He carried a fake birth certificate and appropriated two Social Security numbers.[541]

On his application to work at the BBQ Pit, Church gave a home address and phone number that turned out to be for a company called Mail Receiving Services Inc. Thus, the workers at the store could pass along phone messages, and the mailbox he rented became an apartment number on his application.[542]

When Church was taken to the local FBI office for questioning, he disclosed his true identity, authorities said. One tip-off was that the young-looking Church had listed his age as 33 on his false I.D. Fingerprints and a triangle-shaped scar on his nose confirmed his identity.[543]

While a fugitive, Church even managed to cash about $400 in U.S. savings bonds in Los Angeles with his own Northern Illinois University identification card. There is a three-day waiting period to cash bonds, but it takes much longer to trace them to a central federal government clearinghouse, where authorities can match numbers on the bonds with those on a wanted list. By then, Church had gotten the money and was gone.[544]

While on the run, Church worked at fast-food restaurants, which often do not conduct background checks. He worked manual labor jobs, which often pay in cash, under the table.[545] He used the Social Security numbers of a woman he had dated in Oregon and also of Danny Lee Carson, whose identity he assumed. The real Carson had died at the age of 33.[546] While in Salt Lake City, Church first stayed at a transient hotel, then at a building that only checked references, but not his credit history. He traveled light and did not drive.[547] One friend described him as a "duffel bag and bus man." By avoiding driving, he avoided one of the most common ways that offenders and fugitives from justice are eventually caught—traffic stops.[548]

While Church's day-to-day pre-arrest behavior appeared normal, after his arrest, friends and acquaintances told of some habits that in retrospect seemed suspicious, such as his being nervous when police came in to Bennett's BBQ Pit.[549] One time, when he was working at Bennett's BBQ Pit, it was robbed, and several police officers showed up. Church told a friend, "I can't be here with these cops," and took off.[550]

Law enforcement officials said that Church kept a low profile and did not attract attention. He did not go out often in public and most importantly, did not commit additional crimes. McHenry County Sheriff's Police Lieutenant Eugene Lowery said he believes Church managed to elude police for so long because he lived a low-key life. "He did not attract attention to himself. He didn't go out and commit additional crimes that we know of," Lowery said. "He didn't go out and commit an additional killing spree."[551]

He had a girlfriend who was with him at the time of arrest, one of several women he had dated in the months before his capture. He had worked his way up from a job as a cook to assistant manager, had received three raises in that time period, and had a second job as a maintenance worker at Salt Lake's Delta Center, the home of the Utah Jazz basketball team.[552]

In his application for his job at Bennett's BBQ Pit, Church noted that he was "a born-again Christian" who spent his free time "reading the Bible." "Give me a chance to work for you," Church wrote. "I feel I'm ready." When asked what he expected from his potential employer, he responded, "A fair deal."[553]

While working at Bennett's BBQ Pit, he earned the trust of his employer enough to be given a key to the store and a key and combination to the safe. He had been invited to the home of his bosses for Thanksgiving, which was several days after his capture.[554] His employers had even seen the *America's Most Wanted* episode on Church, but did not draw the connection. One of his employers later stated that two of her sons were joking with each other after seeing the program, saying, "It looks like Danny. It looks like Danny," referring to Church's alias of Danny Lee Carson.[555]

In small-town Woodstock, the district attorney prosecuting the case belonged to the same church as both the Ritter family and the Church family. His son had played on the same high school football team as Rick Church, whom he remembered as a "tough football player" with a bad temper.[556]

Richard Church pled guilty rather than going to trial. By doing so, he was able to avoid the death penalty.[557] Church was sentenced to two life terms—one for each of his murders. He was also sentenced to two separate 30-year sentences for home invasion and the attempted murder of his former girlfriend. The majority of the remainder of the Ritter family agreed to avoid the risks of trial and wanted life in prison for Church, as opposed to seeking the death penalty.[558] The brother of the victim, Raymond Ritter, did indicate that he did feel sorry for the parents of Church, but stated "at least they can go see him" in prison. "I can't go see my brother."[559]

As part of his plea, Church allowed himself to be interrogated and told law enforcement of his life on the run.[560] Church described three "close calls" in which he came close to getting caught and arrested for the homicides. The first was on his way out of Woodstock, when, driving north on Illinois Highway 47, he found police cars coincidentally in front and in back of him. He was not stopped. The second time was in the summer of 1989 when he fled into the woods when federal agents raided the group home of an Alma, Arkansas, religious group, the Alamo, also known as Tony Alamo Christian Ministries, where he was staying. Church stayed with the group and worked on its logging operations in several Western states for about two years before going to Salt Lake City. The third close call came when Church spent more than three weeks in a New York City jail in connection with a domestic dispute involving a friend from the Alamo complex. Even though he was fingerprinted, the connection to the Woodstock homicides was never made.[561]

Church's lawyer, in an effort to convince the court that his client had reformed during his time as a fugitive, stated that Rick Church had even confided in one person from the Tony Alamo group about the crimes, a confession which never came to the attention of authorities.[562] Church stayed and worked with the Tony Alamo group from late 1988 until late 1990, reportedly working ten-hour days sewing, and also at a logging camp with approximately 300 other people.[563] The Alamo group is often classified as a cult[564] and has been raided several times by federal authorities subsequent to the raid from which Church escaped.

Church is representative of one of the most difficult types of fugitives to catch. Although he may have lacked criminal sophistication at the start of the manhunt, he was young, educated, and cautious. He did not have regular involvement with the criminal justice system, but this also meant that he did not have a criminal lifestyle and had infrequent arrests. He was willing to learn how to falsify his identity and work different types of jobs. He led a low-key lifestyle. He kept to himself. It appeared he was sociable, got along with people, and had people who looked out for him. He did not tell people of his past or what he had done.

In 2001, Rick Church tried to appeal his sentence of life without the possibility of parole. Church claimed that the life sentence he received in 1992 for first-degree murder was unconstitutional and should be converted to a maximum 60-year term. If successful, Church could have gone free by his 55th birthday. The appellate court judge held that Church gave up the right to challenge the sentence when he accepted a plea bargain deal to avoid the death penalty.[565]

The Church case is an example of how, even with the most cautious and clever of fugitives, law enforcement getting information on criminal offenders out in the media can lead to successful results.

Today, Richard "Rick" Church, inmate number B35542, is serving a life sentence, without the possibility of parole, in Menard Correctional Center in Menard, Illinois.[566]

Case Study: *America's Most Wanted*

America's Most Wanted, the hit FOX television show, has been on television since its debut on February 7, 1988.[567] It is one of the top-ten longest-running television shows in American history. The show features many of America's most dangerous, notorious, and sought-after fugitives from justice. The first fugitive apprehended after being featured on *America's Most Wanted* was David James Roberts, who was apprehended four days after the show's debut, on February 11, 1988, as the direct result of viewer tips to the show.[568] The show is an excellent example of law enforcement working and cooperating with the media.

The host of the television show is John Walsh, a longtime victims' rights advocate, who endured a parent's ultimate nightmare when his own son, Adam, was abducted and murdered in 1981.[569]

The show has led to the capture of many infamous fugitives, including John List and the Texas Seven, seven prisoners who had escaped from a maximum-security prison in Kenedy, Texas. The show has also led to the recovery of many missing children, including in the headline-capturing Elizabeth Smart case.[570] Smart was a 15-year-old girl who had been kidnapped from her Salt Lake City, Utah, home and later found alive in Sandy, Utah, a suburb, when two people called police after seeing a man and two women walking down the street carrying bedrolls. The callers recognized the man as Brian David Mitchell, aka "Emmanuel," from media reports.[571]

America's Most Wanted has gained a reputation for working well with law enforcement, including the Federal Bureau of Investigation, the United States Marshals, and many local law enforcement agencies.

The show was almost cancelled in 1996 when ratings slipped. Letters and statements from law enforcement poured in, from the chief of the Los Angeles Police, the Drug Enforcement Agency, and the FBI—along with a variety of other law enforcement personnel and agencies.[572] The governors of 37 states also joined in protesting the potential cancellation.[573]

The show was not cancelled. *America's Most Wanted* remains on the air. In May of 2008, the 1,000th fugitive featured on the show was captured.

Case Study: The Andrew Cunanan Killing Spree

In the mid-1990s Andrew Cunanan was an oft-seen figure in San Diego's and San Francisco's gay social scene. At fancy restaurants and bars, he was known as a gay playboy and a loud, gregarious figure. He was renowned for picking up expensive restaurant tabs, a loud laugh, fancy clothes, and big cigars. To some, he was known as Andrew DaSilva, a Hollywood CEO. To others he was known as Naval Lieutenant Commander Drew Cummings, a Yale graduate.[574] He often claimed to be the son of a wealthy plantation owner.[575] He bragged that his bloodlines ran back to the high command of the late dictator Ferdinand Marcos of the Philippines.[576] He was well versed in world affairs, military command structure, and spoke at least conversationally in seven languages.[577]

While some were not really sure of how Cunanan made his living, the truth was that Cunanan was a gay prostitute—a gigolo primarily to older, wealthier men.[578] Cunanan himself was unemployed.[579]

Born to an Italian American mother and a Filipino father, Cunanan was a good student. He was a cross-country runner at an exclusive school in San Diego's upscale La Jolla neighborhood.[580] He made the *San Diego Tribune*'s All Academic Team in 1986 due to his running and his 3.6 grade point average.[581] He was openly gay at a conservative high school, where he spoke frequently about his sexual encounter and was known for seeking attention. He was voted "most likely to be remembered."[582]

His parents broke up when his father, a retired navy man who had studied to be a stockbroker, fled from the United States for his native Philippines after scamming his clients.[583] Cunanan followed him, but soon left after being appalled that his father was living in such poor conditions.[584]

Back in the United States, Cunanan settled back in California. He became a "high-class prostitute," as his mother referred to him.[585] He targeted Gamma Mu members, a fraternity of gay and often wealthy professional men.[586] He looked for benefactors to support his lifestyle. Men would buy him clothes, vacations, and one older man had bought him a $30,000 Infiniti.[587]

Cunanan was known as a party boy. He never had a real job. The beginning of his downfall was when he fell out with a rich benefactor in 1996. He began to sell drug and also to use more drugs.[588] He began to gain weight.[589] Cunanan had kinky tastes in sex, was into bondage and S&M,[590] and he had appeared in several low-budget homosexual pornographic bondage movies.[591] His credit cards were maxed out at $20,000.[592] He had debts in excess of $45,000.[593] Before leaving San Diego, Cunanan attended a farewell dinner party. He told friends that he was flying out to Minnesota for the weekend to "settle some business."[594]

It was in Minnesota that Cunanan's killing spree began. In Minnesota, he met up with a former lover of his, wealthy architect David Madson. He and Madson went out to dinner with friends the first night. He stayed with Madson several days and invited Jeff Trail, a friend and former Navy lieutenant over to the home of Madson. Some reports say Cunanan was obsessed with Trail, but Trail was not interested and strongly disapproved of Cunanan's drug usage.[595] Others, including the brother of Madson, indicated that Trail and Cunanan had been lovers.[596]

At the home of Madson, neighbors heard someone in the apartment scream, "Get the f— out!" followed by loud thuds. Two days later, police discovered Trail's body rolled up in a carpet. He had been beaten up around the face and arms with a claw hammer, and his watch had stopped from the beating.[597]

Madson apparently made no effort to leave; neighbors saw the two men walking Madson's dog the day after Trail's murder.[598] Four days later, Cunanan and Madson drove to a lake north of Minneapolis. Using Trail's .40-caliber pistol, Cunanan shot Madson in the head and back. His body was later discovered by fishermen.[599] Handcuffs, leg irons, and other bondage toys were later found by Minneapolis police in Madson's loft.[600]

Cunanan then fled to Chicago in Madson's Jeep. Police later found a map in the car with the route outlined from Chicago's downtown area to gay bars on Chicago's North Side.[601] It was in Chicago that Cunanan met well-known real-estate mogul Lee Miglin. There is no known evidence that Cunanan knew Miglin.[602] But when police discovered Miglin's body in his garage, his head had been wrapped in masking tape with holes for his nostrils—much like Cunanan's bondage fantasies.[603] The millionaire was riddled with shallow wounds from a gardening tool. It was speculated that Miglin may have been tortured to reveal the whereabouts of his cash and car keys.[604] At Miglin's home, Cunanan ate a half sandwich and shaved with Miglin's razor. He left with Miglin's car, a Lexus, and he also took some coins, about $2,000 in cash, and some of Miglin's clothes.[605]

Law enforcement had been monitoring Cunanan's phone and movements. He headed east and learned his cell phone was being tracked. He ripped out the cellular unit and abandoned the car at a lonely Civil War cemetery in southern New Jersey. Cunanan may have felt the need to get rid of the car he was driving and acquire another car. On May 9, Cunanan killed cemetery caretaker William Reese. He left another corpse when he traded in the Lexus for the red pickup truck of the cemetery's caretaker. He also left a clue: the shell casings from the .40-caliber bullets used to kill Reese matched the .40-caliber shells used to kill Madson.[606]

Cunanan was put on the FBI's Most Wanted List after killing Reese in New Jersey.[607] When FBI officials placed Cunanan on the list, they stated he was "a very dangerous, dangerous person" who was believed responsible for a three-state, four-victim torture and killing series. "We're very fearful that he is going to kill someone else," said FBI Special Agent in Charge William D. Gore. "The main purpose is to get his face out in the public arena.[608] . . . We consider him to be one of the most dangerous people in this country," said Gore.[609] It was announced that Cunanan may have been driving William Reese's 1995 red Chevrolet pickup truck with New Jersey license plate number KH993D.[610] Since he was a person on the Most Wanted List, posters with information about Cunanan were distributed to post offices and law enforcement agencies around the country. The FBI offered a $10,000 reward for information leading to his capture, and he was pictured on the FBI's website.[611] The FBI, considered one of the elite law enforcement organizations worldwide, had a tremendous rate of success with their Most Wanted List. Cunanan, at that time, was the 449th person to be placed on the list since it was created in 1950. Of those, 420 had been located, 131 as a result of tips from the public.[612]

Cunanan stopped in South Carolina to steal plates for the pickup truck he was driving.[613] He then made his way to Miami, Florida. In early June, he parked the red pickup in a South Beach parking garage, where the car sat unnoticed.[614] On July 7, he had to use one of his IDs to pawn some gold coins stolen from Miglin at Cash on the Beach. He left a thumbprint on the receipt.[615] On July 11, a Miami Subs Grill worker identified Cunanan and called police, but by the time police arrived he had disappeared.[616] On July 14, surveillance film showed Cunanan surveying world-famous fashion designer Gianni Versace's regular hangout, the News Café.[617] Later on July 14, Cunanan slipped out of the Normandy Plaza Hotel, where he had stayed since mid-May without paying his bill.[618]

In Miami, on July 15, 1997, Cunanan shot and killed Gianni Versace in the morning hours as Versace returned from purchasing some magazines.[619] Cunanan fled to the red pickup truck he had parked in a garage less than two blocks from Versace's mansion. There, he stashed his bloody clothes and left the car filled with clues, including his passport and the clothing, glasses, and wallet of Lee Miglin.[620] The truck was found less than an hour later.[621]

It has been said that prior to the murder of Gianni Versace, Andrew Cunanan had hidden in plain sight, circulating in Miami's gay community, staying in the city for two months, and selling coins at a pawn shop in his own name. He stayed at Normandy Hotel, an aging, low-rent hotel not far from Miami's swank South Beach section.[622]

After the death of Versace, there were many outraged homosexuals in Miami's gay community, angry at the police and law enforcement. *Newsweek* magazine reported the death of Gianni Versace:

> [It] provoked outraged homosexuals to charge that the FBI was so indifferent to their fate that the Feds didn't bother to warn the South Beach community that Cunanan might be in their midst. The killings also brought unwanted attention to a fraternity of wealthy gay men who are not all out of the closet. Meanwhile, high-profile homosexuals from Venice Beach to Fire Island have begun looking over their shoulders at night.[623]

It is unknown if Versace knew Cunanan. No proof has ever been offered either way. A senior Brazilian law enforcement officer contacted the FBI with information that a Brazilian woman had told local authorities in Sao Paulo that she had attended an informal get-together at the Versace mansion in South Beach the Sunday night before the murder. She claimed Cunanan was at the gathering—and she said she had still photographs and video to prove it. An agent was sent to Brazil to meet with the official.[624]

The FBI was proactive in determining that a possible Cunanan hit list may have been in existence. They worried that he may have worked down a list of wealthy gays and arts patrons. Agents quietly informed possible targets that they should take extra precautions.[625] Nonhomosexual targets like actor Sylvester Stallone were warned of possible Cunanan interest in them.[626]

The first night after the Versace murder, Cunanan hid on a boat. When the owner came to check on the boat in the morning, he saw a man who he believed was Cunanan on the boat. There was a copy of an Italian newspaper that had information about the Versace killing. The man called police. It took the police two days to respond—at that time, they were receiving tips on Cunanan sightings by the hundreds.[627]

Sometime after July 19, Cunanan snuck onto the boat of Torsten Reineck. The fact that Cunanan choose Reineck's boat initially aroused the suspicions of law enforcement. Reineck was a shady businessman who owned a gay bathhouse in Las Vegas.[628]

While hiding on Reineck's boat, Cunanan reached out to associates, looking for help with passports and getting out of the country. He warned that he would out closeted homosexuals he knew unless they assisted him.[629]

On Wednesday, July 23, the houseboat's caretaker dropped by to check out the boat. The 71-year-old Portuguese immigrant carried a cell phone and a .38-caliber pistol. When he entered the houseboat, he noticed the lights were on and saw a pair of unfamiliar sandals. He pulled his gun, and then heard a shot. He ran out and dialed 911.[630]

The FBI obtained a warrant from a judge to search the houseboat. In that time, no one else went in or came out. Police blocked off a 20-block area around the boat. They made an effort to call Cunanan inside the boat, but no one answered. Police on bullhorns shouted, "Andrew, come on out, the world is watching,"[631] perhaps playing on Cunanan's well-known need for attention.

At 8:00 P.M., a decision was made by law enforcement to enter the houseboat. Tear gas was shot in. There was no response. Miami's special response team went in and did a search. The body of Cunanan was found inside, dead from a gunshot wound to his mouth.[632] He was found on a queen-sized bed, on his back, propped up against the headboard by two pillows, clad only in light-blue boxer shorts with blood seeping from both of his ears, his mouth, and nose.[633] A 40-caliber handgun that had been used in three of the five killings rested at his groin, this time used to end his own life.[634]

No connection was ever established between Torsten Reineck and Cunanan. Reineck denied knowing either Cunanan or Versace, although he was known for wearing Versace clothes. Reineck was known to those with whom he came in contact in Las Vegas as "Doc

Ruel," and he passed himself off as a physician.[635] Reineck was also wanted for fraud and tax evasion in Germany.[636]

There has been much speculation on what had been Andrew Cunanan's motive in going on his killing spree. The former prep school graduate had never been arrested in his life. Some speculated that either he had HIV or believed that he had HIV. Others believed that aging, no longer being sought after for his looks and supported by wealthy older men, combined with being a spurned lover, as well as financial pressures were too much for Cunanan to handle.

There were also criticisms in the media on this high-profile case about how Cunanan was able to escape law enforcement. Many in the gay community had complaints. Gay activists said that the police and the FBI did not do enough to alert Miami's gay population.[637]

There has also been much speculation about how and why victims were chosen. Serial killers seldom target celebrities. Quite the contrary, they often target what have been labeled the "less dead." Author Steven Egger defined the "less dead" as:

> . . . marginalized groups of society who comprise the majority of the serial killer's victims. They are called the "less dead" because before their death, they "never were," according to society. In other words, this group is basically ignored and devalued by their own communities or members of their neighborhoods. The "less-dead" victims are not missed and basically ignored by society. Examples of the "less-dead" are prostitutes, the homeless, vagrants, migrant farm workers, homosexuals, the poor, elderly women, and runaways"[638]

While many serial killers seek the types of victims that they perceive will not be missed, Cunanan sought the exact opposite type of victim—high profile, wealthy, with strong community ties—those who would be immediately missed and looked for.

On close inspection, much of the negative criticism of law enforcement's efforts in tracking down Andrew Cunanan seems to be undeserved. If the goal of a manhunt is to get out publicity on the target, this was done. 2,000 flyers were distributed in the Miami area, planting his face everywhere. Cunanan was featured on *America's Most Wanted*. Law enforcement received thousands of calls about Cunanan sightings. Prior to his death, however, there were never any confirmed sightings. Even within the homosexual community, however, there was some reluctance to publicize Cunanan's possible presence. AIDS-awareness activists complain that talking about high-risk sex is considered bad form in South Beach. Even after Versace's death, some nightclub owners did not want to prominently display Cunanan's poster for fear of driving off customers.[639]

If the goal of a manhunt is to stop the killing, once law enforcement had pinpointed Cunanan's location, after the murder of Versace, Cunanan was confined and contained. He never got more than 40 blocks away from the Versace crime scene and was confined to a boat with no way to get out except suicide.[640] There was no more killing. After the boat's caretaker suspected Cunanan was on the boat and heard a gunshot, he called police, and they responded within minutes.

"He managed to get 40 blocks," said Paul R. Philip, special agent in charge of the FBI's Miami office. "That's the best he could do in all this time. I think we did a pretty good job."[641]

Miami Beach Police Chief Richard Barreto stated, "I think he was a desperate person with very little room to move about, not only in this community, but everywhere else in the United States."[642]

In retrospect, Cunanan was not a criminal genius. Despite his efforts, he was unable to get out of the country and unable to obtain a passport that would pass muster. Cunanan did not know how to hotwire a car. He had to kill twice in order to obtain a car for transportation, and then he drove around in that stolen car,[643] which is considered a criminal no-no.

It is believed that Cunanan enjoyed his killing spree. He picked high-profile victims. He taunted law enforcement with a trail of telltale evidence he left behind on purpose. Many speculated that this heightened the thrill for Cunanan and increased his determination to strike again as his killing spree progressed.[644]

Cunanan, while wanted, was able to move about freely in Miami and also in New York. He went to the movies, bought jeans at a Manhattan store, and visited gay nightclubs.[645]

Cunanan's versatility, intelligence, and ability to blend in all contributed to his eluding capture. He checked in to the Normandy Hotel in Miami with a fake identification card. He had a counterfeit French passport.[646] The hotel manager stated that Cunanan always wore a cap and dark glasses.[647] He kept a relatively low profile. "He was always quiet but very polite," said the manager.[648] He never made a phone call.[649] Cunanan was of average height, 5'9", and average weight, from 160–180 pounds. He had no distinguishing features such as a birthmark, buckteeth, or a large nose.[650] While of Caucasian and Filipino decent, Cunanan was able to appear Hispanic. In other words, he was easy to miss. He fit right in. "He didn't argue, he didn't get drunk, he came and went on his own," says Roger Falin, the hotel's owner. "He was like a ghost."

A Miami Beach Police spokesman, speaking on how Cunanan was able to be in the Miami area for over a month undetected, stated:

> We're still trying to answer the question of how Cunanan went undetected during his time in Miami Beach . . . He was not moving about with impunity. Someone at Miami Subs recognized him and called us, but he was gone when we arrived. The problem is Miami Beach's congestion. Sixty percent of the people on the beach are not permanent residents. They're from Miami or New Zealand or wherever. The influx of strangers is so great and Cunanan's look was so average it was hard to pick him out. He fit the description of any number of Latins on the beach. In fact, we grabbed

a guy at Versace's memorial service who turned out to be a *Miami Herald* reporter.[651]

Cataloging all the different ways Cunanan killed—friends and strangers, with guns and tools, quickly and slowly—Thomas Epach, then the chief of criminal prosecutions for the Cook County, Illinois, State Attorney's Office, said, "It's like watching a weather map. This killer is the consummate criminal storm."[652]

CHAPTER 12

HOSTAGE SITUATIONS

One of the most problematic and tension-filled events that law enforcement encounters is a hostage-taking incident. Facing a potential loss of life, the police must not allow any outside interference. The situation can be made more difficult by the fact that the taking of hostages itself can spark intense media interest. Yet there can be no media interference in hostage situations, or for that matter, interference from any outside sources. Police should consider cutting off the utilities to isolate the offender and have him focus his attention on conversations with the police. The police must be careful not to agitate or do anything to set off an offender. The offender should not have access to media coverage of the situation.

The hostage taker holds victims against their will and uses them to try to obtain material gain or personal advantage.[653] Often, an offender will threaten harm or death to his hostages if his demands are not met within a certain specified period of time. The FBI has classified hostage takers into four broad categories: terrorists, prisoners, criminals, and the mentally disordered.[654] There have been studies that have suggested that over half of all hostage incidents are perpetrated by those with mental disorders.[655] Very often, the hostage taker is a young male from a deprived socioeconomic background with little formal education, and he is very willing to kill innocent victims.[656]

It is recommended in a hostage or a barricade situation to deny the offender the excitement and stimulation that they hope to initiate.[657]

This requires that the situation be handled as calmly as possible, with minimal media attention.[658] This may be difficult. Hostage and barricade situations are usually deemed media worthy. Under a high amount of stimulation and in a chaotic situation, the offender is likely to resort to mindless behavior and often violence.[659] Crisis incidents require a well-controlled inner and outer perimeter—a large crowd may often be present that may include the subject's family members, the press, and bystanders. It is important that the hostage taker not be given an audience to play to—as negotiation will not succeed if negotiators are competing with outside influences for the subject's attention.[660]

Often, well-meaning civilians may offer their assistance or may insist upon participating in negotiations with offenders. These may include parents, spouses, lovers, friends, clergy, attorneys, counselors, mental health professionals, and media. As a general rule, civilian participation is unacceptable. The negotiation process is a police operation.[661]

Generally, one of the first actions that should be taken by hostage negotiators is to work with the telephone company to deny the offender the ability to use the phone lines as he wishes. The telephone company will establish a direct line between the negotiator and the subject. This prohibits the offender from talking to friends, family, attorneys, and the press, along with gathering intelligence about police operations from his associates.[662]

Officers are encouraged to initiate conversation, which often is a calming influence, to allow the offender to feel some control of the situation and to consider time an ally. Time promotes some thought process and decreases the likelihood of violence.[663]

Certain guidelines for negotiation are suggested:

- Stabilize and control the situation.
- Take your time when negotiating.

- Allow the subject to speak. It is more important to be a good listener than a good talker.
- Don't offer the subject anything.
- Avoid directing frequent attention to the victims; do not call them "hostages."
- Be as honest as possible; avoid tricks.
- Never dismiss any request as trivial.
- Never say "no."
- Never set a deadline; try not to accept a deadline.
- Do not make alternate suggestions.
- Do not introduce outsiders (non–law enforcement) into the negotiation process.
- Do not allow any exchanges of hostages; especially do not exchange a negotiator for a hostage.[664]

In hostage situations and negotiations, officers should be mindful that no absolutes exist. Law enforcement should be flexible. Each incident takes on a personality of its own.[665] It has been said that commanders can only be sure that their actions will likely be "scrutinized by every Monday morning quarterback from city hall to the city desk."[666] Therefore, they should base their decisions on an understanding of the negotiation process and the many factors that affect it.[667]

Case Study: Tacoma Mall Shootout/Hostage Situation and Media Interference

On Sunday, November 20, 2005, in Tacoma, Washington, 20-year-old Dominick Sergio Maldonado, neatly dressed in a shirt and tie,[668] went on a shooting spree at a crowded mall, shooting six people, one critically. The gunman fired as many as 20 shots as he walked along, yelling and firing his rifle,[669] and smiling as he fired.[670] Maldonado then took hostages after going into a Sam Goody music store. Four hours after taking the hostages, Maldonado surrendered, and the hostages were released unharmed.[671] During the shooting spree and hostage standoff with police, Maldonado sent both his best friend and his former girlfriend text messages reading, "Today is the day that the world will know my anger."[672]

Police were able to establish contact with the hostage taker in this situation, a rarer occasion than one might think for negotiators. "Trained police negotiators more often face suicidal men and women or a suspect barricaded alone in a home," said Tacoma Police Sergeant Daniell Griswold, who acted as the negotiator in this situation.[673] "Very few negotiating teams will actually deal with a true hostage situation such as this," she said. "This is a great learning tool for negotiators as to what worked for us and what didn't work."[674]

Several things didn't work for the team. Among them was the media. Maldonado talked to them, and during the hostage situation, three media outlets called into the Sam Goody store and spoke with hostages.[675] In the hours after Maldonado opened fire in the mall and took hostages in the music store, the store phone rang several times, with calls from the media. Journalists from the Associated Press, FOX News, and KOMO-TV called the store and interfered with the situation.[676]

A Tacoma police spokesman later stated, "Depending on what they said, they could have said things that could have set him off further. We don't know what his triggers were . . . Negotiators are specially trained to deal with subjects and bring it to an end. These folks, they're interested in the story and could possibly make the guy even angrier and start the shooting up all over again."[677]

Kenny Irby, a journalism professor, told the *Seattle Times* that this was a "dangerous precedent . . . Every news organization has to consider a certain level of restraint during an ongoing criminal situation . . . When we move beyond our role as a witness and become participants in the events, that is where a dangerous line is drawn."[678]

Personnel from KOMO-TV and the Associated Press stated that they were only looking for information and did not know there was an active hostage situation. Associated Press news editor Paul Query later stated that his newsroom had a discussion afterwards and "there was a consensus that maybe it [their methods of obtaining information] was a little too aggressive."[679]

When police and sheriff's personnel found out about the calls, they told the media to stop. Ed Troyer, a spokesman for the Pierce County Sheriff, later that day told a group of reporters, "If you do it again, there will be problems." The next day, he stated, "We thought the media was supposed to report, not to participate. We had reporters calling and agitating a man with a rifle. It sure would have been horrible if he had shot somebody. And then they would have been part of the story."[680]

In the Tacoma Mall incident, everything ended up alright for the hostages, with a safe and successful return. In this situation, one of the circumstances that may have led to the safe return of the hostages despite the media interference was the behavior of the hostages themselves. "We just kept talking to him [Maldonado] and kept personalizing everything and kept making him understand that this was not the smartest thing to do . . . It makes it a little harder to kill someone when you know them," said one of the hostages.[681]

Another hostage, a store employee, commented that the gunman told the hostages his name was Dominic, and the hostages gave him their names. The offender told the hostages he had taken methamphetamine that morning, had been mistreated by police as a kid, and felt like no one had paid attention to him, even when he had attempted suicide. The hostages felt that the offender would be less likely to shoot someone they knew, said the store employee. The tension began to ease a bit when the offender's demeanor began to change, and he began asking the hostages how much time they thought he would do, if the state of Washington had a death penalty, and he wondered if the man he had hurt the worst was going to die. "He started to look to us for advice, and we just tried to break him down mentally. We just did a lot of listening."[682]

Sergeant Daniell Griswold was also able to talk to the offender, and the offender allowed the negotiator to speak to the hostages. She coached the hostages about how not to set off the offender, to be calm, not to be overly emotional, to call the hostage taker by his first name, and not to make him mad.[683] In the end, Griswold said her team got the right outcome. "We adapted," she said, "we overcame, and we completed our mission."[684]

CHAPTER 13

NATURAL DISASTERS AND WEATHER CONDITIONS

Police departments work with other governmental agencies and utility companies to ensure the safety of the public and also to maintain order in the event of natural disasters or extreme weather conditions. Reaching out to the media to publicize safety and rescue efforts is one way to ensure that the message reaches as many people as possible.

Law enforcement may speak with the media and provide emergency contact numbers. They may publicize what people should be on the lookout for. In the event of extreme weather conditions, police may issue warnings through the media. The police may issue a warning, for example, in the event of snow—they may urge people to stay off roadways to make it easier to clear roads and make emergency response quicker and safer. Safety tips may be issued through the media. The police may publicize curfew conditions, road closings, or evacuation efforts. The police may issue warnings through the media to stay away from or out of specific areas.

Whenever possible and where safety allows, the media will have access to these areas. If a hazard is created, media access will be restricted. For example, the Los Angeles Police Department may close an area when "a menace to public health or safety is created by a calamity such as a flood, storm, fire, earthquake, explosion, accident, or other disaster."[685] The Chicago Police have a similar policy, in that "access to disaster areas will be restricted when such access will hamper necessary emergency action, volatile circumstances may exist, or the presence of news media would unnecessarily endanger their lives and/or the lives of surviving disaster victims."[686]

Case Study: Police Response in Hurricanes Katrina and Gustav

Hurricane Katrina struck the city of New Orleans in August of 2005. It was the costliest hurricane in United States history, as well as one of the five deadliest. It caused severe damage in the Bahamas, Texas, and Florida. The most severe loss of life and of property, however, was to the city of New Orleans, as it caused the levee system to fail, which led to widespread flooding and destruction. Eighty percent of the city was flooded. Almost 2,000 people lost their lives.[687] The hurricane caused $81.2 billion in damage.

Hurricane Gustav struck New Orleans in the summer of 2008. It caused $15 billion in damages. The hurricane was responsible for 138 deaths. It initially was classified as a Category 4 hurricane, even stronger than Katrina. It was downgraded to a Category 2 hurricane, 1 mph under a Category 3, however, by the time it hit New Orleans. The entire governmental system, including the police, was lauded for their readiness and their response to Gustav, unlike what had happened in response to Katrina.

Many people have been blamed for the problems with Hurricane Katrina, from politicians to government agencies. This case study explores the police response and readiness in both situations, including dealing with the media to get the message out regarding the potential danger and hazards of both hurricanes.

During Hurricane Katrina, the then New Orleans Police Superintendent Eddie Compass stated that 249 New Orleans police officers left their posts without permission.[688] Fifteen percent of the entire police department were deserters during this natural disaster, a time when police were needed the most.[689] Initial reports had 400 to 500 officers unaccounted for,[690] however, lines of communication were poor, and police officials were often unable to establish contact with their members. Telephone and radio communications failed, and some officers were stranded on rooftops for four or five days. "We had to rescue our police officers to get them back in," said Warren Riley after he had become the superintendent.[691]

"Some lost their homes and some were looking for their families . . . some simply left because they said they could not deal with the catastrophe," then Deputy Superintendent and future Superintendent Warren Riley said.[692] Some approximations had 80 percent of the New Orleans police force left homeless after Hurricane Katrina.[693]

Many of the officers who deserted the force came back to find themselves ostracized by those who did not desert their posts, and feelings ran so strong that some of the deserting officers were forced to work out of a local high school rather than at their assigned stations. The high school became known among non-deserters as the "leper colony."[694]

Lieutenant David Benelli, president of the union for New Orleans police officers, called for the firing of the deserters, stating, "For those who left because of cowardice, they don't need to be here . . . If you're a deserter and you deserted your post for no other reason than you were scared, then you left the department and I don't see any need for you to come back . . . We know there were people who flat-out deserted . . . But we also know there were officers who had to make critical decisions about what to do with their families."[695]

Hurricane Katrina was a huge public relations nightmare for many politicians and many branches of government, the police included. The New Orleans Police Department was criticized both for its readiness and its response. The department was widely criticized for failing to control lawlessness after the hurricane struck. Twelve New Orleans police officers were also investigated for their possible involvement in looting. A month and a half after the hurricane had struck, about 400 people had been arrested in New Orleans since the police department had set up a makeshift jail at the city's Amtrak station.[696] Roughly half of those arrests were for felony crimes like looting and burglary.[697] Clearly, many more crimes were involved in the temporarily underpoliced New Orleans.

After four weeks the police chief, Eddie Compass, was forced to retire.[698] Initially, a police spokesman stated that the superintendent was retiring to "spend more time with his family;" however, the superintendent told his officers that the mayor forced him out.[699] In addition to complaints of his officers looting and deserting, two officers who Superintendent Compass referred to as his friends had committed suicide during the devastation in the wake of Hurricane Katrina.[700]

The New Orleans Police Department came under criticism five months after the storm, when internal police statistics showed that the department was still recording more than half of the city's looting complaints under a special code, 21K, developed shortly after the hurricane. The K stood for Katrina, and the 21 signified "lost or stolen," a standard pre-storm designation used mostly in cases in which criminal activity is not clear-cut, such as when there is no forced entry or a when victim cannot recall when he or she last saw the missing property. More significantly, "lost or stolen" cases do not show up in publicly released crime reports.[701]

The police stated the 21K code was developed as Hurricane Katrina's floodwaters receded and residents returned to their waterlogged and windblown property, many of their homes and businesses ripped open to the elements or broken into by rescue crews. The chaotic landscape made it difficult to separate legitimate looting and burglary complaints from storm losses and, to a lesser extent, false insurance claims, Police Superintendent Warren Riley said.[702]

Yet even after most homeowners and merchants had inventoried and secured their property, the "lost or stolen" classification was still used by the police throughout the city, including in areas that didn't flood. The practice drew critics, including some high-ranking police supervisors, who said the 21K designation had outlived its purpose. "If we're not seeing an understandable rise in burglary and looting since the storm, then there's a big problem in how the police department is conducting its business," said Anthony Radosti, a former New Orleans police officer and the vice president of the Metropolitan Crime Commission, a nonprofit watchdog group. "Creating a category for the hurricane might have been a good idea, but there has to be a cut-off date. Now it just looks like they're cooking the statistics."[703]

In an infamous and highly publicized incident involving the New Orleans Police Department, MSNBC correspondent Fred Savidge reported from a New Orleans Wal-Mart and showed New Orleans police officers seemingly joining in on the looting, filling up a shopping cart with clothes while looters went on a rampage throughout the store. Despite the videotape, four New Orleans police officers were later cleared of looting allegations stemming from a news videotape that showed them taking items from the Wal-Mart two days after the hurricane. The officers, however, were suspended for ten days for failing to stop civilians from cleaning out the ransacked store.[704] The four officers were each suspended for ten days without pay for "neglect of duty" because "people can be observed illegally inside the store with property in their possession and you took no police action to prevent or stop the looting" according to their disciplinary letters.[705]

The video, shot by an MSNBC crew inside Wal-Mart, shows the officers filling a shopping cart with shoes, clothes, and other items. In the background, citizens can be seen calmly looting everything from sweaters to bicycles. When a reporter asked the officers what they were doing, one of them responded, "Looking for looters." She then hastily turned her back to the camera.[706]

Despite public outrage over the officers' actions, an internal investigation recently cleared them of looting allegations, said the commander of the Public Integrity Bureau. The commander indicated the officers had permission from their superiors to take necessities for themselves and other officers. The department later informed Wal-Mart management, after the store had been secured, that its officers had taken some needed items.[707]

On top of her ten-day suspension, the officer who was confronted by the MSNBC reporter received an additional three-day penalty for her "discourteous" response to the newsman.[708] Through a spokesman, the superintendent stated, "It was determined that all four officers had received permission from their commanders to get clothing for fellow officers who were soaking wet. They did not steal anything."[709]

Police departments from around the nation were called in to New Orleans to assist. They did a very good job at helping to restore New Orleans and are to be credited for their noble efforts. It was a very difficult situation for these officers, being placed in a seemingly no-win situation, with angry, displaced, homeless citizens and a devastated city. And the majority of police officers in New Orleans are clearly and undoubtedly law-abiding professionals who were put in a horrific situation with failed equipment, disrupted communication, and lack of immediate outside support. "There were wild aspersions that the NOPD had run amok, but a lot of these stories came out before all the facts had been gathered and investigated. We were the whipping boys right after the storm . . . There's no doubt in my mind that not all police officers, unfortunately, honored their oath of office," said Lieutenant David Benelli of the police union. "But it doesn't take away from the fact that the majority, the vast majority, honored that oath. And they don't deserve to be lumped in by the media with the few who didn't do the right thing."[710]

After the tragedy, the devastation, the financial loss, and public relations nightmare of Hurricane Katrina, New Orleans was ready, three years later, for Hurricane Gustav. Before the hurricane even hit, it was termed "the storm of the century."[711] As the storm raged across the Gulf of Mexico, only 10,000 of 239,000 residents of New Orleans remained in the city, the others having evacuated.[712] That was well below the number who remained in New Orleans several years before, when more than 25,000 alone camped out in the Louisiana Superdome during Hurricane Katrina. Thousands more were stranded in homes, hospitals, public buildings, and freeway overpasses.[713]

In the days before Hurricane Gustav hit, New Orleans Mayor Ray Nagin ordered residents of the city to evacuate and imposed a dusk to dawn curfew for those that chose to remain.[714] Mayor Nagin warned residents that looters would be sent to state prison and stated, "Looters will go directly to jail. You will not get a pass this time . . . You will not have a temporary stay in the city. You will go directly to the big house."[715] While few residents remained in the city, 1,400 New Orleans police officers and 2,000 National Guard members patrolled the streets.[716]

Elsewhere in the state of Louisiana, all police officers in Baton Rouge were called to duty the week before the storm hit to prepare for the flooding, traffic, and widespread power outages.[717] Vacations were cancelled for Baton Rouge officers, and police academy class graduations were pushed up by four days to increase manpower on the streets.[718] One approximation had a total of two million persons that were evacuated from coastal south Louisiana, leaving only about 100,000 people behind as of the night before the hurricane hit.[719] A state police spokesman had the numbers of evacuees at 90 percent of the coastal Louisiana population, which was the largest evacuation in state history.[720]

Mayor Nagin referred to the storm before it struck as "the mother of all storms" and "the storm of the century."[721] "This storm is so powerful that I'm not sure we have seen anything like it," he said. "The National Weather Service is saying that it's the worst possible storm that they can imagine. That gives you some idea of what we're dealing with."[722] The mayor warned before Gustav hit that it could be "worse than a Katrina."[723]

Fire Chief Freddy Guidry of Lafourche Parish District 3 said more people left "than with any storm I've ever seen. It seems like Katrina did teach us a lesson."[724]

Police searched for looters. There has been a feeling in post-Gustav times that the government's reaction was to adopt a "better safe than sorry" philosophy. While Gustav may not have lived up to its billing, one news source said:

Gustav—and the frantic response to it by government officials and local residents—made it clear how Hurricane Katrina's legacy is a newfound respect for nature and continuing anxiety over whether the levees designed to keep New Orleans from flooding will do their jobs.[725]

Another factor that is credited for the improved law enforcement response and the improved media image of the department was the decision by New Orleans Police Superintendent Warren Riley to give his city's 1,485 officers paid time off to get their families to safety. It was a lesson learned from Hurricane Katrina, when officers abandoned their posts, saying they were forced to choose between taking care of strangers and taking care of their families. Before Hurricane Gustav hit, the department made sure they had time to do both. Before the hurricane, Riley said 97 percent of the city's officers would stay to respond to Gustav.[726]

New Orleans police also tactically prepared for Gustav differently. The entire force worked through Gustav, with teams of officers set up at five safe houses around the city to prevent the widespread looting that followed Katrina. Unmarked police cruisers patrolled neighborhoods, weaving around downed trees and power lines even before Gustav's heaviest winds died down.[727] "We looked at what caused trouble during Katrina and how we can correct it," City Councilwoman Cynthia Hedge-Morrell said. "And everything was in place."[728]

As was the case with Hurricane Katrina, other outside law enforcement agencies participated in the effort. In the case of Hurricane Gustav, many of the other police agencies were in place before the hurricane hit. The state of New York, for example, sent eight National Guard helicopters, a cargo plane, and about 60 airmen and soldiers to aid in the response to Gustav.[729] New York City also sent several rescue units to help.[730]

The city of New Orleans also got plenty of help from state and federal agencies, which sent buses, boats, planes, and helicopters to evacuate those without cars, the homebound, the sick, and the stragglers. The

Federal Emergency Management Agency said 9,000 people were medically evacuated ahead of Hurricane Gustav, including 8,000 from nursing homes.[731] The National Guard mobilized about 7,000 troops for Hurricane Gustav,[732] and an additional 4,000 were ready to arrive if needed. It called up roughly 5,500 for Katrina, said Captain Taysha Deaton Gibbs, a National Guard spokeswoman. "We operated quicker, we had our troops pre-positioned earlier," she said. "These were lessons learned from Katrina."

In Baton Rouge, special teams were set up to deal with different problems that could arise during the storm, such as an expected increase in the number of calls from residents seeking assistance. Much of the police response was based on lessons learned. "Experience is the best teacher and we had one heck of an experience in 2005," said Baton Rouge Police spokesman Sergeant Don Kelly shortly before the storms hit. "I think we've learned from it and I think we're much better prepared."[733]

CHAPTER 14

INFORMING THE PUBLIC AND INTERACTING WITH THE MEDIA IN OTHER CRIMES

Police departments should consider putting together news releases for such events as major organizational changes and promotions, new programs, community service work, projects, campaigns, changes in department policy, enforcement policies, police service, or awards or recognition programs honoring citizens and/or officers.[734] Police also need to notify the public in the case of any major crime patterns.

News releases, much like a good police report, should respond directly to the six basic questions that any audience would want answered: Who? What? Why? Where? When? How?[735]

Departments should also consider putting out community alerts and public service announcements in the case of crime patterns and problems. This is reflective of a proactive department. Departments should offer prevention and safety tips, along with ways to notify the appropriate personnel in the event that one comes in contact with a criminal offender or the source of a problem.

On occasion, a news conference may be necessary. This will be the case when media attention reaches the point where an individual can no longer respond to media demands on a one-on-one basis. This would be the case when an incident is of considerable interest, such as the following:

- Disasters resulting in deaths or injuries and/or significant property loss
- Any situation that results in multiple deaths
- Mass arrests and civil disturbances involving large numbers of people
- Big vice or drug busts
- Anytime help is needed from the public on an important case
- When there is a crisis or a danger that the public should be made aware of
- When the department has a major new program or project to unveil
- When there have been major personnel or organizational changes within the police agency
- When there are going to be major changes in the way that police respond to citizen requests for service
- When there will be award or recognition ceremonies for officer and citizen honorees
- When the department feels it must answer police misconduct allegations of major proportions[736]

Case Study: New Methods and Programs: High Point, North Carolina's "Hug a Thug" Program

Criminals are always trying to stay one step ahead of the law. They learn about police procedures, strategies, and law enforcement methods. They talk to each other about crime techniques, how they got caught, how not to get caught, the law, their cases, their sentences, what makes for a weak case against them, and what makes for a strong case. Criminals are changing with the times. Police should be willing to change with the times as well.

Some criminals put a great deal of thought and effort into their criminality. Were they to put that effort toward something positive, they could achieve something that mainstream society could be proud of.

As a prosecutor, I once had a gang member who I was questioning for shooting a rival gang member ask me if he would be more likely to be charged with attempted murder than aggravated battery with a firearm since he had shot the victim multiple times above the waist, where the victim's vital organs were. The gang member, who had not graduated from high school, was able to state for which crimes someone convicted would be required to serve 50 percent of his time and for which crimes the offender would be required to serve 85 percent of his time—information that I did not know until I consulted a law book.

I have had gang members who were able to rattle off to me which police worked which shifts. When I was a police officer, I had a gang member question me about whether I could make an arrest on the side of the street on which I was making it, since it was on the other side of the street from the district I worked in. I have had offenders tell me that their favorite shows were *Forensic Files*, *New Detectives*, and *Cold Case Files*, and brag how much they had learned from the shows.

I have interviewed a drug dealer arrested for selling narcotics to undercover police officers in a complex conspiracy operation, who told me that he knew he was in trouble after making the sale when he was stopped by police officers he had never seen before. He assumed, correctly, that these police officers were from a specialized narcotics unit and this was something bigger than a normal street stop. He had correctly guessed that the purpose of the police stopping him was that they just wanted to identify him and then release him, waiting to arrest him while they built narcotics cases on other individuals he was conspiring with.

Several drug dealers have told me they kept up with the latest police technology and surveillance methods from watching HBO's cops and criminals drama, *The Wire*.

In order for those who enforce the law to stay ahead of those who break the law, sometimes the police have to use their imaginations. They have to be flexible. They have to be innovative. They have to take chances. Instituting a new program may not always be popular with the general public. In order to generate publicity for a new program, get the message out, help explain the purpose of the program, and gain public support, it helps for the police to have a good relationship with members of the media. The police and the media can work together toward publicizing a new crime-fighting program.

One such program is that which was instituted in High Point, North Carolina. The Overt Drug Market Strategy, also dubbed by some as "Hug a Thug," represented a nontraditional way of fighting the crime associated with the drug trade in High Point. The program focused on a combination of scaring the offenders and holding them accountable for their actions, but also supporting them and guiding them toward something positive—that final step being the twist. Old methods of arrest and incarceration had not been working, so the department tried something new. While not everyone might be supportive of the new program, it represented an example of taking a chance, being open-minded, and working not only with the media, but also with the community. The program has had some success, and thanks to help from the media in publicizing the program, some positive feedback. Such policies are now being tested in many other areas of the country.

The Overt Drug Market Strategy incorporates a three-phase intervention approach to cutting crime:

- Phase I: Using detailed crime-mapping tools and relationships with neighborhood policing programs, officers identify strong criminal cases against the offenders that present the largest threat to the community.

- Phase II: Community leaders publicly confront such offenders and offer viable lifestyle alternatives to drug dealing. Neighborhood support organizations follow up with help obtaining employment, transportation, food, and shelter assistance to ensure that offenders have every opportunity to change for the better.

- Phase III: Police lay out the alternative, lengthy prison sentences that await criminals if they do not amend their behavior and take advantage of community support.[737]

In the High Point, North Carolina, program, police investigated more than 20 dealers operating in the city's West End neighborhood, where crack cocaine was openly sold for over three months. The police made dozens of undercover buys and videotaped many other drug purchases.[738]

The police also did something nonconventional: determining who the influential persons were in the drug dealers lives—their mothers, relatives, and mentors—and they cultivated relationships with them.[739] The police built what they felt to be ironclad legal cases against the offenders and then, in another twist, they refrained from arresting most of the dealers.[740]

There were two police goals here: to shut down the open-air drug markets and to give the drug dealers, especially the younger ones with less of a criminal background, a second chance.[741] Open-air drug markets, where drugs are sold on the street or in drug houses, create numerous problems for law enforcement and the community. Property values go down. Violent drug gangs fight over turf. Addicts commit robberies and thefts to get the money to purchase narcotics. Businesses and families leave the community.[742] Often, the police method of enforcement is to conduct sweeps, arresting large numbers of drug sellers, potential drug buyers, or both. This practice has had limited effectiveness in eliminating drugs and violence. The High Point Program has not eliminated illegal drug use, nor was it designed to do so.[743] "This is not a war on drugs," said Police Chief James Fealy. Rather, he says, the goal was shut down overt drug markets because "street-level dope dealing is what drives a significant amount of crime."[744]

In May 2004, after building solid cases against some drug dealers, the police invited 12 narcotics dealers to a meeting at the police station, along with a promise that they would not be arrested that night. The police had the help of the dealers' families and mentors. Those selected for the program were those without violent criminal histories—the offenders with violent histories had already been arrested.[745]

Nine of the 12 dealers showed up. First, they were met by a room filled with clergy, social workers, and community activists who confronted them with the harm they were doing, urged them to stop, and offered help.[746] One pastor noted that the suspects "were slouching in their seats and one guy even seemed to be dozing off . . . Their attitude was, 'This is just another program and it will blow over.'"[747]

The next room the dealers were brought to was filled with police, prosecutors, and federal agents. Evidence relating to each particular dealer was laid out in front of them. There were also arrest warrants for the dealers, filled out, but missing only the signature of a judge.[748] An ultimatum was issued to stop drug dealing or go to jail.[749] Maximum penalties and federal prosecutions were threatened.[750] It was noted by the same pastor that the drug dealers "seemed to be paying a lot more attention."[751]

One pastor involved in the project, who was also a leader in community anticrime efforts, summed up the message that was delivered: "We're against what you're doing, but we're for you." City employees also worked to help find ex-offenders and suspects employment.[752]

The High Point police chief stated that this particular drug market closed overnight and has not reopened. The city's two other major drug markets were also closed using the same strategy, police stated.[753]

Other police departments have since tried the same strategy, with success. Still others are preparing programs to try this strategy. One professor who specialized in narcotics-related issues referred to it as "the hottest thing in drug enforcement."[754]

The program does have its critics. They say it is too lenient and object to treating the drug dealers softly. The critics distinguish the drug dealer from the drug user, who they say would benefit from programs and treatment.

Others question whether such a program could work in a major city. Some major cities have instituted versions of the program in designated areas. Similar programs have been instituted in Nashville, Tennessee; Raleigh, North Carolina; Providence, Rhode Island; and Rockford, Illinois.[755]

Yet despite the critics, the High Point, North Carolina, program appears to have had great success. The strategy combines the "soft" pressure from families and community with the "hard" threat of aggressive, ready-to-go criminal cases.[756] Violent crime, which is defined as murder, rape, robbery, aggravated assault, prostitution, sex offenses, and weapons violations, dropped in High Point. More than two years later, violent crime remains more than 25 percent lower in the area, according to police statistics.[757] Drug-related crime has dropped 35 percent in High Point.[758] Of the 75 people who have been through the intervention program, 74 percent are doing well or have moved off the police radar, High Point Police Major Marty Sumner said. The other 26 percent have returned to the streets.[759]

In 2007, the Ash Institute for Democratic Governance and Innovation at Harvard University's John F. Kennedy School of Government named the Overt Drug Market Strategy of North Carolina's High Point Police Department as a 2007 Innovations in American Government Award winner. The program received $100,000 to promote replication of its crime reduction efforts and share best practices around the country.[760]

In law enforcement, to keep up with the criminal offenders, one has to be innovative, take a chance, and change with the times. With these hard measures, it is important to work with the media to get the message out as to what you are doing. Once laughed at by some, and downplayed as "Hug a Thug," the Overt Drug Market Strategy appears to have been a success, and positive media attention has helped publicize and popularize this novel approach to law enforcement.

Case Study: Drunk Driving and
Other Checkpoints

Checkpoints are systematic methods for stopping vehicles to determine whether the drivers are driving under the influence of drugs or alcohol, or for other important matters, without regard to whether there is reasonable suspicion for the stop. The United States Supreme Court has upheld these stops under limited circumstances. Checkpoints for driving under the influence are constitutional as long as police follow the proper administrative procedures in setting them up.

The question of whether DUI roadblocks were per se unconstitutional pursuant to the United States Constitution was addressed in *Michigan Department of State Police v. Sitz*. The government had acknowledged that a roadblock was a seizure; thus, the Court focused its examination on whether such a seizure was unreasonable. In examining whether a DUI roadblock was an unreasonable seizure, the Court utilized a three-pronged balancing test. The United States Supreme Court balanced 1) the state's interest in preventing accidents caused by drunk drivers, 2) the effectiveness of sobriety checkpoints in achieving that goal, and 3) the level of intrusion on an individual's privacy caused by the checkpoints. Ultimately, the Court concluded that the momentary seizure of a DUI roadblock was not unreasonable, stating that "the balance of the State's interest in preventing drunken driving, the extent to which this system can reasonably be said to advance that interest, and the degree of intrusion upon individual motorists who are briefly stopped, weighs in favor of the state program."[761] Checkpoints for narcotics, however, are not constitutional.[762]

Courts have looked at some of the following factors as criteria to determine whether necessity to permit the checkpoint outweighs the rights of the citizens in states: 1) there is an absence of unlimited discretion on the part of individual officers, 2) there are procedural guidelines, 3) the decision is made by supervisory/policy level personnel to establish the roadblock, 4) the selection of the site is made by supervisory/policy level personnel, 5) the showing of official authority at the site is apparent, 6) there is advance publicity, 7) the method to stop vehicles is preestablished and systematic, and there is no safety risk.[763] The more of these factors that are present, the more likely that a court will determine that a roadblock is legal.

Often, police will seek to publicize the fact that they may be cracking down on drunk driving or enforcing DUI laws. It is not unusual to see an article in the newspaper, a television news story, or a press release such as the following:

> *Michigan State Police to Step Up Patrols for Thanksgiving Holiday Weekend*
>
> November 27, 2002
>
> EAST LANSING: Throughout the Thanksgiving holiday weekend, Michigan State Police troopers will again team up with other state police and highway patrol agencies across the nation and Canada for Operation C.A.R.E. (Combined Accident Reduction Effort). Additionally, troopers will continue to unite with Mothers Against Drunk Driving (MADD) and local Michigan law enforcement for the "Tie One On for Safety" campaign throughout the entire holiday season.
>
> The Thanksgiving holiday weekend is, traditionally, one of the most traveled holiday weekends of the year. State Police will have extra patrols on the roads this holiday weekend beginning at 6:00 P.M., Wednesday, November 27, through midnight, Monday, December 2. "Troopers will continue to take a zero-tolerance approach to unbuckled motorists as part of the statewide 'Click It or Ticket' campaign," stated Lt. Col. Tadarial J. Sturdivant, Deputy Director, Uniform Services Bureau, Michigan State Police. "In addition, they will be paying special attention to drivers who are speeding and driving under the influence of alcohol or drugs."

> Last year during this same holiday weekend there were 11 fatal crashes in Michigan, resulting in 12 deaths. Of these 12 persons killed, 30 percent were not wearing safety belts. Alcohol was a factor in 55 percent of those crashes.
>
> Lt. Colonel Sturdivant stressed, "Thanksgiving is an occasion to enjoy spending time with your family. Please, Drive Michigan Safely; always wear your safety belts, buckle your children, don't drink and drive, and obey all of Michigan's traffic laws."[764]

Courts approve of and strongly encourage such advance publicity for DUI roadblocks. The courts have noted that advance publicity of the intention of the police to establish DUI roadblocks, without designating specific locations at which they will be conducted, also serves to minimize any apprehension motorists may otherwise experience upon encountering one. In fact, if a major goal of a roadblock searching for drunken drivers is deterrence, that goal is promoted by publicity. The more aware drivers are that they may be stopped at such a roadblock, the more likely they will be to seek alternate means of transportation when they are drinking or to refrain from drinking when they know they will be driving.[765]

Case Study: Gang Names in the Media

There has long been a debate, both within law enforcement and within the media, as to whether or not to publicize the names of street gangs. Members of both police and the media are divided as to the appropriate way to handle this issue. Critics of publicizing gang names feel that such a practice gives the gangs publicity and glory, making them more attractive to potential recruits. Others feel that the public needs to be educated on identifying and recognizing gang members and that the crimes committed by gang members have news value.

One *Albuquerque Tribune* reporter wrote of the grief she received after writing a story about the gang violence between two New Mexico gangs, TCK (short for Thugs Causing Kaos or True City Kings[766]) and the West Side Locos, which had led to 11 homicides in a four-year period.[767] Local police did not approve of gang names making it into media reports.[768] Police stated that the media was just giving the gangs what they wanted, which was notoriety and attention.[769] Naming the gangs, police stated, would just make the gang members bolder and more appealing to vulnerable youths. Those gang members who were not talked or written about would feel the need to step up the violence in a sense of competition.[770]

The *Albuquerque Tribune* editor defended his newspaper's practice: "I'm still not clear how not naming them has added to the public security."[771] *Albuquerque Tribune* editor Phil Casaus said, "I'm not unmindful of their [police] concerns, but I think the public's right to know balances that . . . these gangs have been tied to 11 homicides and people have been caught in the cross fire; people who aren't involved in gangs puts it directly in the public's interest."[772] A *Detroit News* reporter agreed, stating, "If you've got another John Dillinger living next door, you're going to want to know about it.[773] If an incident is gang-related, write that into the story," he advised. "Name the gang and its location. Let the public know about the gang."[774]

Critics of releasing gang names to the media cite the example of Los Angeles mega-gang, the Crips, which had its first bona fide gang homicide in 1972. A *Los Angeles Times* story described the Crips's key attire as black leather jackets. In the homicide, a 16-year-old high school quarterback, who was not in a gang, was beaten to death over a black leather coat. Before this report, gang members hadn't yet crossed over to killing. The story and subsequent publicity of the killing gave the Crips such notoriety that its ranks swelled. Rival gangs formed, and Los Angeles soon became one of the United State's most gang-infested cities.[775]

Some newspapers and media outlets have differing philosophies regarding the printing of gang names in crime stories. One school of thought equates reporting gang activity with publicizing bomb threats. The coverage, they maintain, gives attention to the perpetrator and does little to benefit the public.[776]

There does appear to be a trend, however, involving another school of thought toward law enforcement educating the public about gang and publicly naming gangs. Law enforcement agencies have long avoided giving names of gangs to the media because it was a source of pride to the gangs. But the Los Angeles Police Department and L.A. Mayor Antonio Villaraigosa are going against the grain. As part of a broader plan that aimed to stem the spurt of gang violence in the region, the LAPD released a list of the city's 11 Top Targeted Street Gangs.[777] A Los Angeles Police spokesman said part of the idea was to "deputize the public to stand up to the gang culture. We want the public to be more aware of who they are and to call us and let us know what they're up to."[778] Critics, however, including many within law enforcement, felt that naming the top gangs can spark competition, with different gangs wanting to be the top gang, wanting identification, advertisement, and bragging rights.[779]

In Dane County, Wisconsin, where state capital Madison is located, law enforcement officials and social workers had generally declined to name gangs because they did not want to feed the gangs' desire for publicity. However, officials abandoned that approach because they believed the public needed to be alerted to the growing threat of youth gang activity in Dane County.[780]

Additionally, television shows such as the History Channel's *Gangland* and Black Entertainment Television's (BET) *American Gangster* have done critically acclaimed documentary-style episodes on street gangs and gang members, with cooperation from a variety of law enforcement sources—police, prosecutors, judges, and federal agents. While entertaining, they also act to educate the public, and cooperation with law enforcement increases their accuracy.

The debate will continue. The public has a need to know about the dangers of gangs and an interest in being able to recognize signs of gang activity. Besides the need for public safety, violence in the community is news and does need to be reported. On the other hand, there is also no doubt that giving the gangs publicity does increase their attractiveness to some vulnerable youths.

It should be noted that in urban areas, where gangs are stronger, more organized, and more sophisticated, gang members often go out of their way to keep a lower profile, and deny gang membership as they attempt to go undetected by law enforcement in their effort to make money from their illegal activities. This is much like organized crime members have done in the past and continue to do. These gangs are less likely to be influenced by newspaper articles about their gangs; in fact, they may shun such attention.

In smaller towns, in suburban areas, the gangs are less criminally sophisticated and less established. These gangs will often seek publicity, utilize gang graffiti, and look to establish a reputation through gang violence. These gangs may be more prone to increase in membership and prestige through media attention.

Case Study: Attempting to Reduce the Prostitution Problem: Publicizing Prostitutes and Johns

Prostitution is illegal in every state except in certain parts of Nevada. Yet prostitution exists in almost every city in the United States. Street-level prostitution, where transactions take place in the open as opposed to a brothel, is illegal in all parts of the United States. Far more law enforcement attention is paid to street "hookers" than to more expensive "call girls," who usually operate out of the yellow pages, the Internet, and hotel rooms. Street-level prostitution generates far more complaints from the public. Persons who prostitute themselves on the street or exchange sex for money or something of value, frequently have sexually transmitted diseases. Prostitutes are likely to have drug problems. And where there are prostitutes, there are often both other crimes and nuisance offenses, such as drug sales, street robberies, pimps, public drinking, and littering of used condoms, crack pipes, and hypodermic needles.

Most street prostitutes have severe drug habits. It is generally agreed that if prostitutes are using drugs, get arrested, but do not get help for their addiction, then they will quickly return to prostitution. For many years, law enforcement efforts were spent on arresting prostitutes, who often spent a short amount of time in jail, if at all, and then returned to the streets, drugs, and prostituting themselves. In recent years, an effort has been made to focus on the customers of prostitutes. These customers, almost always men, are known as johns. The strategy is to cut down on prostitution by reducing demand and the client base. Techniques such as arresting the johns, fining them, and towing or seizing their cars have been utilized, with varying levels of success.

One technique that has been utilized as of recent years is working with the media, publicizing the identity of those soliciting or patronizing prostitutes, making an effort to shame the john. The city of Chicago posts the names and pictures of those who have been arrested for the solicitation of prostitution on their police department's website.[781] The city council of Newark, New Jersey, had published in its own newspaper a "Who's Who" of names and addresses of alleged prostitutes and their customers in an effort to use shame to cut down on their business. "We can't print enough copies. There's a great demand for these things. People are looking for their husbands, for their neighbors," said one councilman of the *Newark City Council Monitor News Supplement*, a quarterly publication that was mailed to voters and had a circulation of 60,000.[782]

A two-year study for the U.S. Justice Department's National Institute of Justice, led by researcher Michael Shively and released in March of 2008, found more than 200 communities nationwide have tried targeting customers of prostitution in print, on TV, the Internet, billboards, or by sending "Dear john" letters home. Chicago, New York, Denver, St. Louis, and Madison, Wisconsin, are among the cities that publicize arrests or send letters home.[783]

Among the programs are:

- New Haven, Connecticut, where police kicked off a prostitution crackdown on August 14, 2008, in the Fair Haven neighborhood with 12 arrests of clients whose names and photos were released to news media. News outlets including WTNH-TV, WVIT-TV, and the *New Haven Register* used them.

- Elgin, Illinois, on July 23, 2008, approved releasing the names of clients to news media.

- Warren, Michigan, started posting online pictures of people arrested as prostitutes and customers as of August of 2008, and it expects to expand to the city TV station, the police commissioner stated.

- Asheville, North Carolina, where police began showcasing arrested prostitutes and their clients on the city's website and television channel in February 2008.[784]

Some newspapers will not print the names of those arrested, but have worked with the police in printing the names of those who have been convicted. The Fort Wayne, Indiana, *News-Sentinel* has tracked people charged with soliciting prostitutes and published their names when they're convicted. In 1995, managing editor Richard Battin was presented with a petition signed by 1,000 members of the Southwest Area Partnership, a neighborhood group. The concerned residents wanted the newspaper to print the names of those who were arrested, but executive editor Joseph Weiler balked. "We don't want to embarrass people by printing their names if they're innocent," he said. "But once they are convicted, we feel that publishing their names will be a deterrent and will help neighborhoods become safer."[785]

But these practices are not without their critics. Critics point out that the job of the newspaper is not law enforcement, and the two roles should be separate.[786] Critics state that printing pictures of johns "elevates the question of prostitution beyond the importance to the community and elevates the potential penalty or harm to an individual beyond what may be appropriate." In other words, given the embarrassment they could cause, printing pictures of johns can be construed as an additional punishment.[787] These critics point out that publication is not done to punish the person, but to inform the public.[788] They argue that if a newspaper is going to print pictures or names of johns who are arrested, it would be only fair to report the outcome of the case; the city would make its point by having the photos published, but the newspaper would have the chore of seeing that the outcome of each case is reported.[789]

It should be noted that this is not an abnormal practice to newspaper reporting, however. While there are some landmark and high-profile cases that attract a great deal of media attention up to and including the trial, in most cases, the majority of media attention is generated by the arrest. Many cases, as they move through the criminal justice system, no longer generate the same amount of public attention or media coverage. There are many situations in which a criminal offender is arrested or even accused, and the story makes the news, but the eventual disposition or resolution of the case does not. Thus far, publicizing the names of johns arrested for prostitution and putting them online or in newspapers has been held as lawful and not unconstitutional and appears to be a practice growing in popularity.

Case Study: Confidence Games

Confidence games are titled as such because they involve the offender gaining the trust and confidence of the victim. Many con artists are able to be successful for long periods of time not only because of their initial presentation to victims, but also because their victims may experience embarrassment, grief, or shame after being taken. Reaching out to the media is a good way to publicize these con games. It lets victims know that they are not alone and do not need to feel shamed by what has happened. This may encourage victims to come forward. It also acts to educate possible victims and let them recognize a con game that may be about to be perpetrated against them. Victims should always be strongly advised to document the incident in the report, identifying information from the victim should be taken, and the victim should be encouraged to prosecute.[790] Among some of the more common con games are:

- Ruse entry: These cases involve thefts, usually from senior citizens, by criminals posing as tradesmen or laborers. The thieves usually work in groups, but the victim will likely only see one. Their goal is to get into the home. They may present themselves as utility workers, city workers, or construction workers. They will try to gain the victims' confidence. Victims may hear that the workers were sent by a relative of the victim or that they are working in the neighborhood. One offender will then create a distraction while the partner goes through the home. If a vehicle is seen, it will most likely be a work type vehicle, which appears to fit in.[791]

- Pigeon drop: In this con, a stranger, often a woman, who may appear more trustworthy to a potential victim, will approach with a story. It is often represented to the victim that the stranger discovered a wallet with a large sum of money or other valuables. In many areas, the offender will be outside of an ethnic grocery store, approach someone of the same ethnicity, and give the sad story. The stranger may claim that she has won the lottery, but is unable to personally collect, as she is in the country illegally. The stranger will express a willingness to split the newfound wealth with the victim if everyone involved will put up some "good faith" money while the con artist exchanges the goods for cash. The victim turns over the "good faith" money and never sees the money or the strangers again. Often, this scam will involve multiple offenders, but one will be playing the role of a "good faith" money giver.[792]

- Unknown caller or visitor: People, often a woman and a child, come to the victim's door asking to enter the house for a favor, such as to use the restroom or get a drink of water. One person distracts the victim while another person steals cash or jewelry. Another scam is a person who comes to the victim's door, often at odd hours, and may claim to be a neighbor who needs money right now for his sick mother's medicine and who vows to repay the money. Other forms of this scam include persons approaching on the street who claim to need to get to the hospital, to be stranded, or to be out of gas.[793]

• Telemarketing, telephone, and Internet fraud: These scams take many forms. They may involve solicitation for donations for a good cause, such as "police widows," which is fraudulent. These can include travel scams, business opportunities, sweepstakes, credit repair scams, or anything that requires one to pay money to enter. They can involve a caller demanding or requesting credit card or identifying info or wanting a quick decision or money paid right now. These scams are often conducted over the Internet as well, where persons may request the victim's password for security purposes.[794]

• Bank examiner swindle: Someone posing as either a bank or police official asks for help, in person or via the telephone, to catch a dishonest bank employee. The victim is told to withdraw money from a bank account, turn it over to them so the serial numbers can be checked or the money marked. The victim turns the money over and it is switched, or the victim is told that it is evidence and given a receipt. A reimbursement check is promised, which of course never comes.[795]

• Nigerian computer/advance fee scams: A letter or email asks for help to transfer money out of Nigeria or another country through an overseas bank account. There is a promise of large sums of money if the victim will help. The request may ask for a bank and account number or other personal information or for some type of "good faith" advance fee.[796]

There are many people particularly susceptible to falling victim to confidence games. Offenders pick and choose who they select as victims—the elderly, single women, illegal aliens, and lonely hearts are often among those who are targeted. Using the media to educate and reach out to potential victims, along with community outreach and policing programs, is the best way to ensure that these offenders do not succeed in their criminal endeavors and get identified and caught.

WHAT THE PROS SAY

"The successful media officer understands the importance of his or her role in the law enforcement process. The media relations officer serves several contrasting roles concurrently throughout a criminal investigation. Balancing the needs of the criminal investigation as well as the prosecution and serving the needs of the community by keeping them informed can prove to be a challenge to even the best media relations officer.

The media officer does not want to compromise a criminal investigation. Providing specific details of the crime can be counterproductive to the successful prosecution of the case. Releasing too much information regarding the progress of the case can alert the offender to leads, witnesses, and evidence that the police have or are searching for. Seasoned detectives understand that a criminal investigation is fluid in nature, with many twists and turns throughout. Oftentimes, initial hypotheses or leads can turn cold quickly. To the untrained citizen, these twists and turns are viewed as incompetence, especially when television crimes are cleared within the hour of a television show. Releasing information too soon gives the media and the public the impression that the police don't know what they are doing and that a dangerous person remains at large. Then the story turns to the police investigation rather than the crime

(Continued)

itself. When this occurs, elected or appointed officials are vulnerable for replacement.

A responsible police agency appears in control, professional, and calculated, in sharing information with the community and assuring the public that the police are actively engaged in the investigation of the crime. Small, general, nonspecific information regarding the crime or event should be released. The purpose of this release is to acknowledge the event and to assure the community that the police investigation, with all of its resources, is currently underway. Properly administered, it informs the community that their police force is highly trained, competent, and responsive to their needs.

Media relations officers should be particularly understanding to the feelings and concerns of the community. The *Dragnet* style of releasing information comes across as cold, indifferent, and arrogant. In today's society of partnerships between the police and the community, the best release is delivered in a sensitive manner with empathy and commitment.

In July of 1999, the Skokie Police Department was thrust into the international media spotlight when a man named Benjamin Smith gunned down former Northwestern University basketball coach Ricky Birdsong as he walked with his children on a residential neighborhood street. Benjamin Smith had connections to the World Church of the Creator and was suspected in several other shootings that occurred in Chicago's North Side, targeting Jews who were walking home from religious services earlier that same night. As the evening progressed, we found out that Smith's shooting rampage was targeting minorities in other communities throughout Illinois. Skokie Chief of Police Barry Silverberg, then a detective commander in charge of the case, understood the importance of solving this crime quickly and calming the fears of his community. He fully supported the efforts of the media officer and focused his attention to the criminal investigation. As the media officer, I released basic information, which could not harm the case. I relied on good relationships, which I had built over time in order to keep media focused, assure the community that we were actively involved, and were utilizing all available resources to solve this crime and bring the killer to justice. The case had many twists and turns, as it occurred over a July 4th holiday weekend. Smith was traveling throughout the Midwest shooting at minorities. When a vehicle description was confirmed, police were notified via a nationwide broadcast. A short time later, the information was released to the public requesting their assistance in locating the vehicle and the suspect. Within hours of the release of his vehicle description, the gunman dumped his car and carjacked another. Ultimately, Benjamin Smith was killed in a shootout with police. Inside of his car, we discovered evidence indicating that he was reading about his crimes and the progress of police toward his capture.

The community responded well to the openness and accessibility of their police force. Community meetings were held to assure residents that it was safe to walk their children in the neighborhood. Working in partnership with the local newspapers, we were able to give greater depth to the case, once it was over. We were also able to present our side of the story and to dispel any misunderstandings that had taken place. We were able to encourage greater partnerships within the neighborhood. Those relationships still exist today. Oftentimes, good community stories are given media attention following a bad event.

Understanding the media is also important for the media officer. Knowing the roles, duties, and responsibilities of the reporter, field reporter, news editor, and camera crew will help you understand their point of view and where to turn if wrong information has been released. If you release no information or take the 'no comment' route, the story will turn from the crime itself to the police department. The media will hint about incompetence or cover-up. If the media cannot cover the story, they will report anything they can find. This includes the man on the street interviews, community reaction to the police, or if all else fails, they will just make something up. This will be done in an attempt to force the story

(Continued)

to the surface. The media officer will be forced to defend the agency and its members, department head, or elected officials." **Commander Mike Ruth, Skokie Police Department**

Michael R. Ruth, a 30-year law enforcement veteran, currently serves as a police commander for the Skokie, Illinois, Police Department. He is the former media officer for the Skokie Police Department. He previously served as a police officer in Hometown, Illinois, and a communications dispatcher for the Alsip, Illinois, Police Department. He serves as an adjunct faculty member at the University of Illinois at Chicago and Governors State University. He also serves as academic chair for Kaplan University.

"To simply say that the media is a valuable tool to law enforcement is a gross understatement. If anyone in law enforcement has the unique opportunity of working for a nonpolitical department, then they do not need the media. However, we all know that a nonpolitical department is as rare as a unicorn. It does not exist. Any branch of law enforcement is accountable to a political process. You may work for the governor, mayor, city council, etc., but whomever it is, that individual reports to and is responsible to the public in one way or another. The media becomes the lightning rod to those individuals who control the ebb and flow of those departments. A classic example of this would be the case in Chicago that eventually led to the retirement of Superintendent Phil Cline. In that case, an off-duty Chicago police officer had his actions captured on videotape and was accused of beating up a female bartender who refused to continue to serve him. The case is a classic example of what happens when perception outweighs reality.

Please note, I am not saying the media was the only reason why this catastrophic set of circumstances took place; this is not the case. To fully examine what took place is another study for another time. I am simply using this reference to show what happens in the media and how it affects the movers and shakers and their response to what is in the media.

Any tradesman or any individual who uses tools on a daily basis knows that if your tools are neglected and left in the tool box, they will rust and eventually become useless. The very same applies to law enforcement. The media tool must be used on a frequent basis. This means that in good times, and most importantly in difficult times, the media has to be used. Law enforcement needs to use the media more than the media uses them. This can be very difficult without proper planning and relations with the media.

The media, very much like law enforcement, is truly a necessary evil. Just like those in law enforcement, the media has a job to do, and a good reporter will pursue that end just as a good detective will pursue a homicide offender. The relationship between the media and law enforcement can become amicable if the efforts needed in any relationship are applied. This is an ongoing process and will not happen overnight.

It is important to note that media relations does not equate to censorship. Just because there is an ongoing dialogue between the media and law enforcement does not imply that control of what is written or broadcast will be censored by law enforcement. What it does mean is that by having a relationship, you can have input as to the facts of whatever the story is, at least from the law enforcement side of the story.

How is this tool developed? When do you put it to use? How is this relationship with the media initiated? Now is the time to start this relationship. When looking at the media, it is extremely important to realize that like politics, everything is local. The local daily community paper is the most important chain in this link. I am not referring to the *Today Show* or *Good Morning America*. This section of the media will follow the lead of the local paper. Stories that are used in these programs will generally start out from the local paper or news broadcast, then go national.

(Continued)

In most communities, the local paper runs a police blotter or some form of local news of what crimes or arrests are taking place in the community. This is the reporter that is the key to the relationship with the media. He or she is the mainstream connection to the community. Have this individual do a ride-along with someone from your agency. Ideally, it should be the department spokesperson if one is in place. If not, the officer that is going to do the ride-along must be an officer that is competent and trusted by management. It would be useless to put a reporter with an officer who has absolutely no use for the media. Common sense should prevail. You want the reporter to see everything and at the same time, realize that crime scenes and investigations take priority and must be handled according to policy. Set the ground rules for the ride-along beforehand. If this is strictly for background information for the individual reporter, tell him exactly that and do not allow cameras or tape recorders on the ride-along. On the other hand, if the law enforcement agency is doing a roadside safety check for seat belts, by all means make it a news event. The bottom line becomes getting the relationship started. Sit down and have your spokesperson or whoever deals with the media get the opportunity to meet and greet this reporter.

This is just the start of the relationship foundation with the media. The next step is one of common courtesy. If a reporter calls your desk sergeant looking for information on a particular incident, and the desk sergeant becomes indignant over the questions or is discourteous in his response, what do you think the reaction of the reporter will be in the printed story about this incident?

A common complaint of law enforcement is, 'Those reporters never get the facts right.' If you don't provide the facts or refuse to talk to the media, how do you expect them to get the facts of the case? I am not talking about giving away all the details of a crime; always remember, the investigation supersedes the First Amendment. The media has a right to be in the vicinity of the crime, but they do not have a right to interfere with an investigation or to access all the information about that crime at that particular moment. The ultimate responsibility of law enforcement is to thoroughly investigate the crime, protect the victims, and apprehend the offenders.

The media needs basic information at a crime scene. What is the crime? How did it happen? Can you identify the victim? Does the community have anything to fear? Is there anyone in custody? Obviously, there will be many more questions asked and all the answers may not be releasable at that point. If there is information that cannot be released, inform the reporter of those facts. NEVER use the term 'no comment.' When an individual takes the Fifth Amendment, a constitutional right, what is the first impression everyone has? He is guilty and hiding something. The same thing applies to 'no comment'; it gives the impression you know the facts, but they are being withheld. Confront the issue directly with, 'That information would affect the integrity of the investigation and cannot be released at this point in time.' That translates to a very nice way of saying no comment.

In any relationship you must take the good with the bad. It is hardest to deal with the media when there is negative news about your agency. Those are the times that your efforts and work and the relationship should pay off. No, it is not going to make the bad news go away, but it might make it last a shorter period of time in the news cycle. The hardest time to call a press conference is when the news is negative about your agency. First and foremost, these are the times that you must make lemonade out of the lemons that you have. Whatever the problem is, no matter how terrible the news, there has to be something positive your agency is doing to rectify the situation. Secondly, your agency is the one releasing the facts. It is not an exclusive to any one news source; everyone gets the information at the same time. You control the message. Plan the news conference to include the facts of what took place, how it came to light, and what is being done by your agency to correct the problem. This will not make the bad news

(Continued)

disappear, but it should limit the amount of time it is covered in the news cycle.

Earlier, the negative result of the media was briefly discussed in the off-duty police beating case. Let's take a moment to look at just one instance of positive results.

In May of 1997, an incident that happened with Ken Herzlich, of Network Video Productions, is an example of positive relations with the media. Ken is known as a 'stringer.' This is an individual with a video camera, a video journalist if you will, who is out on the streets of Chicago from about 10:00 P.M. to the early hours of the morning. He makes a living by capturing videotape of major incidents, fires, police-involved shootings, accidents, etc., that take place during the late night and early morning hours. He then contacts the major media outlets and sells the video that he has captured. Ken has been doing this for some time and is very good at what he does.

On this particular night in May, Ken heard what he thought was an unusual radio transmission on the police network. A police officer, Olive Dickey, was calling for a supervisor at Astor and Scott, in regards to a parking violation.

Ken thought this was a little out of the ordinary and proceeded to the scene. Once he was there, he observed a red Jeep with multiple parking tickets and Minnesota license plates. Ken contacted a news station in Minnesota, figuring the vehicle might be stolen, and it turned out the vehicle was wanted in a double homicide in Minnesota, and the information known to the police at that time was that it might be connected to the homicide of Lee Miglin, a well-known Chicago real estate mogul. Miglin was another murder in the Andrew Cunanan killing spree. As it turned out, this was the case. Ken was on the scene very early in the morning and was asked a rather unusual request by Chicago Police detectives who were processing the vehicle. The detectives asked Ken to delay releasing the tape so they could have some additional time to follow up on potential leads before the information was made public. Ken sat on one of the top stories of the year until 6:00 A.M. that morning. Without the relationship between Ken and the department, this would not have happened.

It takes work from both sides to maintain a healthy relationship. Work with the local reporter from the community paper as he is covering the latest police story. When the opportunity presents itself to promote your department, reach out to that reporter and let him know what is going on so he can adequately cover the story. The hardest part of any relationship is when the news is bad. Now, more than ever, reach out to the reporter and give him the bad news firsthand and what the department is doing to correct the problem. It may sound crazy, but if you call the reporter and give him the facts firsthand, the story will not go away, but it may not last as long as it would when the story comes from another source. Be proactive in you relationship with the media; in the long run it pays off." **Deputy Director (Retired) Patrick T. Camden, News Affairs, Chicago Police Department**

Patrick T. Camden was the deputy director of News Affairs of the Chicago Police Department (1998–2008). After retiring as a sworn police officer with 29 years of service in 1998, Pat was appointed the deputy director by then Superintendent Terry G. Hillard. One of the first things Pat did was to expand the unit to a 24/7 operation by having nine sworn police officers assigned to the unit. Prior to 1998, the unit was an 8 to 5 operation, closed on the weekends. This unit was the liaison between the Chicago Police Department and the media. The Chicago Police Department is the second largest department in the United States and the city of Chicago is the third largest media market in the country. Deputy Camden responded to approximately 325 police-involved shootings and numerous major incidents while he was the deputy director. Pat is currently an adjunct professor with Northwestern University, Center for Public Safety and teaches media relations to police officers who attend the School of Police Staff and Command. Pat is an adjunct professor at Lewis University, Romeoville,

(Continued)

Illinois, and is also involved in the Executive Training Program for the Chicago Police Department.

When he was a sworn police officer, Pat worked in the Special Operations Group and Patrol Division for 15 years prior to being assigned to News Affairs. Pat is a media relations consultant and trainer for Camden Consulting and can be contacted at 773-543-2340 or pcamden@comcast.net.

ENDNOTES

1. William L. Harvey, "Media Relations for Beginners: Media Relations 101 for New Chiefs," Policelink.com, July 8, 2008.

2. Jane Hansenchildren, "Hardwick Baby Death Only Part of the Big Story," *Atlanta Journal-Constitution*, August 4, 1992.

3. Gerald W. Garner, *Chief, the Reporters Are Here!: The Police Executive's Personal Guide to Press Relations*, Springfield: Thomas Books, 1987, 15–17.

4. Ibid.

5. Ibid., 17–18.

6. Iowa City, Iowa, Police Department, General Order 01–07, Issued November 20, 2001.

7. Chicago Police Department, D.S.O 04–14, October 1, 2004, 2.

8. Gerald W. Garner, *Chief, the Reporters Are Here!: The Police Executive's Personal Guide to Press Relations*, Springfield: Thomas Books, 1987, 7–8.

9. Ibid., 8–9.

10. Ibid., 163–166.

11. William L. Harvey, "Media Relations for Beginners: Media Relations 101 for New Chiefs," Policelink.com, July 8, 2008.

12. Richard Weinblatt, "How History Makes the Future of Police Media Relations Clearer," Weinblatt's Tips, Policeone.com, April 4, 2005.

13. Ibid.

14. Ibid.

15. Gerald W. Garner, *Chief, the Reporters Are Here!: The Police Executive's Personal Guide to Press Relations*, Springfield: Thomas Books, 1987, 40–42.

16. David Kazak, North East Multi-Regional Training Handout, Media Matters.

17. First Amendment, U.S. Constitution.

18. Sixth Amendment, U.S. Constitution.

19. *Sheppard v. Maxwell*, 384 U.S. 333 (1966).

20. Ibid.

21. 720 ILCS 5/1–5, 720 ILCS 5/1–6

22. 725 ILCS 5/114–6

23. Ibid.

24. Ibid.

25. *People v. Aprile*, 15 Ill. App. 3d 327 (4th Dist. 1973).

26. *People v. Hariston*, 10 Ill. App. 3d 678 (1st Dist. 1973).

27. *People v. Kirchner*, 194 Ill. 2d 502 (2000).

28. *Irvin v. Dowd*, 366 U.S. 717 (1961).

29. Ibid.

30. American Bar Association Criminal Justice Section Standards, Fair Trial and Free Press, Part I, Conduct of Attorneys in Criminal Cases. Conduct of Law Enforcement Officers, Judges, and Court Personnel in Criminal Cases, Standard 8–2.1, "Release of Information by Law Enforcement Agencies."

31. American Bar Association Criminal Justice Section Standards, Fair Trial and Free Press, Part I, Conduct of Attorneys in Criminal Cases. Conduct of Law Enforcement Officers, Judges, and Court Personnel in Criminal Cases, Standard 8–3.1, "Prohibition of Direct Restraints on Media."

32. John Brewer, "Judge Issues Gag Order in Olga Franco Trial," *St. Paul Pioneer Press*, July 23, 2008.

33. *Hanlon v. Berger*, 526 U.S. 808 (1999), *Wilson v. Layne*, 526 U.S. 603 (1999).

34. David Kazak, North East Multi-Regional Training Handout, Media Matters.

35. Ibid, 20.

36. Ibid.

37. Ibid.

38. Ibid.

39. Ibid.

40. Ibid.

41. Ibid.

42. Ibid.

43. Ibid.

44. Los Angeles Police Department Media Relations Handbook, 2007–2008, 2.

45. Chicago Police Department D.S.O 04–14, 1, "News Media Guidelines," October 2004, 1.

46. Los Angeles Police Department Media Relations Handbook, 2007–2008, 5.

47. Ibid.

48. Chicago Police Department D.S.O 04–14, October 1, 2004, 2.

49. Ibid.

50. Ibid., 4.

51. Ibid.

52. Ibid.

53. Los Angeles Police Department Media Relations Handbook, 2007–2008, 2.

54. Ibid., 2–3.

55. Ibid., 3.

56. Ibid., 3–4.

57. Chicago Police Department D.S.O 04–14, October 1, 2004, 4.

58. Ibid., 5.

59. Ibid.

60. Chicago Police Department D.S.O 04–14, October 1, 2004, 3.

61. Chicago Police Department D.S.O 04–14, October 1, 2004, 1.

62. Ibid., 3.

63. Gerald W. Garner, *Chief, the Reporters Are Here!: The Police Executive's Personal Guide to Press Relations*, Springfield: Thomas Books, 1987, 143–147.

64. Ibid., 140–142.

65. Chicago Police Department D.S.O 04–14, October 1, 2004, 6.

66. Bob Secter, "July 13, 1966: 8 Student Nurses Slain in Their Townhouse," *Chicago Tribune*, September 18, 1997, reprinted from *Chicago Days: 150 Defining Moments in the Life of a Great City*, edited by Stevenson Swanson, Contemporary Books.

67. Ibid.

68. Ibid.

69. Ibid.

70. Jerry Crimmins, "This Is Optional Sidebar," *Chicago Daily Law Bulletin*, May 4, 2006.

71. Steve Johnson, Sharman Stein, Bob Merrifield, Helaine Olen, Rob Karwath, and Jerry Shnay, "Speck's Death Fails to End the Pain of Victim's Relatives," *Chicago Tribune*, December 6, 1991.

72. John Anderson, "Horror: Richard Speck Sparked an Industry That Finds Big Money in Murder," *Chicago Tribune*, May, 19, 1996.

73. Bob Secter, "July 13, 1966: 8 Student Nurses Slain in Their Townhouse," *Chicago Tribune*, September 18, 1997, reprinted from *Chicago Days: 150 Defining Moments in the Life of a Great City*, edited by Stevenson Swanson, Contemporary Books.

74. Jerry Crimmins, "This Is Optional Sidebar," *Chicago Daily Law Bulletin*, May 4, 2006.

75. Ibid.

76. Ibid.

77. David Lohr, "Richard Speck," Crimemagazine.com—An Encyclopedia of Crime, August 20, 2003.

78. Steve Johnson, Sharman Stein, Bob Merrifield, Helaine Olen, Rob Karwath, and Jerry Shnay, "Speck's Death Fails to End the Pain of Victim's Relatives," *Chicago Tribune*, December 6, 1991.

79. Ibid.

80. *www.crimeandjustice.us*

81. "Speck's Death Fails to End the Pain of Victim's Relatives.

82. "Horror: Richard Speck Sparked an Industry That Finds Big Money in Murder"

83. Bob Secter, "July 13, 1966: 8 Student Nurses Slain in Their Townhouse," *Chicago Tribune*, September 18, 1997, reprinted from *Chicago Days: 150 Defining Moments in the Life of a Great City*, edited by Stevenson Swanson, Contemporary Books.

84. Jerry Crimmins, "This Is Optional Sidebar," *Chicago Daily Law Bulletin*, May 4, 2006.

85. Jack R. Greene, "O.W. Wilson," *Encyclopedia of Police Science*, CRC Press, 2006, 1,362.

86. Jerry Crimmins, "This Is Optional Sidebar," *Chicago Daily Law Bulletin*, May 4, 2006.

87. Ibid.

88. Steve Johnson, Sharman Stein, Bob Merrifield, Helaine Olen, Rob Karwath, and Jerry Shnay, "Speck's Death Fails to End the Pain of Victim's Relatives," *Chicago Tribune*, December 6, 1991.

89. Jerry Crimmins, "This Is Optional Sidebar," *Chicago Daily Law Bulletin*, May 4, 2006.

90. Ibid.

91. Steve Johnson, Sharman Stein, Bob Merrifield, Helaine Olen, Rob Karwath, and Jerry Shnay, "Speck's Death Fails to End the Pain of Victim's Relatives," *Chicago Tribune*, December 6, 1991.

92. Ibid.

93. Ibid.

94. Ibid.

95. Ibid.

96. Ibid.

97. Ibid.

98. Ibid.

99. *Rideau v. Louisiana*, 373 U.S. 723 (1963).

100. Seamus Toomey, "Will a Comment Hurt? Lawyers Debate Relevance of Police Chief's 'People Without Souls' Remark on Jury Selection," *Chicago Daily Herald*, May 22, 2002.

101. Michael Sneed, "Even in Death, Richard Speck Still Shocks," *Chicago Sun-Times*, May 12, 1996.

102. Ibid.

103. Bob Greene, "Speck's High Life Shouldn't Have Been a Shock," *Chicago Tribune*, May 19, 1996.

104. Ibid.

105. Ibid.

106. Ibid.

107. Ibid.

108. Richard Roeper, "Tapes Reveal Speck at His Freakish Worst," *Chicago Sun-Times*, May 16, 1996.

109. "Mass Killer Partied in Prison," *Washington Post*, May 14, 1996.

110. Ibid.

111. Richard Roeper, "Tapes Reveal Speck at His Freakish Worst," *Chicago Sun-Times*, May 16, 1996.

112. Ibid.

113. Ibid.

114. "Mass Killer Partied in Prison," *Washington Post*, May 14, 1996.

115. Bob Secter, "July 13, 1966: 8 Student Nurses Slain in Their Townhouse," *Chicago Tribune*, September 18, 1997, reprinted from *Chicago Days: 150 Defining Moments in the Life of a Great City*, edited by Stevenson Swanson, Contemporary Books.

116. "Tapes Reveal Speck at His Freakish Worst."

117. "Speck's Death Fails to End the Pain Of Victim's Relatives."

118. Jerry Crimmins, "This Is Optional Sidebar," *Chicago Daily Law Bulletin*, May 4, 2006.

119. Patrick Morley, *Report Writing for Criminal Justice Professionals,* New York: Kaplan Publishing, 2008.

120. *Smith v. Doe*, 538 U.S. 84 (2003).

121. Natalie Mikles, "Internet an Aid in Locating Area Sex Offenders," *Tulsa World*, June 12, 2002.

122. Ibid.

123. Ibid.

124. Eric Russell, "100 Attend Bangor Forum Urging Residents to Use Sex Offender Registry," *Bangor Daily News* (Maine), October 22, 2008.

125. Ibid.

126. Brian DeBose, "Sex Offenders Registered Online," *Washington Afro-American*, March 16, 2001.

127. Allison Samuels and Paul Tolme, "Who Is the Real Kobe?" *Newsweek*, July 28, 2003.

128. Ibid.

129. "Chronology of Events in Kobe Bryant Sexual Assault Case," *Associated Press*, August 11, 2004.

130. Jeralyn Merrit, "Live Online with Jeralyn Merrit," Washingtonpost.com, September 2, 2004.

131. Patrick Morley, *Report Writing for Criminal Justice Professionals,* New York: Kaplan Publishing, 2008.

132. Allison Samuels and Paul Tolme, "Who Is the Real Kobe?" *Newsweek*, July 28, 2003.

133. Ibid.

134. Ibid.

135. Ibid.

136. "Chronology of Events in Kobe Bryant Sexual Assault Case," *Associated Press*, August 11, 2004.

137. Ibid.

138. Richard Hoffer and Lester Munson, "Bad Defense; Kobe Bryant's Rape Case Started Ugly, and It Will Only Get Worse," *Sports Illustrated*, October 20, 2003.

139. K. Jackson, "Questions Abound in Kobe Case," *Mansfield News Journal*, October 22, 2003.

140. Ibid.

141. Jeralyn Merrit, "Live Online with Jeralyn Merrit," Washingtonpost.com, September 2, 2004.

142. Lance Pugmire, "Sheriff Supports Filing Charged; The Woman who Accused Kobe Bryant of Sexual Assault Is 19 and a Hotel Employee," *Orlando Sentinel*, July 9, 2003.

143. Ibid.

144. Ibid.

145. Ibid.

146. Ibid.

147. David Kelly, "Decision on Bryant in Limbo; Colorado Officials Leave All Options Open as They Hope to Decide by Friday Whether to File Criminal Charges against the Laker Star Guard," *Los Angles Times*, July 8, 2003.

148. Mike McKibbin, "Sheriff Backs Investigators in Bryant Case," *Cox News Service*, September 2, 2004.

149. Ibid.

150. Amy Herdy, "Weak Case Closes with a Whimper; Legal Observers Say Prosecutors Never Had Much of a Chance against Kobe Bryant and His Lawyers, and They Wonder Why It Took So Long to Make an Obvious Decision," *Denver Post*, September 2, 2004.

151. Michelle McPhee, "Kobe Who? Asked Sheriff Quick to Get a Warrant, Slow to Realize Impact," *Daily News*, August 10, 2003.

152. "Chronology of Events in Kobe Bryant Sexual Assault Case," *Associated Press*, August 11, 2004.

153. Jennifer Hamilton, "Kobe Bryant's Defense Team Well-Regarded, Familiar with High-Profile Cases," *Associated Press*, July 24, 2003.

154. Ibid.

155. Ibid.

156. "Chronology of Events in Kobe Bryant Sexual Assault Case," *Associated Press*, August 11, 2004.

157. Steve Lipsher and Howard Pankratz, "Judge Halts Bryant Hearing, Move Comes After NBA Star's Defense Raises Issue of Accuser's Sexual History," *Denver Post*, October 10, 2003.

158. "Chronology of Events in Kobe Bryant Sexual Assault Case," *Associated Press*, August 11, 2004.

159. Ibid.

160. Ibid.

161. Ibid.

162. Steve Lipsher and Howard Pankratz, "Judge Halts Bryant Hearing, Move Comes After NBA Star's Defense Raises Issue of Accuser's Sexual History," *Denver Post*, October 10, 2003.

163. Ibid.

164. Ibid.

165. Ibid.

166. Ibid.

167. Ibid.

168. Ibid.

169. Ibid.

170. Ibid.

171. Ibid.

172. K. Jackson, "Questions Abound in Kobe Case," *Mansfield News Journal*, October 22, 2003.

173. Ibid.

174. Dianne Williamson, "Myths Part of Bryant Rape Case; Victims of Sex Assault Still Face Tough Hurdles," *Sunday Telegram* (Massachusetts), July 27, 2003.

175. Jeralyn Merrit, "Live Online with Jeralyn Merrit," Washingtonpost.com.

176. Jeff Benedict and Steve Henson, "The Case against Kobe Bryant Unraveled in a Mock Trial. The Accuser, Already Frustrated by Court Errors and Strife in the Legal Team, Buckled Under Tough Practice Questioning," *Los Angeles Times*, November 6, 2004.

177. Ibid.

178. Ibid.

179. Ibid.

180. Michelle McPhee, "Kobe Who? Asked Sherriff Quick to Get a Warrant, Slow to Realize Impact," *Daily News*, August 10, 2003.

181. Jeff Benedict and Steve Henson, "The Case against Kobe Bryant Unraveled in a Mock Trial. The Accuser, Already Frustrated by Court Errors and Strife in the Legal Team, Buckled Under Tough Practice Questioning," *Los Angeles Times*, November 6, 2004.

182. Ibid.

183. Ibid.

184. Ibid.

185. Ibid.

186. Ibid.

187. Ibid.

188. Ibid.

189. Ibid.

190. Ibid.

191. Ibid.

192. Ibid.

193. Ibid.

194. Ibid.

195. Marcia Smith, "Case Dismissed; Prosecutors Say Bryant's Accuser Unwilling to Proceed," *Orange County Register*, September 2, 2004.

196. *http://sports.espn.go.com/nba/news/story?id=1872928*

197. Allison Samuels and Paul Tolme, "Kobe Bryant: 'A Long Sigh of Relief,'" *Newsweek*, August 16, 2004.

198. Marcia Smith, "Case Dismissed; Prosecutors Say Bryant's Accuser Unwilling to Proceed," *Orange County Register*, September 2, 2004.

199. Amy Herdy, "Weak Case Closes in a Whimper. Legal Observers Say Prosecutors Never Had Much of a Chance against Kobe Bryant and His Lawyers, and They Wonder Why It Took So Long to Make an Obvious Decision," *Denver Post*, September 2, 2004.

200. Howard Pankratz and Steve Lipsher, "Late Deal Ends Kobe Bryant Criminal Case; NBA Star Avoids Criminal Trial when Alleged Victim Won't Testify," *Kansas City Star*, September 2, 2004.

201. Jeff Benedict and Steve Henson, "The Case against Kobe Bryant Unraveled in a Mock Trial. The Accuser, Already Frustrated by Court Errors and Strife in the Legal Team, Buckled Under Tough Practice Questioning," *Los Angeles Times*, November 6, 2004.

202. *www.cnbc.com/id/23810523*

203. *http://blogs.telegraph.co.uk/brendan_gallagher/blog/2008/06/14/top_15_most_popular_nba_jerseys*

204. Model Penal Code, Section 222.1, "Robbery."

205. Patrick Morley, *Report Writing for Criminal Justice Professionals,* New York: Kaplan Publishing, 2008.

206. Ibid.

207. Ibid.

208. Dwayne Rodgers, "Shootout Deaths," *City News Bureau*, Los Angeles, April 10, 1997.

209. Patrick McGreevy, "19 LAPD Officers Receive Medal of Valor," *The Daily News of Los Angeles*, September 10, 1998; Julia Scheeres, "LAPD Honors 19 for Valor on Duty, Awards: Seventeen of the Officers Were Singled Out for Their Roles in the 1997 North Hollywood Bank Shootout," *Los Angeles Times*, September 3, 1998.

210. Dwayne Rodgers, "Shootout Deaths," *City News Bureau*, Los Angeles, April 10, 1997.

211. Patrick McGreevy, "19 LAPD Officers Receive Medal of Valor," *The Daily News of Los Angeles*, September 10, 1998.

212. Scott Glover, "Suit Tarnishes Anniversary of Bank Shootout," *Los Angeles Times*, February 28, 1998

213. Dwayne Rodgers, "Shootout Deaths," *City News Bureau* (Los Angeles), April 10, 1997.

214. Ibid.

215. Julia Scheeres, "LAPD Honors 19 for Valor on Duty, Awards: Seventeen of the Officers Were Singled Out for Their Roles in the 1997 North Hollywood Bank Shootout," *Los Angeles Times*, September 3, 1998.

216. Ibid.

217. Scott Glover, "Suit Tarnishes Anniversary of Bank Shootout," *Los Angeles Times*, February 28, 1998.

218. Julia Scheeres, "LAPD Honors 19 for Valor on Duty, Awards: Seventeen of the Officers Were Singled Out for Their Roles in the 1997 North Hollywood Bank Shootout," *Los Angeles Times*, September 3, 1998.

219. Patrick McGreevy, "19 LAPD Officers Receive Medal of Valor," *The Daily News of Los Angeles*, September 10, 1998.

220. Ibid.

221. Julia Scheeres, "LAPD Honors 19 for Valor on Duty, Awards: Seventeen of the Officers Were Singled Out for Their Roles in the 1997 North Hollywood Bank Shootout," *Los Angeles Times*, September 3, 1998.

222. Patrick McGreevy, "19 LAPD Officers Receive Medal of Valor," *The Daily News of Los Angeles*, September 10, 1998.

223. Ibid.

224. Dominic Berbeo, "Parks Defends Officers' Actions in North Hollywood Bank Shootout," *Metropolitan News Enterprise* (Los Angeles), April 22, 1998.

225. Scott Glover, "Suit Tarnishes Anniversary of Bank Shootout," *Los Angeles Times*, February 28, 1998.

226. Edward J. Boyer, "Look Ahead: The Bloody 1997 North Hollywood Shootout Will Be Replayed as… Trial Starts in Claim that Officers Let Robber Die," February 14, 2000.

227. Scott Glover, "Suit Tarnishes Anniversary of Bank Shootout," *Los Angeles Times*, February 28, 1998.

228. Ibid.

229. Ibid.

230. Patrick McGreevy, "Review Backs Use of Force in 1997 Shootout, North Hollywood Actions 'In Policy,'" *The Daily News of Los Angeles*, February 4, 1998.

231. Ibid.

232. Michael Sniffen, "FBI Focusing on Photos in Olympic Bombing Investigation", *Associated Press*, August 30, 1996.

233. Kevin Sack, "Richard Jewell, 44, Hero of Atlanta Attack, Dies," *New York Times*, August 30, 2007.

234. Ibid.

235. Brendan Williams, "Defamation as a Remedy for Criminal Suspects Tried Only in the Media," *Communication and the Law*, September 1997.

236. Kevin Sack, "Richard Jewell, 44, Hero of Atlanta Attack, Dies," *New York Times*, August 30, 2007.

237. Brian Duffy, Stephen J. Hedges, Richard J. Newman, Tim Zimmermann, Philippe B. Moulier, Doug Podolsky, Douglas Pasternak, Fred Coleman, Jamie McNeely, Laura Koss-Feder, "Clues from the Sky," U.S. *News and World Report*, July 29, 1996.

238. Ibid.

239. Kevin Sack, "Richard Jewell, 44, Hero of Atlanta Attack, Dies," *New York Times*, August 30, 2007.

240. Brendan Williams, "Defamation as a Remedy for Criminal Suspects Tried Only in the Media," *Communication and the Law*, September 1997.

241. James Collins, reported by Adam Cohen, Andrea Sachs, and Elaine Shannon, "The Strange Saga of Richard Jewell," *Time*, November 11, 1996.

242. Brendan Williams, "Defamation as a Remedy for Criminal Suspects Tried Only in the Media," *Communication and the Law*, September 1997.

243. Ibid.

244. Ibid, quoting *Atlanta Constitution-Journal*, July 30, 1996.

245. Ibid.

246. Ibid.

247. "The Notorious Serial Killers," *USA Today*, May 11, 1994.

248. David Kindred, "A Long Wait in the Shadows After His Moment in the Sun," *Atlanta Constitution-Journal*, August 1, 1996.

249. James Collins, reported by Adam Cohen, Andrea Sachs, and Elaine Shannon, "The Strange Saga of Richard Jewell," *Time*, November 11, 1996.

250. Ibid.

251. Ibid.

252. Ibid.

253. Ibid.

254. Ibid.

255. Brendan Williams, "Defamation as a Remedy for Criminal Suspects Tried Only in the Media," *Communication and the Law*, September 1997.

256. James Collins, reported by Adam Cohen, Andrea Sachs, and Elaine Shannon, "The Strange Saga of Richard Jewell," *Time*, November 11, 1996.

257. Brendan Williams, "Defamation as a Remedy for Criminal Suspects Tried Only in the Media," *Communication and the Law*, September 1997.

258. *Chicago Tribune* News Services, "Leno's Wisecracks No Gems to Jewell," *Chicago Tribune*, November 12, 1996.

259. Kevin Sack, "Richard Jewell, 44, Hero of Atlanta Attack, Dies," *New York Times*, August 30, 2007.

260. Larry Reibstein, Daniel Pedersen, Daniel Klaidman, "A Tarnished Jewell," *Newsweek*, October 7, 1996.

261. Carol Woodford, "Jewell Drops Suit vs. Old Employer," *Chicago Sun-Times*, August 27, 1997.

262. Ibid.

263. Ibid.

264. Brendan Williams, "Defamation as a Remedy for Criminal Suspects Tried Only in the Media," *Communication and the Law*, September 1997.

265. Ibid.

266. Ibid.

267. Ibid.

268. James Collins, reported by Adam Cohen, Andrea Sachs, and Elaine Shannon, "The Strange Saga of Richard Jewell," *Time*, November 11, 1996.

269. Ibid.

270. Ibid.

271. Brendan Williams, "Defamation as a Remedy for Criminal Suspects Tried Only in the Media," *Communication and the Law*, September 1997.

272. James Collins, reported by Adam Cohen, Andrea Sachs, and Elaine Shannon, "The Strange Saga of Richard Jewell," *Time*, November 11, 1996.

273. Ibid.

274. "Magazine Settles with Richard Jewell," *Chicago Sun-Times*, August 20, 1997.

275. Carol Woodford, "Jewell Drops Suit vs. Old Employer," *Chicago Sun-Times*, August 27, 1997.

276. James Collins, reported by Adam Cohen, Andrea Sachs, and Elaine Shannon, "The Strange Saga of Richard Jewell," *Time*, November 11, 1996.

277. Kevin Sack, "Richard Jewell, 44, Hero of Atlanta Attack, Dies," *New York Times*, August 30, 2007.

278. Harry Weber, "Richard Jewell Honored at Georgia Capital for Heroism During 1996 Olympic Bombing," *Associated Press*, August 1, 2006.

279. Holly Edwards, "Bomb Suspect Upset by Abortion, Homosexuals," *The Tennessean*, June 1, 2003.

280. Ibid.

281. "UPI NewsTrack Top News," June 24, 2005.

282. Kristen Wyatt, "Authorities Arrest Olympic Park Bombing Suspect Eric Rudolph in Western N.C.," *Associated Press*, May 31, 2003.

283. "Excerpts from the 11 Page Statement from Eric Rudolph," *Associated Press*, April 14, 2005.

284. Ellen Perry and Jenny Jarvie, "Rudolph Admits Bombing 1996 Olympic Park, The Defiant Ex-Fugitive Cites Hatred of Abortion, Government Sanctions. A U.S. Plea Agreement Lets 'Cold, Callous' Killer Avoid Death Penalty," *Los Angeles Times*, April 14, 2005.

285. Kevin Sack, "Richard Jewell, 44, Hero of Atlanta Attack, Dies," *New York Times*, August 30, 2007.

286. Harry Weber, "Autopsy: Heart Disease Killed Former Security Guard Jewell, Wrongly Accused in Olympic Bombing," *Associated Press*, August 30, 2007.

287. Eric W. Hickey, *Serial Murderers and Their Victims*, Thomson/Wadworth Publishing, 4th Edition, 2006, 18; quoting Steven Egger, *A Working Definition of Serial Murder and the Reduction of Linkage Blindness*, 1984, 351.

288. Eric W. Hickey, *Serial Murderers and Their Victims*, Thomson/Wadworth Publishing, 4th Edition, 2006, 326.

289. Ibid.

290. Steven Eggers, *The Killers Among Us: An Examination of Serial Murder and Its Investigation*, Prentice Hall, 2nd Edition, 306.

291. Eric W. Hickey, *Serial Murderers and Their Victims*, Thomson/Wadworth Publishing, 4th Edition, 2006, 326; citing J. D. Glover and D. C. Witham, "The Atlanta Serial Murderers," *Policing,* 1989.

292. Ibid.

293. Ibid, p. 306, citing H. L. Marsh, "Newspaper Crime Coverage in the U.S.: 1983–1988", Criminal Justice Abstracts, p. 511.

294. Ibid.

295. Steven Eggers, *The Killers Among Us: An Examination of Serial Murder and Its Investigation*, Prentice Hall, 2nd Edition, 106.

296. Ibid.

297. Ibid.

298. Ibid.

299. Ibid.

300. Ibid., 107.

301. "The Green River Case," *Tacoma News Tribune*, November 6, 2003.

302. Gene Johnson, "Longtime Suspect Arrested in Connection with 1980's Green River Killing Case," *Associated Press*, December 1, 2001.

303. "Newspaper Reveals Letter from Green River Killer in 1984," *Associated Press*, November 7, 2005.

304. Michael Ko and Duff Wilson, "When Reichert Met Ridgway, an Unusual Bond Formed. 21 Year Green River Story Unfolds in Just-Released Tapes," *Seattle Times*, February 10, 2004.

305. Ibid.

306. Ibid.

307. Mia Pienta, "Ridgway, a Top Suspect for Two Decades, Appeared to Live Normal Life," *Associated Press*, November 30, 2001.

308. Ibid.

309. Duff Wilson and Craig Welsh, "Ridgway: Nice But a Bit Odd; Associates Call Him Smart, Meticulous, and Maybe a Bit Too Friendly," *Seattle Times*, December 2, 2001.

310. Mia Pienta, "Ridgway, a Top Suspect for Two Decades, Appeared to Live Normal Life," *Associated Press*, November 30, 2001.

311. Ibid.

312. Ibid.

313. Duff Wilson and Craig Welsh, "Ridgway: Nice But a Bit Odd; Associates Call Him Smart, Meticulous, and Maybe a Bit Too Friendly," *Seattle Times*, December 2, 2001.

314. Mia Pienta, "Ridgway, a Top Suspect for Two Decades, Appeared to Live Normal Life," *Associated Press*, November 30, 2001.

315. Duff Wilson and Craig Welsh, "Ridgway: Nice But a Bit Odd; Associates Call Him Smart, Meticulous, and Maybe a Bit Too Friendly," *Seattle Times*, December 2, 2001.

316. "The Green River Case," *Tacoma News Tribune,* November 6, 2003.

317. Mia Pienta, "Ridgway, a Top Suspect for Two Decades, Appeared to Live Normal Life," *Associated Press*, November 30, 2001.

318. Mike Barber, "Letter from a Serial Killer, 19 Years Ago, Ridgeway Offered Tantalizing Clues," November 7, 2005.

319. Ibid.

320. Ibid.

321. Mike Barber and Vanessa Ho, "Agent Missed Killer's Clues, Former FBI Profiler Admits Error on Ridgway Letter," *Seattle Post-Intelligencer*, November 27, 2003.

322. Mike Barber, "Letter from a Serial Killer, 19 Years Ago, Ridgeway Offered Tantalizing Clues," November 7, 2005.

323. Mike Barber and Vanessa Ho, "Agent Missed Killer's Clues, Former FBI Profiler Admits Error on Ridgway Letter," *Seattle Post-Intelligencer*, November 27, 2003.

324. Ibid.

325. Ibid.

326. Ibid.

327. Ibid.

328. Mike Barber, "Letter from a Serial Killer, 19 Years Ago, Ridgeway Offered Tantalizing Clues," November 7, 2005.

329. Mike Barber and Vanessa Ho, "Agent Missed Killer's Clues, Former FBI Profiler Admits Error on Ridgway Letter," *Seattle Post-Intelligencer*, November 27, 2003.

330. Ibid.

331. Ibid.

332. "Lover's Lanes Cleared," *Washington Post*, August 7, 1977.

333. Tracy Connor, "Breslin: Berkowitz 'Sticks to Me': Columnist Looks Back at Messages That Linked Him to Son of Sam," *New York Daily News*, July 15, 2007.

334. *www.nydailynews.com/features/sonofsam/manhunt.html*

335. Rick Hampson, "Remembering the Terror: I Am a Monster, The Son of Sam," *Associated Press*, April 12, 1987.

336. Ibid.

337. Ibid.

338. Ibid.

339. Ibid.

340. Ibid.

341. Tracy Connor, "Breslin: Berkowitz 'Sticks to Me': Columnist Looks Back at Messages That Linked Him to Son of Sam," *New York Daily News*, July 15, 2007.

342. Jack Egan, "Son of Sam: Big Story; Arrest Dominates Headlines Around the World; Controversy Over Coverage, News Analysis," *Washington Post*, August 13, 1977.

343. Rick Hampson, "Remembering the Terror: I Am a Monster, The Son of Sam," *Associated Press*, April 12, 1987.

344. *www.nydailynews.com/features/sonofsam/manhunt.html*

345. Rick Hampson, "Remembering the Terror: I Am a Monster, The Son of Sam," *Associated Press*, April 12, 1987.

346. Ibid.

347. Ibid.

348. David Alpern, Betsy Carter, and Tony Schwartz, "How They Covered Sam," *Newsweek*, August 22, 1977.

349. Ibid.

350. Ibid.

351. Ibid.

352. Rick Hampson, "Remembering the Terror: I Am a Monster, The Son of Sam," *Associated Press*, April 12, 1987.

353. *www.nydailynews.com/features/sonofsam/manhunt.html*

354. Richard Pienciak, *Associated Press*, May 9, 1978.

355. Malcolm Carter, *Associated Press*, June 12, 1978.

356. David Goldiner, "Son of Sam Sez, 'Honor Sam's Law," *New York Daily News*, May 22, 2006.

357. Jennifer Jordan, "Governor Proposes Expansion of State's Son of Sam Laws," *Associated Press*, April 5, 2000.

358. Julie C. Hilden, FindLaw Columnist, Special to CNN.com, "When Crime Pays, Who Should Get the Money?" CNN.com, March 3, 2004.

359. Tarron Lively, "Sniper Tipsters Get Reward of $500,000; Information Put an End to Shooting Spree That Took 10 Lives and Terrorized the Area," *Washington Times*, March 21, 2004; T. Trent Gegax, "Caught Sleeping," *Newsweek*, October 24, 2002.

360. Jo Becker and Serge F. Kovaleski, "Ghostwriters Work with Moose; FBI Profilers Specify Wording of Public Statements," *Washington Post*, October 23, 2002.

361. "Sniper Unlike Killers in the Past; Even Jack the Ripper Sought Publicity for His Murders," *The Toronto Sun*, October 23, 2002; "Dialogue with Police Heightens Sniper Mystery; Serial Killers Have Long Shown an

Interest in Communicating with Authorities. The Gunman May Get a Thrill Out of Staying Ahead," *The Nation*.

362. Richard Pienciak, "Your Children Are Not Safe: Snipers Threat Released After He Kills Again," *New York Daily News*, October 23, 2002.

363. T. Trent Gegax, "Caught Sleeping," *Newsweek*, October 24, 2002.

364. Frank Green, "Communicating with a Killer, Media Play Middleman in Cat-and-Mouse Game," *Richmond Times-Dispatch*, October 23, 2002.

365. "Dialogue with Police Heightens Sniper Mystery; Serial Killers Have Long Shown an Interest in Communicating with Authorities. The Gunman May Get a Thrill Out of Staying Ahead," *The Nation*.

366. Ibid.

367. Frank Green, "Communicating with a Killer, Media Play Middleman in Cat-and-Mouse Game," *Richmond Times-Dispatch*, October 23, 2002.

368. "Dialogue with Police Heightens Sniper Mystery; Serial Killers Have Long Shown an Interest in Communicating with Authorities. The Gunman May Get a Thrill Out of Staying Ahead," *The Nation*.

369. Ibid.

370. Richard Pienciak, "Your Children Are Not Safe: Snipers Threat Released After He Kills Again," *New York Daily News*, October 23, 2002.

371. Ibid.

372. "Dialogue with Police Heightens Sniper Mystery; Serial Killers Have Long Shown an Interest in Communicating with Authorities. The Gunman May Get a Thrill Out of Staying Ahead," *The Nation*.

373. Ibid.

374. Richard Pienciak, "Your Children Are Not Safe: Snipers Threat Released After He Kills Again," *New York Daily News*, October 23, 2002.

375. Jo Becker and Serge F. Kovaleski, "Ghostwriters Work with Moose; FBI Profilers Specify Wording of Public Statements," *Washington Post*, October 23, 2002.

376. Frank Green, "Communicating with a Killer, Media Play Middleman in Cat-and-Mouse Game," *Richmond Times-Dispatch*, October 23, 2002.

377. Ibid., quoting Dr. Alan Fox, Northeastern University.

378. Jo Becker and Serge F. Kovaleski, "Ghostwriters Work with Moose; FBI Profilers Specify Wording of Public Statements," *Washington Post*, October 23, 2002.

379. Ibid.

380. T. Trent Gegax, "Caught Sleeping," *Newsweek*, October 24, 2002.

381. Evan Thomas, reported by Pat Wingert, Suzanne Smalley, T. Trent Gagax, Daniel Klaidman, Mark Hosenball, John Barry, Mark Miller, Anne Bellie Gesalman, Julie Scelfo, Andrew Murr, Ana Figueroa, Kevin Peraino, Catherine Skipp, Arian Campo-Flores, Sarah Downey, Michael Iskoff, and Seth Mnookin. "Decent Into Evil," *Newsweek*, November 4, 2002.

382. Stephanie Simon and P. J. Huffstutter, "Clues Were Clear but Slow to Add Up; The BTK Killer Seemed Intent on Giving the Police What They Needed for an Arrest. The Man Behind Bars Paints a Logical yet Unexpected Portrait," *Los Angeles Times*, March 6, 2005.

383. Ibid.

384. David Twiddy, "BTK Suspect Hid for Years Around the City He Allegedly Terrorized," *Associated Press*, February 27, 2005.

385. Stephanie Simon and P. J. Huffstutter, "Clues Were Clear but Slow to Add Up; The BTK Killer Seemed Intent on Giving the Police What They Needed for an Arrest. The Man Behind Bars Paints a Logical yet Unexpected Portrait," *Los Angeles Times*, March 6, 2005.

386. Brad Regan, "The Digital Detectives," *Popular Mechanics*, May 1, 2006.

387. David Twiddy, "BTK Suspect Hid for Years Around the City He Allegedly Terrorized," *Associated Press*, February 27, 2005.

388. Brad Regan, "The Digital Detectives," *Popular Mechanics*, May 1, 2006.

389. Stephanie Simon and P. J. Huffstutter, "Clues Were Clear but Slow to Add Up; The BTK Killer Seemed Intent on Giving the Police What They Needed for an Arrest. The Man Behind Bars Paints a Logical yet Unexpected Portrait," *Los Angeles Times*, March 6, 2005.

390. Eagle Staff, "Police Reveal Details of BTK Investigation," *Wichita Eagle*, July 9, 2005.

391. Ron Sylvester, "Sentencing of BTK Serial Killer Begins Wednesday," *Wichita Eagle*, August 17, 2005.

392. Brad Regan, "The Digital Detectives," *Popular Mechanics*, May 1, 2006.

393. Ibid.

394. Eric Taub, "Deleting May Be Easy, But Your Hard Drive Still Tells All," *New York Times News Service*, April 7, 2006.

395. Brad Regan, "The Digital Detectives," *Popular Mechanics*, May 1, 2006.

396. Stephanie Simon and P. J. Huffstutter, "Clues Were Clear but Slow to Add Up; The BTK Killer Seemed Intent on Giving the Police What They Needed for an Arrest. The Man Behind Bars Paints a Logical yet Unexpected Portrait," *Los Angeles Times*, March 6, 2005.

397. Eagle Staff, "Police Reveal Details of BTK Investigation," *Wichita Eagle*, July 9, 2005.

398. "Kansas BTK Killer Given 10 Life Sentences," *United Press International*, August 18, 2005.

399. Sgt. Jeff DeYoung, "Police Pulling the Trigger Don't Soon Forget," *Greensboro N.C. News & Record*, April 13, 2008.

400. Bill Church, "Public Has the Right to Know Details of the Shooting," *Statesman Journal* (Salem, Oregon), July 13, 2008.

401. Glenn Nelson, Arthur Santana, and Tracy Jan, "Demetrius DuBose: 1971–1999—Lost After Football—But Former Local Star's Demise Shocks Many," *Seattle Times*, August 8, 1999.

402. *http://und.cstv.com,* "The Official Athletic Site" (Notre Dame University).

403. Ibid.

404. Glenn Nelson, "Puzzling End to Life of Intensity," *Seattle Times*, August 8, 1999; Glenn Nelson, Arthur Santana, Tracy Jan, "Demetrius DuBose: 1971–1999—Lost After Football—But Former Local Star's Demise Shocks Many," *Seattle Times*, August 8, 1999.

405. Ibid.

406. Ibid.

407. Ibid.

408. Glenn Nelson, Arthur Santana, and Tracy Jan, "Demetrius DuBose: 1971–1999—Lost After Football—But Former Local Star's Demise Shocks Many," *Seattle Times*, August 8, 1999.

409. "Notre Dame Silent on DuBose Situation," *Houston Chronicle*, September 1, 1992.

410. *Associated Press* Reports, September 2, 1991.

411. Glenn Nelson, Arthur Santana, and Tracy Jan, "Demetrius DuBose: 1971–1999—Lost After Football—But Former Local Star's Demise Shocks Many," *Seattle Times*, August 8, 1999.

412. Ibid.

413. Steve Kelly, "Snapshots of a Life Lost Reveal the True Demetrius DuBose," *Seattle Times*, August 8, 1999; Glenn Nelson, "Puzzling End to Life of Intensity," *Seattle Times*, August 8, 1999.

414. Glenn Nelson, "Puzzling End to Life of Intensity," *Seattle Times*, August 8, 1999.

415. Glenn Nelson, Arthur Santana, and Tracy Jan, "Demetrius DuBose: 1971–1999—Lost After Football—But Former Local Star's Demise Shocks Many," *Seattle Times*, August 8, 1999; Glenn Nelson, "Puzzling End to Life of Intensity," *Seattle Times*, August 8, 1999; Rick Morrissey, "A Life Left Unfulfilled," *Chicago Tribune*, July 27, 1999; David Haugh, "How Do You Explain This: DuBose Tragedy Stuns N.D. Family," *South Bend Tribune*, July 27, 1999.

416. Ibid.

417. Ibid.

418. Alan Grant, "John Lynch Likes Confrontation, But He Will Never Understand the One That Took His Best Friend's Life," *Chicago Sun-Times* (reprinted from *ESPN: The Magazine*), November 19, 2000.

419. Michael Stetz and Gregory Allen Gross, "It Was Like a Tale of Two Beings: Slain Man's Antics Mystify," *San Diego Union Tribune*, July 27, 1999.

420. "Family of Demetrius DuBose Files Lawsuit," *South Bend Tribune*, October 26, 1999.

421. Ken Ellingwood, "Probe of Police Urged in Ex-Football Player's Death; Protest: Black Leaders Say San Diego Officers Unnecessarily Tried to Handcuff Demetrius DuBose," *Los Angeles Times*, August 3, 1999.

422. Ibid.

423. Ibid.

424. Ibid.

425. Tony Perry, "Police Shooting Was Justified, D.A. Finds; Investigation: Vowing Full Disclosure, Officials Post Entire Report on San Diego Slaying on the Internet," *Los Angeles Times*, November 2, 1999.

426. Ibid.

427. Ibid.

428. Tony Perry, "Protesters Demand Special Session on Police Shooting," *Los Angeles Times*, November 6, 1999.

429. "FBI Clears San Diego Police in Shooting of Ex-NFL Player," *Associated Press*, November 26, 1999.

430. Ibid.

431. "Citizen's Review Board Finds Officers Acted Within Police Policy," *Associated Press*, May 3, 2000.

432. Tony Perry, "Police Panel Criticizes Officers in Athlete's Death," *Los Angeles Times*, May 4, 2000.

433. "Police Chief Opposes Settling Civil Lawsuit in Former NFL Player's Death," *Associated Press*, July 19, 2000.

434. "Week in Review," *San Diego Union-Tribune*, February 23, 2003.

435. Marisa Taylor, "Police Officers Cleared in DuBose Shooting; Action Was Justified; Federal Jurors Decide," *San Diego Union-Tribune*, February 19, 2003.

436. Chief David Bejarano, "Policing for America's Finest City," *Opinion*, March 30, 2003.

437. Patrick J. Morley, *Report Writing for Criminal Justice Professionals*, New York: Kaplan Publishing, 2008, section by James Marsh, "Guidelines for Documentation of a Use-of-Force Encounter," 205.

438. For more details of this case, see Patrick J. Morley, *Report Writing for Criminal Justice Professionals*, New York: Kaplan Publishing, 2008, section by James Marsh, "Guidelines for Documentation of a Use-of-Force Encounter."

439. Sharon Theimer, "A Case More Gruesome than Any Could Have Imagined," *Associated Press*, November 29, 1994.

440. Ibid.

441. Ibid.

442. Ibid.

443. Ibid.

444. Ibid.

445. Anthony Shadid, "Dahmer Testifies Boy Had Drill Hole in Skull When Cops Questioned Him," *Associated Press*, April 6, 1993.

446. Ibid.

447. Ibid.

448. Ibid.

449. Sharon Theimer, "A Case More Gruesome than Any Could Have Imagined," *Associated Press*, November 29, 1994.

450. Ibid.

451. "Family of Dahmer Victim Reaches Tentative Settlement," *Associated Press*, March 21, 1995.

452. Ibid.

453. Linda Deutsch, "Vegas Police Talked of Getting O. J. On Recording," *Associated Press*, September 19, 2008.

454. Ibid.

455. Ibid.

456. Kenneth Ritter, "O. J. Simpson Transferred from Vegas to Nevada Prison," *Associated Press*, December 8, 2008.

457. "March 3, 12:39 A.M., After Breaking Up a Quarrel That Reportedly Involved Blacks, Los Angeles Policemen Laurence M. Powell and Timothy E. Wind Use Their Portable Communications Computer to Conduct a Team of Officers on a Burglary Stakeout: Sounds Almost as Exciting as Our Last Case. It Was Right Out of Gorillas in the Mist." *Time Magazine*, April 1, 1991.

458. Linda Deutsch, "Judge: Police Remarks in King Case Were Racist," *Associated Press*, June 10, 1991.

459. Ibid.

460. Marshall Ingwerson, "Miami: A Magnet for Adventure and Profit," *Christian Science Monitor*, May 7, 1987.

461. P. Taylor, "Miami—The Capitalist's Cuba," *Herald*, December 17, 1987.

462. Marshall Ingwerson, "Miami: A Magnet for Adventure and Profit," *Christian Science Monitor*, May 7, 1987.

463. Ibid.

464. Ibid.

465. Ibid.

466. Ibid.

467. "1987 Dade Homicides Plunge Far Below 'Murder Capital' Days," *Associated Press*, December 31, 1987.

468. Reuters News Service, "Corruption Probe Rocks Miami Force," *The Globe and Mail* (Canada), January 9, 1988.

469. "1987 Dade Homicides Plunge Far Below 'Murder Capital' Days," *Associated Press*, December 31, 1987.

470. Paul Eddy, Michael Graham, Hugo Sabogal, Sara Walden, "Miami: City on the Edge of Anarchy," *Sydney Morning Herald* (Australia), December 27, 1986.

471. "Drug Related Corruption Study Could Help Other Police Departments," *United Press International*, May 23, 1988.

472. Ibid.

473. Ibid.

474. Paul Eddy, Michael Graham, Hugo Sabogal, Sara Walden, "Miami: City on the Edge of Anarchy," *Sydney Morning Herald* (Australia), December 27, 1986.

475. P. Taylor, "Miami—The Capitalist's Cuba," *Herald*, December 17, 1987; Paul Eddy, Michael Graham, Hugo Sabogal, Sara Walden, "Miami: City on the Edge of Anarchy," *Sydney Morning Herald* (Australia), December 27, 1986.

476. Ibid.

477. Paul Eddy, Michael Graham, Hugo Sabogal, Sara Walden, "Miami: City on the Edge of Anarchy," *Sydney Morning Herald* (Australia), December 27, 1986.

478. Marshall Ingwerson, "Miami: A Magnet for Adventure and Profit," *Christian Science Monitor*, May 7, 1987.

479. Ibid.

480. P. Taylor, "Miami—The Capitalist's Cuba," *Herald*, December 17, 1987.

481. "Drug Related Corruption Study Could Help Other Police Departments," *United Press International*, May 23, 1988.

482. Ibid.

483. Ibid.

484. Ibid.

485. P. Taylor, "Miami—The Capitalist's Cuba," *Herald*, December 17, 1987.

486. "Drug Related Corruption Study Could Help Other Police Departments," *United Press International*, May 23, 1988.

487. Richard Cole, "Principal Miami Corruption Witness Gets 10 Years," *Associated Press*, March 11, 1988.

488. Ibid.

489. Reuters News Service, "Corruption Probe Rocks Miami Force," *The Globe and Mail* (Canada), January 9, 1988.

490. Richard Cole, "Principal Miami Corruption Witness Gets 10 Years," *Associated Press*, March 11, 1988.

491. Reuters News Service, "Corruption Probe Rocks Miami Force," *The Globe and Mail* (Canada), January 9, 1988.

492. Ibid.

493. "Drug Related Corruption Study Could Help Other Police Departments," *United Press International*, May 23, 1988.

494. Tom Morgenthau, with Erik Calonius, Charles Lane, David L. Gonzalez, and Cheryl Miller, "Miami," *Newsweek*, January 25, 1988.

495. Ibid.

496. Reuters News Service, "Corruption Probe Rocks Miami Force," *The Globe and Mail* (Canada), January 9, 1988.

497. Tom Morgenthau, with Erik Calonius, Charles Lane, David L. Gonzalez, and Cheryl Miller, "Miami," *Newsweek*, January 25, 1988.

498. Reuters News Service, "Corruption Probe Rocks Miami Force," *The Globe and Mail* (Canada), January 9, 1988.

499. Tim Feran, "Media, Public Pay Growing Role in Tracking Down Fugitives," *Columbus Dispatch* (Ohio), March 19, 2004.

500. Tim Feran, "Media, Public Pay Growing Role in Tracking Down Fugitives," *Columbus Dispatch* (Ohio), March 19, 2004, quoting Tom Rosensteil.

501. Tim Feran, "Media, Public Pay Growing Role in Tracking Down Fugitives," *Columbus Dispatch* (Ohio), March 19, 2004.

502. Ibid.

503. Ibid.

504. *www.woodstock-il.com*

505. *www.woodstock-il.com*

506. Charles Mount, "Grisly Tale Unfolds as Church Enters Guilty Plea," *Chicago Tribune*, July 24, 1992.

507. Colin McMahon, "Church Was Clever in Eluding the Police," *Chicago Tribune*, November 25, 1991.

508. David Young and John O'Brien, "Woodstock's Suspect's Truck Is Found, Fugitive Trail Leads to California," *Chicago Tribune*, September 28, 1988.

509. Susan Kuczka, Flynn McRoberts, Joseph Kirby, John O'Brien, and Jack Houston, "3 Year Manhunt Ends Suddenly; Slain Couple's Daughter Says Ordeal Is Over," *Chicago Tribune*, November 22, 1991.

510. Charles Mount, "Grisly Tale Unfolds as Church Enters Guilty Plea," *Chicago Tribune*, July 24, 1992.

511. Jack Houston, "Woodstock Fugitive's Trail Now Ice Cold," *Chicago Tribune*, September 3, 1991.

512. Charles Mount, "Grisly Tale Unfolds as Church Enters Guilty Plea," *Chicago Tribune*, July 24, 1992.

513. Jack Houston, "Woodstock Fugitive's Trail Now Ice Cold," *Chicago Tribune*, September 3, 1991.

514. Ibid.

515. Ibid.

516. Charles Mount, "Grisly Tale Unfolds as Church Enters Guilty Plea," *Chicago Tribune*, July 24, 1992.

517. Ibid.

518. Ibid.

519. Colin McMahon, "Church's Blood, Hair Sought," *Chicago Tribune*, January 8, 1992.

520. Phillip Franchine, "Woodstock Man Pleads Guilty in Slayings," *Chicago Sun-Times*, July 24, 1992.

521. Jack Houston, "Woodstock Fugitive's Trail Now Ice Cold," *Chicago Tribune*, September 3, 1991; David Young and John O'Brien, "Woodstock's Suspect's Truck Is Found, Fugitive Trail Leads to California," *Chicago Tribune*, September 28, 1988.

522. Jack Houston, "Woodstock Fugitive's Trail Now Ice Cold," *Chicago Tribune*, September 3, 1991.

523. Ibid.

524. Ibid.

525. Colin McMahon, "Church Was Clever in Eluding the Police," *Chicago Tribune*, November 25, 1991.

526. Colin McMahon, "Church's Blood, Hair Sought," *Chicago Tribune*, January 8, 1992.

527. Jack Houston, "Woodstock Fugitive's Trail Now Ice Cold," *Chicago Tribune*, September 3, 1991.

528. Ibid.

529. Charles Mount and Joseph Kirby, "Church to Tell of Life on the Lamb," *Chicago Tribune*, July 26, 1992.

530. Susan Kuczka, Flynn McRoberts, Joseph Kirby, John O'Brien, and Jack Houston, "3 Year Manhunt Ends Suddenly; Slain Couple's Daughter Says Ordeal Is Over," *Chicago Tribune*, November 22, 1991.

531. Jack Houston, "Woodstock Fugitive's Trail Now Ice Cold," *Chicago Tribune*, September 3, 1991.

532. Susan Kuczka, Flynn McRoberts, Joseph Kirby, John O'Brien, and Jack Houston, "3 Year Manhunt Ends Suddenly; Slain Couple's Daughter Says Ordeal Is Over," *Chicago Tribune*, November 22, 1991.

533. Ibid.

534. Colin McMahon, "Fugitive Church Returns to Face Murder Charges in Woodstock," November 26, 1991.

535. Ibid.

536. Susan Kuczka, Flynn McRoberts, Joseph Kirby, John O'Brien, and Jack Houston, "3 Year Manhunt Ends Suddenly; Slain Couple's Daughter Says Ordeal Is Over," *Chicago Tribune*, November 22, 1991.

537. Ibid.

538. Ibid.

539. Ibid.

540. Ibid.

541. Colin McMahon, "Fugitive Church Returns to Face Murder Charges in Woodstock," November 26, 1991.

542. Colin McMahon, "Church Was Clever in Eluding the Police," *Chicago Tribune*, November 25, 1991.

543. "3 Year Manhunt Ends Suddenly; Slain Couple's Daughter Says Ordeal Is Over."

544. Charles Mount and Joseph Kirby, "Church to Tell of Life on the Lamb," *Chicago Tribune*, July 26, 1992.

545. Colin McMahon, "Church Was Clever in Eluding the Police," *Chicago Tribune*, November 25, 1991.

546. Ibid.

547. Ibid.

548. Ibid.

549. Ibid.

550. Colin McMahon, "That Wasn't Danny, Friends Say," *Chicago Tribune*, November 24, 1991.

551. James Kimberly, "Local Authorities Know Frustrations of Manhunt, No Rest for Officials until Hunt Is Over," *Chicago Daily Herald*, July 19, 1997.

552. Ibid.

553. Ibid.

554. Ibid.

555. Ibid.

556. Charles Mount, "Grisly Tale Unfolds as Church Enters Guilty Plea," *Chicago Tribune*, July 24, 1992.

557. Charles Mount and Joseph Kirby, "Church to Tell of Life on the Lamb," *Chicago Tribune*, July 26, 1992.

558. Charles Mount, "Grisly Tale Unfolds as Church Enters Guilty Plea," *Chicago Tribune*, July 24, 1992.

559. Ibid.

560. Ibid.

561. Ibid.

562. Charles Mount and Joseph Kirby, "Church to Tell of Life on the Lamb," *Chicago Tribune*, July 26, 1992.

563. Ibid.

564. James Kimberly, "Local Authorities Know Frustrations of Manhunt, No Rest for Officials until Hunt Is Over," *Chicago Daily Herald*, July 19, 1997.

565. Charles Keesham, "Killer Loses Plea to Cut Term," *Chicago Daily Herald*, July 27, 2001.

566. *www.idoc.state.il.us.*

567. *www.amw.com.*

568. Ibid.

569. Ibid.

570. Ibid.

571. Tim Feran, "Media, Public Pay Growing Role in Tracking Down Fugitives," *Columbus Dispatch* (Ohio), March 19, 2004.

572. Sharon Bernstein, "Crime Doesn't Pay Enough: 'America's Most Wanted' Is No Longer Wanted by Fox; Viewers, L.A.'s Police Chief, the DEA, Even the FBI Are Upset," *Los Angeles Times*, August 31, 1996.

573. Tim Feran, "Media, Public Pay Growing Role In Tracking Down Fugitives," *Columbus Dispatch* (Ohio), March 19, 2004.

574. Evan Thomas, with Brook Larmer, Peter Katel, Daniel Klaidman, Jamie Reno, Andrew Murr, John McCormik, Gregory Beals, Patricia King, Marcus Mabry, Steve Rhodes, John Engen, Ginny Carroll, Jennifer Tanaka, and bureau reports, "Facing Death," *Newsweek*, July 28, 1997; Evan Thomas, with Brook Larmer, Peter Katel, Jamie Reno, John McCormick, Andrew Murr, Peter Annin, Gregory Beals, Steve Rhodes, Jennifer Tanaka, Patricia King, and Frappa Stout, "End of the Road," *Newsweek*, August 4, 1997.

575. Evan Thomas, with Brook Larmer, Peter Katel, Daniel Klaidman, Jamie Reno, Andrew Murr, John McCormik, Gregory Beals, Patricia

King, Marcus Mabry, Steve Rhodes, John Engen, Ginny Carroll, Jennifer Tanaka, and bureau reports, "Facing Death," *Newsweek*, July 28, 1997.

576. Evan Thomas, with Brook Larmer, Peter Katel, Jamie Reno, John McCormick, Andrew Murr, Peter Annin, Gregory Beals, Steve Rhodes, Jennifer Tanaka, Patricia King, and Frappa Stout, "End of the Road," *Newsweek*, August 4, 1997.

577. Kelly Thorton, "Suspected Serial Killer Added to FBI Top Ten Most Wanted List," *Copley News Service*, June 13,1997.

578. Ibid.

579. Ibid.

580. Evan Thomas, with Brook Larmer, Peter Katel, Daniel Klaidman, Jamie Reno, Andrew Murr, John McCormik, Gregory Beals, Patricia King, Marcus Mabry, Steve Rhodes, John Engen, Ginny Carroll, Jennifer Tanaka, and bureau reports, "Facing Death," *Newsweek*, July 28, 1997.

581. William Recktenwald and Andrew Martin, "New Twist in Miglin Case; A Jeep Illegally Parked Near Lee Miglin's Home Becomes a Possible Link to His Murder and 2 Other Deaths," *Chicago Tribune*, May 8, 1997.

582. Ibid.

583. Ibid.

584. Ibid.

585. Ibid.

586. Tod Simons, "Inside Gamma Mu—Secrecy of Gay Social Club Gamma Mu," *The Advocate*, September 2, 2007.

587. Ibid.

588. Ibid.

589. Ibid.

590. Ibid.

591.   Evan Thomas, with Brook Larmer, Peter Katel, Jamie Reno, John McCormick, Andrew Murr, Peter Annin, Gregory Beals, Steve Rhodes, Jennifer Tanaka, Patricia King, and Frappa Stout, "End of the Road," *Newsweek*, August 4, 1997.

592.   "Twisted Trail: San Diego to Miami: Slayings Yield Clues That Paint Portrait of Cunanan," *St. Louis Post-Dispatch*, July 20, 1997.

593.   Kelly Thorton, "In Storm's Eye, Cunanan Read, Shopped," *San Diego Union-Tribune*, January 3, 1998.

594.   Evan Thomas, with Brook Larmer, Peter Katel, Daniel Klaidman, Jamie Reno, Andrew Murr, John McCormik, Gregory Beals, Patricia King, Marcus Mabry, Steve Rhodes, John Engen, Ginny Carroll, Jennifer Tanaka, and bureau reports, "Facing Death," *Newsweek*, July 28, 1997.

595.   Ibid.

596.   John H. White, "Auto Fuels Murder Manhunt; Stolen Jeep found near Miglin home", *Chicago Sun-Times*, May 8, 1997.

597.   Evan Thomas, with Brook Larmer, Peter Katel, Daniel Klaidman, Jamie Reno, Andrew Murr, John McCormik, Gregory Beals, Patricia King, Marcus Mabry, Steve Rhodes, John Engen, Ginny Carroll, Jennifer Tanaka, and bureau reports, "Facing Death," *Newsweek*, July 28, 1997.

598.   Ibid.

599.   Ibid.

600.   Evan Thomas, with Brook Larmer, Peter Katel, Jamie Reno, John McCormick, Andrew Murr, Peter Annin, Gregory Beals, Steve Rhodes, Jennifer Tanaka, Patricia King, and Frappa Stout, "End of the Road," *Newsweek*, August 4, 1997.

601.   Evan Thomas, with Brook Larmer, Peter Katel, Daniel Klaidman, Jamie Reno, Andrew Murr, John McCormik, Gregory Beals, Patricia King, Marcus Mabry, Steve Rhodes, John Engen, Ginny Carroll, Jennifer Tanaka, and bureau reports, "Facing Death," *Newsweek*, July 28, 1997.

602.   Ibid.

603. Ibid.

604. Ibid.

605. Ibid.

606. Ibid.

607. Ibid.

608. Kelly Thorton, "Suspected Serial Killer Added to FBI Top Ten Most Wanted List," *Copley News Service*, June 13, 1997.

609. Ibid.

610. Ibid.

611. Ibid.

612. Ibid.

613. Ibid.

614. Ibid.

615. Evan Thomas, with Brook Larmer, Peter Katel, Jamie Reno, John McCormick, Andrew Murr, Peter Annin, Gregory Beals, Steve Rhodes, Jennifer Tanaka, Patricia King, and Frappa Stout, "End of the Road," *Newsweek*, August 4, 1997.

616. Ibid.

617. Ibid.

618. Ibid.

619. Evan Thomas, with Brook Larmer, Peter Katel, Jamie Reno, John McCormick, Andrew Murr, Peter Annin, Gregory Beals, Steve Rhodes, Jennifer Tanaka, Patricia King, and Frappa Stout, "End of the Road," *Newsweek*, August 4, 1997.

620. "Twisted Trail: San Diego to Miami: Slayings Yield Clues That Paint Portrait of Cunanan," *St. Louis Post-Dispatch*, July 20, 1997.

621. Evan Thomas, with Brook Larmer, Peter Katel, Jamie Reno, John McCormick, Andrew Murr, Peter Annin, Gregory Beals, Steve Rhodes, Jennifer Tanaka, Patricia King, and Frappa Stout, "End of the Road," *Newsweek*, August 4, 1997.

622. Ibid.

623. Evan Thomas, with Brook Larmer, Peter Katel, Daniel Klaidman, Jamie Reno, Andrew Murr, John McCormik, Gregory Beals, Patricia King, Marcus Mabry, Steve Rhodes, John Engen, Ginny Carroll, Jennifer Tanaka, and bureau reports, "Facing Death," *Newsweek*, July 28, 1997.

624. Ibid.

625. Ibid.

626. "Cunanan Houseboat Link Being Probed," *United Press International*, July 28, 1997.

627. Evan Thomas, with Brook Larmer, Peter Katel, Jamie Reno, John McCormick, Andrew Murr, Peter Annin, Gregory Beals, Steve Rhodes, Jennifer Tanaka, Patricia King, and Frappa Stout, "End of the Road," *Newsweek*, August 4, 1997.

628. Ibid.

629. Ibid.

630. Ibid.

631. Howard Chua-Eoan, "Dead Men Tell No Tales; America's Most Wanted Man, Seen Everywhere, Ended His Life in a Houseboat a Couple Miles Away from His Last Crime Scene. Andrew Cunanan's Life May Be Over but Questions Remain," *Time Magazine*, August 4, 1997.

632. Donald P. Baker and Audrey Gillian, "Police Check if Cunanan Had Help," *Washington Post*, July 25, 1997.

633. Kelly Thorton, "In Storm's Eye, Cunanan Read, Shopped," *San Diego Union-Tribune*, January 3, 1998.

634. Evan Thomas, with Brook Larmer, Peter Katel, Jamie Reno, John McCormick, Andrew Murr, Peter Annin, Gregory Beals, Steve Rhodes,

Jennifer Tanaka, Patricia King, and Frappa Stout, "End of the Road," *Newsweek*, August 4, 1997.

635. Tyler Bridges, "Houseboat Owner's True Identity Surprises Las Vegas Crowd," *Miami Herald*, July 27, 1997.

636. Donald P. Baker and Audrey Gillian, "Police Check if Cunanan Had Help," *Washington Post*, July 25, 1997.

637. Evan Thomas, with Brook Larmer, Peter Katel, Daniel Klaidman, Jamie Reno, Andrew Murr, John McCormik, Gregory Beals, Patricia King, Marcus Mabry, Steve Rhodes, John Engen, Ginny Carroll, Jennifer Tanaka, and bureau reports, "Facing Death," *Newsweek*, July 28, 1997.

638. Steven Egger, *The Killers Among Us: An Examination of Serial Murder and Its Investigation,* 2nd Edition, Prentice Hall, 2002, 88.

639. Ibid.

640. Ibid

641. Donald P. Baker and Audrey Gillian, "Police Check if Cunanan Had Help," *Washington Post*, July 25, 1997.

642. Ibid.

643. Evan Thomas, with Brook Larmer, Peter Katel, Daniel Klaidman, Jamie Reno, Andrew Murr, John McCormik, Gregory Beals, Patricia King, Marcus Mabry, Steve Rhodes, John Engen, Ginny Carroll, Jennifer Tanaka, and bureau reports, "Facing Death," *Newsweek*, July 28, 1997.

644. Ibid.

645. Evan Thomas, with Brook Larmer, Peter Katel, Jamie Reno, John McCormick, Andrew Murr, Peter Annin, Gregory Beals, Steve Rhodes, Jennifer Tanaka, Patricia King, and Frappa Stout, "End of the Road," *Newsweek*, August 4, 1997.

646. Evan Thomas, with Brook Larmer, Peter Katel, Daniel Klaidman, Jamie Reno, Andrew Murr, John McCormik, Gregory Beals, Patricia King, Marcus Mabry, Steve Rhodes, John Engen, Ginny Carroll, Jennifer Tanaka, and bureau reports, "Facing Death," *Newsweek*, July 28, 1997.

647. Ibid.

648. Ibid.

649. Ibid.

650. Ibid.

651. Pat Jordan, "Versace's Paradise: in a World of Pleasure, Murder Can Be the Most Powerful Memory.; Miami Beach, Florida; Designer Gianni Versace," *Playboy*, December 1, 1997.

652. Evan Thomas, with Brook Larmer, Peter Katel, Daniel Klaidman, Jamie Reno, Andrew Murr, John McCormik, Gregory Beals, Patricia King, Marcus Mabry, Steve Rhodes, John Engen, Ginny Carroll, Jennifer Tanaka, and bureau reports, "Facing Death," *Newsweek*, July 28, 1997.

653. Curt R. Bartol and Anne M. Bartol, *Criminal Behavior: A Psychosocial Approach*, 8th edition, Pearson Prentice Hall, 2008, 500.

654. Ibid., 501.

655. Ibid.

656. Ibid.

657. Ibid., 503.

658. Ibid.

659. Ibid., 502.

660. Bruce Wind, "Guide to Crisis Negotiation," *Lectric Law Library*, taken from FBI's *Monthly Magazine*, October 1995.

661. Ibid.

662. Ibid.

663. *Criminal Behavior: A Psychosocial Approach*, citing G. D. Fuselier and G. W. Noesner, "Confronting the Terrorist Hostage Taker," *FBI Law Enforcement Bulletin*, 10.

664. Ibid.

665. Bruce Wind, "Guide to Crisis Negotiation," *Lectric Law Library*, taken from FBI's *Monthly Magazine*, October 1995.

666. Ibid.

667. Ibid.

668. Jake Ellison, Christine Frey, and Athima Chansanchai, "Shooting at Mall Leaves 7 Injured, Man Fires on Tacoma Shoppers, Gives Up; Hostages Stay Cool, Emerge Unharmed," *Seattle Post-Intelligencer*, November 21, 2005.

669. Emily Heffter, Julia Summerfeld, and Mike Carter, "Mall Shooter; 'World Will Feel My Anger'; Man Frees Hostages, Surrenders After 6 Shot in Tacoma," *Seattle Times*, November 21, 2005.

670. Rachel LaCorte, "Man Arrested in Tacoma Mall Shooting," *Associated Press*, November 20, 2005.

671. Rachel LaCorte, "Reports: Suspect in Tacoma Mall Shooting Spree Sent Angry Text Messages Before the Rampage," *Associated Press*, November 21, 2005.

672. Ibid.

673. Stacy Mullick, "Negotiators Will Analyze Incident," *The News Tribune* (Tacoma, Washington), November 27, 2005.

674. Ibid.

675. Ibid.

676. Sharon Pian Chan, "Police Upset by Media's Calls to Store Where Hostages Held," *Seattle Times*, November 22, 2005.

677. Ibid.

678. Ibid.

679. Ibid.

680. Ibid.

681. Jake Ellison, Christine Frey, and Athima Chansanchai, "Shooting at Mall Leaves 7 Injured, Man Fires on Tacoma Shoppers, Gives Up; Hostages Stay Cool, Emerge Unharmed," *Seattle Post-Intelligencer*, November 21, 2005.

682. Adam Lynn and Stacy Mullick, "Hostage, Negotiator Remember Hours of Fear; A Police Sergeant and a Man Taken Hostage in Last Sunday's Shooting at Tacoma Mall Recount Three Tense Hours While a Gunman Held Three Captive," *The News Tribune* (Tacoma, Washington), November 27, 2005.

683. Ibid.

684. Stacy Mullick, "Negotiators Will Analyze Incident," *The News Tribune* (Tacoma, Washington), November 27, 2005.

685. Los Angeles Police Department Media Relations Handbook, 2007–2008.

686. Chicago Police Department, D.S.O 04–14, October 1, 2004, 3.

687. Rick Jervis, Marisol Bello, and Andrea Stone, "New Storm, New Lessons; Fear of Another Katrina Heightened Sense of Urgency," *Gannett News Service*, September 2, 2008.

688. Julia Silverman, "Police Chief: 249 New Orleans Officers Left Their Posts Without Permission During Katrina," *Associated Press*, September 27, 2005.

689. Ibid.

690. Jack Dunphy, "Rebuilding a Police Department," *National Review*, October 11, 2005.

691. Nicole Gaouette, "A Shattered Gulf Coast; New Orleans Police Investigating Possible Looting by Officers; Some Are Suspected of Stealing, or Standing By While Others Did. A Video Is at the Center of the Inquiry. It's the Latest Blow to the Department," *Los Angeles Times*, September 30, 2005.

692. Julia Silverman, "Police Chief: 249 New Orleans Officers Left Their Posts Without Permission During Katrina," *Associated Press*, September 27, 2005.

693. Jack Dunphy, "Rebuilding a Police Department," *National Review*, October 11, 2005.

694. Ibid.

695. Julia Silverman, "New Orleans Police Chief Resigns After Four Turbulent Weeks," *Associated Press*, September 27, 2005.

696. "Hurricane Aftermath; New Orleans; Crime Rises as Residents Come Back; Police Form a Looting Squad to Patrol the City," *Houston Chronicle*, October 10, 2005.

697. Ibid.

698. Julia Silverman, "New Orleans Police Chief Resigns After Four Turbulent Weeks," *Associated Press*, September 27, 2005.

699. Nicole Gaouette, "A Shattered Gulf Coast; New Orleans Police Investigating Possible Looting by Officers; Some Are Suspected of Stealing, or Standing By While Others Did. A Video Is at the Center of the Inquiry. It's the Latest Blow to the Department," *Los Angeles Times*, September 30, 2005.

700. Julia Silverman, "New Orleans Police Chief Resigns After Four Turbulent Weeks," *Associated Press*, September 27, 2005.

701. Michael Perlstein, "Police Reports Conceal Looting," New Code Could Conceal Level of Crime in Katrina's Aftermath," *New Orleans Times-Picayune*, February 7, 2006.

702. Ibid.

703. Ibid.

704. Michael Perlstein, "NOPD Clears Cops in Looting Probe; They Had OK to Take Clothing, Officials Said," *New Orleans Times-Picayune*, March 18, 2006.

705. Ibid.

706. Ibid.

707. Ibid.

708. Ibid.

709. Ibid.

710. Ibid.

711. Erin Calabrese and Andy Geller, "Big Easy Braces for Katrina Two—Orleans Nearly Empty, Holdouts Locked and Loaded as Gustav Nears," *New York Post*, September 1, 2008.

712. Ibid.

713. Rick Jervis, Marisol Bello, and Andrea Stone, "New Storm, New Lessons; Fear of Another Katrina Heightened Sense of Urgency," *Gannett News Service*, September 2, 2008.

714. Erin Calabrese and Andy Geller, "Big Easy Braces for Katrina Two—Orleans Nearly Empty, Holdouts Locked and Loaded as Gustav Nears," *New York Post*, September 1, 2008.

715. Ibid.

716. Ibid.

717. Jared Janes, "All BR Police Called Up . . . Officers Notified of Schedules, Deployment for Gustav," *The Advocate*, August 30, 2008.

718. Ibid.

719. Erin Calabrese and Andy Geller, "Big Easy Braces for Katrina Two—Orleans Nearly Empty, Holdouts Locked and Loaded as Gustav Nears," *New York Post*, September 1, 2008.

720. Becky Bohrer, "As Gustav Nears, New Orleans Becomes a Ghost Town," *Associated Press*, August 31, 2008.

721. Erin Calabrese and Andy Geller, "Big Easy Braces for Katrina Two—Orleans Nearly Empty, Holdouts Locked and Loaded as Gustav Nears," *New York Post*, September 1, 2008.

722. Ibid.

723. Rick Jervis, Marisol Bello, and Andrea Stone, "New Storm, New Lessons; Fear of Another Katrina Heightened Sense of Urgency," *Gannett News Service*, September 2, 2008.

724. Ibid.

725. Ibid.

726. Erin Calabrese and Andy Geller, "Big Easy Braces for Katrina Two—Orleans Nearly Empty, Holdouts Locked and Loaded as Gustav Nears," *New York Post*, September 1, 2008.

727. Rick Jervis, Marisol Bello, and Andrea Stone, "New Storm, New Lessons; Fear of Another Katrina Heightened Sense of Urgency," *Gannett News Service*, September 2, 2008.

728. Ibid.

729. Erin Calabrese and Andy Geller, "Big Easy Braces for Katrina Two—Orleans Nearly Empty, Holdouts Locked and Loaded as Gustav Nears," *New York Post*, September 1, 2008.

730. Ibid.

731. Rick Jervis, Marisol Bello, and Andrea Stone, "New Storm, New Lessons; Fear of Another Katrina Heightened Sense of Urgency," *Gannett News Service*, September 2, 2008.

732. Ibid.

733. Jared Janes, "All BR Police Called Up . . . Officers Notified of Schedules, Deployment for Gustav," *The Advocate*, August 30, 2008.

734. Gerald W. Garner, *Chief, the Reporters Are Here!: The Police Executive's Personal Guide to Press Relations*, Springfield: Thomas Books, 1987, 118.

735. Ibid., 119–121.

736. Ibid., 106–107.

737. "High Point's Overt Drug Market Strategy Honored as Innovations in American Government Award Winner; Harvard University's Ash Institute Honors Collaboration with Community Leaders and Law Enforcement to Halt Neighborhood Crime," *Business Wire*, September 25, 2007.

738. Mark Schoofs, "Novel Police Tactic Puts Drug Markets Out of Business," *Wall Street Journal*, September 27, 2006.

739. Ibid.

740. Ibid.

741. Ibid.

742. Ibid.

743. Ibid.

744. Ibid.

745. Ibid.

746. Ibid.

747. Ibid.

748. Ibid.

749. Ibid.

750. Ibid.

751. Ibid.

752. Ibid.

753. Ibid.

754. Ibid.

755. Rachel Stilts, "Police Put Pressure on E. Nashville Drug Dealers," *The Tennessean*, March 21, 2008.

756. Mark Schoofs, "Novel Police Tactic Puts Drug Markets Out of Business," *Wall Street Journal*, September 27, 2006.

757. Ibid.

758. Rachel Stilts, "Police Put Pressure on E. Nashville Drug Dealers," *The Tennessean*, March 21, 2008.

759. Ibid.

760. "High Point's Overt Drug Market Strategy Honored as Innovations in American Government Award Winner; Harvard University's Ash Institute Honors Collaboration with Community Leaders and Law Enforcement to Halt Neighborhood Crime," *Business Wire*, September 25, 2007.

761. *Michigan v. Sitz*, 496 U.S. 444 (1990).

762. *Indianapolis v. Edmond*, 531 U.S. 32 (2000). (In this case, officers set up a checkpoint to stop vehicles to determine if the vehicle contained drugs. After the vehicle was stopped, the officers would circle it with a narcotics dog. The United States Supreme Court ruled that officers may not set up a roadblock the sole purpose of which is to catch lawbreakers. Therefore, the roadblock was unconstitutional.)

763. *Illinois v. Bartley*, 109 Ill. 2d 273 (1985).

764. "Michigan State Police to Step Up Patrols for Thanksgiving Holiday Weekend," *Michigan State Police Press Release*, November 27, 2002.

765. *Illinois v. Bartley*, 109 Ill. 2d 273 (1985).

766. Jolene Gutierrez Krueger and Maggie Sheppard, "Surprise Sweep Rounds Up Several in Effort to End Feud," *The Albuquerque Tribune*, April 12, 2007.

767. Maggie Sheppard, "TCK, West Side Id'd to Give Public Full Story," *The Albuquerque Tribune*, April 14, 2007.

768. Ibid.

769. Ibid.

770. Ibid.

771. Ibid.

772. Ibid.

773. Tony Case, "Covering Youth Gangs—Panelists Discuss Whether a Newspaper Should Identify the Gang and Name Its Members in a Crime Story," *Editor and Publisher Magazine*, October 8, 1994.

774. Ibid.

775. Ibid.

776. Ibid.

777. Bethiana Palma, "LAPD Shift on Gangs Gets Mixed Reviews," *Pasadena Star-News*, February 25, 2007.

778. Ibid.

779. Ibid.

780. Andy Hall, "A Primer on Local Gangs," *Wisconsin State Journal* (Madison), June 19, 2005.

781. *www.chicagopolice.org*

782. Todd Richissin, "Newark 'Vice News' Lists Alleged Druggies, Prostitutes, Customers," *Associated Press*, April 3, 1990.

783. Jordan Schrader, "To Reduce Prostitution, Communities Try Shaming Clients," *USA Today*, August 29, 2008.

784. Ibid.

785. "Fort Wayne Paper Names 'Johns,'" *Editor and Publisher Magazine*, September 9, 1995.

786. Gina Lubrano, Opinion, "Prostitution Is a Problem: But Is Publishing Photos of 'Johns' News or Punishment?" *San Diego Union-Tribune*, August 15, 1994.

787. Ibid.

788. Ibid.

789. Ibid.

790. Patrick J. Morley, *Report Writing for Criminal Justice Professionals*, New York: Kaplan Publishing, 2008.

791. Ibid.

792. Ibid.

793. Ibid.

794. Ibid.

795. Ibid.

796. Ibid.

INDEX

ABOUT THE AUTHOR

Patrick Morley is a prosecutor for the Cook County State Attorney's Office, where he is assigned to the Cold Case Homicide Unit. He has been a prosecutor since 2000 and has worked in the Complex Narcotics Litigation Unit, Narcotics Special Prosecutions, Felony Trial Division, Homicide/Sex Unit, and Felony Review. He was a Chicago police officer and sergeant for seven years (1993–2000). He is an adjunct instructor for Northwestern University's Center for Public Safety and teaches for their School of Police Staff and Command. He has also been an adjunct instructor at Kaplan University since 2005. He is an instructor for North East Multi-Regional Training, where has also taught over 200 seminars to Chicago-area police officers, on search and seizure, criminal law, and other legal issues. He was an adjunct instructor at the University of Illinois—Chicago (UIC) from 2000–2008, teaching Criminal Investigations and Criminal Law. He has also taught criminal justice–related classes at Loyola University in Chicago, Harold Washington College, Calumet College, and at the Chicago Police Academy. He is the author of the textbook *Report Writing for Criminal Justice Professionals: Learn to Write and Interpret Police Reports* (Kaplan Publishing, 2008).